MERCHANDISING LIBRARY
MATERIALS TO YOUNG ADULTS

Libraries Unlimited Professional Guides for Young Adult Librarians Series

C. Allen Nichols and Mary Anne Nichols,
Series Editors

Merchandising Library Materials to Young Adults
Mary Anne Nichols

Library Materials and Services for Teen Girls
Katie O'Dell

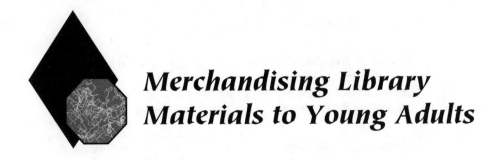

Merchandising Library Materials to Young Adults

MARY ANNE NICHOLS

2002
LIBRARIES UNLIMITED
A Division of Greenwood Publishing Group, Inc.
Greenwood Village, Colorado

To Allen, Evan, and Bennett—I am truly blessed.

The author gratefully acknowledges the permission of the following companies for allowing photographs of their products to be included in this work: **Brodart Co.**, P.O. Box 300, McElhatten, PA 17748; **Demco, Inc.**, P.O. Box 1488, Madison, WI 53707; **Displays 2 Go**, 55 Broad Common Road, Bristol, RI 02809; **Gaylord Bros.**, P.O. Box 4901, Syracuse, NY 13221; **Gressco, Ltd.**, P.O. Box 339, Waunakee, WI 53597; **Highsmith, Inc.**, P.O. Box 800, Fort Atkinson, WI 53538; **Library Display Shelving**, 173 W. Ohio Avenue, Lake Helen, FL 32744; **Literature Display Products**, P.O. Box 501790, Indianapolis, IN 46250; **Texwood Library Furniture**, P.O. Box 431, Taylor, TX 76574.

Libraries Unlimited
A Division of Greenwood Publishing Group, Inc.
7730 East Belleview Avenue, Suite A200
Greenwood Village, CO 80111
1-800-225-5800
www.lu.com

Library of Congress Cataloging-in-Publication Data

Nichols, Mary Anne, 1967-
    Merchandising library materials to young adults / Mary Anne Nichols.
        p. cm. -- (Libraries Unlimited professional guides for young adult librarians series, ISSN 1532-5571)
    Includes bibliographical references and index.
    ISBN 0-313-31382-2 (alk. paper)
    1. Libraries and teenagers--United States. 2. Young adults' libraries--United States. 3. Teenagers--Books and reading--United States. 4. Library exhibits--United States. I. Title. II. Series.

Z718.5 .N53 2002
027.62'6--dc21
                                                            2001054545

Contents

Tables and Illustrations

Tables

Illustrations

Series Foreword

We firmly believe in young adult library services and advocate for teens whenever we can. We are proud of our association with Libraries Unlimited and grateful for their acknowledgment of the need for additional resources for teen-serving librarians. We intend for this series to fill those needs, providing useful and practical handbooks for library staff. Readers will find some theory and philosophical musings, but for the most part, this series will focus on real-life library issues with answers and suggestions for front-line librarians.

Our passion for young adult librarian services continues to reach new peaks. As we travel to present workshops on the various facets of working with teens in public libraries, we are encouraged by the desire of librarians everywhere to learn what they can do in their libraries to make teens welcome. This is a positive sign since too often libraries choose to ignore this underserved group of patrons. We hope you find this series to be a useful tool in fostering your own enthusiasm for teens.

Mary Anne Nichols
C. Allen Nichols
Series Editors

Introduction

Having served teens in a public library setting for fourteen years, as well as playing an active role in the lives of my teenage nephews and "tween" nieces, I am always in awe of their energy (and sometimes lethargy!), curiosity, and unique outlook on life. Their hectic schedules certainly keep all of us on our toes. Over the years, it has become obvious to me that in order for libraries to attract and keep busy teens as customers, old ways of thinking must change. Teens are being courted by advertisers of billion-dollar companies scrambling for a portion of their millions of dollars in disposable income. They are also turned on by the instant gratification and attractiveness of the Internet. Let's face it, to these forward-thinking teens, dusty library books shelved spine out are not going to cut it.

Having earned a B.S. in marketing, it was an easy extension for me to apply retail/business concepts to a library situation. While some people may feel intimidated with words such as *marketing* and *merchandising* or other business terminology, you will see that many libraries are using these concepts, just not calling them by such formal names. Successfully marketing and merchandising a library collection to teens does not require a special education. It takes a dedicated staff member playing an active role in creatively thinking out of the box in order to offer a current collection that teens will like and use. Merchandising is not for the faint-hearted—it requires a commitment to be on top of trends that teens are setting and working day to day to fill their needs with an attractive and appealing YA collection, area, and service plan. It also requires that the YA staff member become an advocate in teen services and in merchandising to work with other staff members in the library, including administrators, in order to offer a full-service plan aimed at teens.

This guide is meant to give you a basic understanding of merchandising so that you can begin to apply these concepts in your library setting. Some of the ideas are inexpensive, while others require a larger budgetary commitment. You can start small and slowly increase your merchandising efforts. You will see that your co-workers will notice and be impressed—but most important, the teens that use your collection will know that you are working for them.

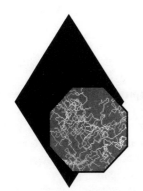

1

Marketing—An Introduction

Teens are a growing segment of the population. Their number has been on the rise since the early 1990s, and by the year 2010 the number of people aged twelve to nineteen years will reach 34 million. Teens are courted by all sorts of advertisers such as Nike, Claire's, Pepsi, and Revlon, who are scrambling for a share of the $141 billion teens spend yearly.[1]

Libraries need to be just as active in pursuing teens and gear their collections and services to them. Statistics show that almost one out of every four people who enter a library is a teenager.[2] If library staffs serving young adults become aware of marketing and its tenets, teens will notice and begin to use library collections and services more than they do now. Peter Zollo is a researcher and marketing consultant with Teenage Research Unlimited. He states in his book *Wise Up to Teens* that there are two keys to success in marketing to teens: first, acknowledge the importance of teenage consumers; and second, recognize their uniqueness.[3]

This chapter provides a brief introduction to the subject of marketing. While an in-depth discussion of the subject cannot be covered in one chapter, it is necessary to gain a rudimentary understanding of marketing in order to understand its relative, merchandising. At the broadest corporate level, the function of marketing activities is to bring buyers and sellers together. To relate this to libraries, YA patrons become "buyers" and the library "sells" or offers services to them. Once the definition of marketing is broadened to include non-profit organizations, the primary characteristic becomes the exchange or transfer of goods, services, or ideas so that both the marketer and the customer profit in some way.[4] In essence, this is what librarians do every day.

Librarians who understand marketing have changed the definition of what they do. Before, emphasis was placed on collections and services, whereas the shift now is to become customer-oriented. A true marketing approach determines the needs and wants of its customers and uses resources available to deliver the products and services. A library today must be willing to adapt collections and services to satisfy the customer.[5] This active, not passive, role involves purchasing materials such as comic books and popular music, as well as more traditional YA books and magazines— despite the fact that they are often the targets of theft and vandalism.

One of the key elements of marketing is knowing who your customers are and then being able to deliver to them what you have (which also happens to be what they need and want). Library staff has the opportunity to excel at this point. Librarians, who are in close daily contact with young adults at the reference and circulation desks or are available to the after-school crowd, know what materials are requested. Another informal way of finding out what teens want is to ask them for suggestions while on school visits or while they are in the library. Also, contacting schools for summer reading lists or lists of required reading for the school year can provide answers. These suggestions and requests should be the driving force in the development of YA collections.[6]

Successful marketers truly understand their customers and what they need and want. It is important to study the lives of teens in the community and to know the answers to the following questions:

- What is the makeup of the community?

- Do teens have jobs?

- How do they spend their spare time?

- Where do they hang out?

- What extracurricular activities are out there for them?

- What businesses or services do they frequent?

- Are there latchkey programs in the community or large church youth groups?

Knowing what teens do in the community will allow the librarian to plan collections and services accordingly. For example, it is senseless to spend money on a large collection of college catalogs or ACT or SAT testing books if most of the teens in a community attend trade or two-year colleges.

Marketing is not solely for the purpose of providing YA patrons with new services, but also to reinforce and improve existing services. Librarians need to be prepared to capitalize on and expand strengths in the collection and remedy weaknesses. The key to successful marketing also includes constant evaluation and monitoring. The book *Output Measures and More: Planning and Evaluating Public Library Services* by Virginia Walter is an invaluable tool to help with evaluating and analyzing users and usage.

There are certain elements that play a role in the marketing of YA services. These elements can be grouped into what the business world calls the "four Ps" of marketing—product, price, place, and promotion.

PRODUCT

Product is the services offered by the library: the YA collection, programming services, reader's advisory services, Internet access (including the use of MUD [multi-user dimension games] and chat rooms), homework centers, and Infotrac, just to name a few. YA librarians need to concern themselves with product design in that they plan and arrange their products and services in a way that will attract teens to the library.

PRICE

The price element can be defined as what it costs the library to offer the services. It also involves the cost of staff time involved in the preparation of programs and services. Ideas to consider in this element are ways to cut costs. Belonging to a standing order plan for series paperbacks can save both time and money. A standing order plan allows a librarian to choose which paperback series and how many copies of each title he or she would like to receive from a distributor. The ordering can be done on a quarterly or annual basis, thus saving time regularly researching new additions to series. Developing a good relationship with Friends of the Library groups that can provide money toward a collection or furniture is essential in helping to stretch library budgets. Membership in a regional library system and using the resources of the state library can help with program development and professional resources. Tools such as a good desktop publishing program or an Ellison machine can provide low-cost ways to create displays.[7]

PLACE

Place is where YA services are offered. Young adults should have a space they can call their own. It does not have to include a spacious room. At the bare minimum, the YA collection should be separated from the rest of the library collection. If the library does not have a separate room, it is necessary that young adults be able to find their collection and know that the space belongs to them. Yellow YA spine stickers ordered from Demco at least make the YA books stand out from the rest of the collection. Eye-catching posters near the collection or a bulletin board posting middle or high school news, highlighting teens, or displaying teen book reviews will label the area for teens. If a YA room does exist, it should be geographically placed far away from the children's room. Comfortable chairs and tables provide a place to work on homework. Library computers and Internet stations should also be present. All of these considerations should be included to provide a section of a library that appeals to teens and can be easily recognized as designed for them. The element of place can also occur outside of the library. School visits, visits to the institutionalized, and drop collections at housing or apartment developments bring the YA place somewhere else.

PROMOTION

Promotion is the one element that people easily associate with marketing. Promotion can occur both inside and outside the library. Promotion inside the library occurs when library tours take place or when flyers or booklists are developed and distributed at the time of checkout. Flyers or posters should be brightly colored and use graphics that appeal to teens in order to grab their attention. Programming can also promote library services. All library staff needs to be aware of library events. For example, a teen that approaches the circulation desk and asks a question should be given a straight answer or referred to the correct staff member. Displays can also be used to promote YA collections inside the library.

Promotion outside of the library occurs while making school visits to talk about books, make presentations to classes, or to attend meetings with media specialists. Giving a presentation at a school open house or having a display table at parent/teacher conference nights counts as promotion also. Networking with community agencies or planning programs co-sponsored by local businesses or the local parks and recreation department also gains exposure for the library. Displaying flyers throughout the community at places where teens hang out will advertise library events to teens that might not normally attend them.

Providing incentives or giveaways for contests or reading programs indirectly promotes the library. Librarians who hand sell or are able to give short book talks (one or two sentences) to entice young adults to check out books while working the reference desk or performing reader's advisory services are also executing a form of promotion. If preregistration for programs is necessary, the names and addresses can be used as a mailing list to alert teens of library events. Distributing a newsletter highlighting YA services or having a section in the library newsletter of special interest to young adults can also help with promotion. Preparing a newsletter highlighting YA services can be a rewarding project for a teen advisory board or for an active junior Friends of the Library group as well as a positive form of promotion for the librarian. These newsletters can be mailed to teens using the aforementioned mailing list.

Promotion includes paid advertising plus all aspects of public relations. Public relations involves relationships with news media, community organizations, and patrons. Obtaining the support of the news media is important because it provides credibility to the services the library provides. Identifying editors and reporters from local newspapers is necessary. It is important to know the deadlines for their publications, how they would like copy to be prepared, and what person handles the publicity. After the material is sent to the appropriate person, a follow-up phone call verifying receipt of it and being available to answer any questions is important. Press releases should be written on library letterhead with the contact person from the library identified as well as the date of the release. The information should be kept simple and typed double-spaced. News releases should answer these fundamental questions: Who is the organization involved? What will happen? When will it happen? Where will it happen? Why is it happening? How did it all come about?[8]

All of these ideas for promotion accomplish the same goals: gaining the attention of the customers, giving them a positive feeling, and influencing them to use the product or service.

Merchandising is related to marketing—especially the promotion element—but is basically concerned with the distribution or placement of the collection. It includes the concepts of displays, shelving techniques, furniture, and non-traditional shelving units. The rest of the book will cover these important topics and how library staff can incorporate them to entice teens to use the collection. Librarians need to draw upon their marketing knowledge in order to merchandise their YA collections well. The good news is that one does not need to have a marketing background in order to market the YA library collection. In fact, many of the most successful marketing activities in corporations such as Harley Davidson and Iams pet food are executed by individuals who know exactly what their customers want and are able to provide it to them. Some of the ideas practiced by executives in these companies that have made them successful are things that libraries have been doing for years: meeting face to face with the people who matter most—the customers, hiring only people who are passionate about what they do, loving and respecting the customers, and creating a sense of community for the customers.[9]

NOTES

1. Peter Zollo, *Wise Up to Teens: Insights into Marketing and Advertising to Teenagers,* 2d ed. (Ithaca, NY: New Strategist Publications, Inc., 1999), 6.

2. U.S. Department of Education, Office of Educational Research and Improvement, National Center for Education Statistics, *Services and Resources for Children and Young Adults in Public Libraries* (Washington D.C.: GPO, 1995).

3. Zollo, *Wise Up to Teens,* 6.

4. William Zikmund and Michael D'Amico, *Marketing,* 6th ed. (Cincinnati, OH: South-Western College Publishing, 1999), 9.

5. Mary Anne Nichols and C. Allen Nichols, eds., *Young Adults and Public Libraries: A Handbook of Materials and Services* (Westport, CT: Greenwood Press, 1998), 145.

6. Mary Anne Nichols, "Who Are You and What Do You Want: Marketing Young Adult Services," *Ohio Libraries* (Fall 1999): 19.

7. Nichols and Nichols, *Young Adults and Public Libraries,* 148.

8. Ibid, 149.

9. Sam Hill and Glenn Rifkin, *Radical Marketing: From Harvard to Harley, Lessons from Ten That Broke the Rules and Made It Big* (New York: HarperCollins, 1999).

2

Knowing the Teen Patron

Chapter 1 introduced the keys to successful marketing and merchandising—knowing who the customer is, what it is the customer wants, and being able to provide it to him or her. While this may appear as a simple equation, the first part of it is often overlooked. It is very important to know who is using the library and checking out the materials in the YA collection or attending programs and using other services. Often these are not the same people. Hordes of young adults may be milling around after school, but what is their purpose? Are they completing homework assignments or using the reference collection, magazine databases, or the Internet? Or are they looking for recreational reading, magazines, and/or comic books?

It will be easier to predict what kinds of materials to include in the YA collection if the librarian knows something about who she is trying to serve. Employing market segmentation can do this. Market segmentation divides the total group, in this case young adults aged twelve through eighteen years, into groups with unique characteristics and needs. This makes working with such a large group of youths with different developmental ages and stages more manageable. The YA population of a library community can be broken down further by age, grade, gender, genre favorites of readers, public school attendees versus private school attendees, and so forth. This list is endless.

Read any article on high school today and you will find that almost every school across the nation has athletes, cheerleaders, the hip-hop crowd, punks, nerds, the people in the band, and Goths. Each one of these groups has different likes and dislikes. Often what pleases one group will abhor another. The old adage "You can't be all things to all people" is correct. Breaking down the YA users of a library will allow the YA collection to be a bit more tailored to a segment's liking.

The best way to find out who uses the library is to roam the areas after school or whenever the majority of young adults are in the building. Direct observation can be the easiest and cheapest way to find out who visits the library and uses the collection. Often these are the avid library users seen day-to-day or week-to-week. A good librarian knows these familiar faces and talks to these best customers every day.

To survey teens, nothing too formal needs to be done. Teens will not participate in a survey that asks too many questions and requires much thought. They do not have the time. Ask simple, direct questions such as,

- What is the one thing you would like to see change in the YA area?

- Which of the following types of books do you like to read? Include a list of genres with this question.

- What is the title of one magazine you would like to see in the teen section?

Placing a suggestion box in the YA area provides teens with another forum that allows teens to tell you what they want. Have teens use this as a way to mention titles of materials (magazines, books, and audio-visual) that they would like to see purchased. Most likely, they will know about the new releases of audio and video titles before you will. Show teens that you are reading and acting upon their suggestions by typing a list of responses to their suggestions. Post your responses next to the suggestion box for all to see.

Members of teen advisory boards or student volunteers are also good indicators of who is using the YA section. Teen Advisory Boards (TABs) have become quite popular in libraries. A TAB is made up of a group of teens interested in providing input and assistance to the library services provided to them. TABs usually have designated meeting times. You may start by inviting a group of teens who you have observed to frequent the library and who you think would like to become involved in making the YA section of the library a better place. After an introductory meeting to gauge their interest level, the TAB can establish a meeting schedule.

It is fine to start with a small number of teens and meet once a month or every other month or just during the school year. The teen members will dictate how often they would like to meet and what they would like to do. Once a TAB is established, the teens can advise you on materials to add to the collection or what programs to host. The TAB members can decorate the YA area and help with the programs. The Young Adult Library Services Association publication *Youth Participation in School and Public Libraries: It Works*, edited by Carolyn Caywood (1995), will help to lay the groundwork in implementing a youth participation program at your library.

The number of teens who want to be involved can determine the need for a more formal structure, which could include bylaws, officer elections, and so forth. Participation may vary from meeting to meeting because of teens' busy schedules. If this is the case, you may want to develop some sort of mechanism for determining which teens are truly interested (such as an application process) versus those who are not and just want to eat the free pizza. At any rate, turning away teens does not foster goodwill. The formal aspects of an application form, rules, expulsion of members, and so forth will depend on the personality of the librarian in charge and his or her idea of what the group should be like.

The other key element to knowing who the young adults are is knowing what makes them tick. Any book on marketing library services to young adults is not complete until characteristics of the teen market segment are discussed. Extensive literature exists on understanding this age group, what they think, the problems they face, and the characteristics of their development. The Search Institute has gathered data on the lives of sixth through twelfth graders across the United States.[1] This research supplies a framework that allows those working with teens to provide external assets, such as providing caring and supportive relationships, boundaries and limits, and a structured use of time. In turn, this increases the chances of teens developing internal assets, such as educational commitment, positive values, and social competencies that will guide them for the rest of their lives. The more of these internal assets teens develop, the more likely they are to succeed at school and avoid problems stemming from substance abuse and sexual behavior.[2]

Staff who work with teens everywhere are often passionate about what they do, and those who are successful in their job have developed great rapport and relationships with the teens they serve. Some libraries have a clear set of rules or structure to which teens (and hopefully all patrons) must adhere. Programs or services such as teen advisory boards or teen volunteers allow for structured use of time and positive social interaction with others. Libraries have much to contribute to healthy adolescent development.

Although the various tragedies at U.S. high schools have pushed the study of teenagers onto the front covers of news magazines, the troubled nature of adolescents has been around for a long time. Americans have been speaking and fretting about "juvenile delinquents" for nearly two centuries. The generation gap between parents and children has always been present. Long ago, parents would try to cling to the traditional ways and values of the "old country" while their children learned and invented other ways to live. Parents both applauded and deplored their children's participation in a different way of life.[3] Today the same dichotomy occurs as parents and seniors resist advances in technology and look to teens to program the VCR and teach them how to establish an e-mail account while librarians utilize teen volunteers to troubleshoot computer problems and teach Internet training to seniors.

The major differences between teens today and past teenagers have to do with societal changes. Anorexia and self-mutilation seem more prevalent. Gangs, school shootings, and AIDS can be deadly. But the emotional struggles, such as the drive to become independent, remain the same. Teens continue to search for themselves and ask, "Who am I?" and "How do others perceive me?" By beginning to recognize the experiences they have shared with today's teenagers, adults working with teens can strengthen their compassion and acceptance of them. The respect, challenges, and admiration offered to them will follow.[4]

TEENS TODAY

The habits and likes of teens have been newsworthy of late because the teen market rules the world of commerce. Companies such as Teenage Research Unlimited (TRU) specialize in analyzing the growing teenage market. In Peter Zollo's (a TRU researcher and marketing consultant) *Wise Up to Teens*, he provides great insight into the minds of teens and offers ideas on how they spend their time and what makes a product brand appealing to them. Companies such as Coca-Cola, Revlon, McDonald's, and others are sitting up and taking notice of how teens are spending more than $140 billion a year on their products. The book is based on a syndicated study of teenagers, titled the "Teenage Marketing and Lifestyle Study."[5] While it may seem that Zollo's information is only important to marketing professionals, other people who deal with teens, such as those in the library field, have much to gain from the studies.

The book identifies teen activities and interests throughout the week, favorite magazines and recommended media of teens, music preferences, and so on. It also talks about the essence of being a teen and what teen life is like. Digesting this type of material can be very helpful in understanding characteristics of the teen library customer and how to market library services to him or her.

Unfortunately, many libraries have lagged behind businesses that realize that the teen market segment is too powerful to ignore. The United States is enjoying the largest teen population in its history. This is in addition to the 27 million children aged eight to fourteen years (labeled "tweens") who will be soon, or who are already, knocking on the library's doors wanting to check out the YA books and join the programs. Only naïve librarians think that the same tactics used to attract preschoolers and elementary-aged kids can be applied to the teen market. Teens are a tougher audience and creativity and perseverance are required in order to demonstrate that the library has something to meet their wants and needs. While libraries around the country are adding YA specialist positions, the number of staff whose job is solely to work with teens and understand their developmental differences is still below par. The most recent study shows that only 11 percent of the libraries in the United States employ a librarian dedicated to YA services.[6] Those in library management need to realize the importance of having a staff member work to provide quality YA services and act as a library advocate for teens. It will be necessary to hire more people to work with and for teens as this population trend continues to rise until the year 2010.

Studies have shown that teens today are extremely busy. Most start the school day early—before their brain is ready to function. After eight or so hours at school, practice for a sport or extracurricular activity usually begins. After a quick dinner at home, a teen may run to a job and work a few hours until closing. The rest of the evening hours can be occupied by homework, television, listening to music (usually all at the same time). Weekends aren't any less busy, with more extracurricular activities, work, and hanging out with friends.[7] Much of this schedule is self-inflicted, but important for those in the library field to know about. Teen schedules explain why their use of the library tends to lessen after the age of fifteen. Young adults have so little time to actually spend in the library. As a result librarians need to be active, not passive, in their role in vying for a teen's time. This means employing techniques such as savvy merchandising efforts (known before only to bookstores) that help teens choose the material they want and need.

It cannot be stressed enough that to be successful in working with teens one needs to be aware of the world in which the teens live. Patricia Hersch, author of *A Tribe Apart*, suggests some obvious advice on how to have better relationships with this next generation of adults. First and foremost, be real. Their world is not what you would expect, so get out and get informed. Young adults will never accept guidance from someone who is unaware of their reality. Also be available to them and be involved with them through communication. It is also important to be the adult that you are and not to be intimidated by them.[8]

How does one become informed about the fast-paced lives that teens live? One way is to read what teens read. YA magazines such as *Teen People*, *YM*, and *Rolling Stone*, among others, make excellent lunchtime reading for librarians. This will give you a window into their world. It is a way to become familiar with trends and what is hot in the teen world. Make yourself familiar with the school and community life of teens in your service area. Read the school newspaper and monitor what is happening in the teen community. Frequent the coffeehouses or music stores where they shop. Ask TAB members or teen library employees. Set up a TAB that provides you with information on what they need and want. Or find a more informal way of talking to the teens in the library. Just ask, and they will not let you down. Many librarians who run book discussion groups or hold TAB meetings know that it is necessary to have a social time before they get down to business. After all, with teens so much has happened since school let out two or three hours ago. There is plenty to talk about. Social time provides an excellent opportunity to just listen and to take in their language and what is going on in their lives.

Tracking teen pop culture can be very hard because some trends may disappear before a magazine can hit the shelves. That is why keeping track of who is a hot superstar or what is a new fashion trend needs to be an ongoing process. Reading *Teen People* once a year will not work. Erin Helmrich and Wendy Woltjer (two librarians who write for *Voice of Youth Advocates* [*VOYA*]) give the following suggestions on how to become more teen savvy:

1. Watch one teen television show per week.

2. Look at one teen magazine per week.

3. Watch any MTV news show for a quick dose of music news.

4. Talk to teens to find out what they like.

5. Check out teen-friendly and teen-informative websites.[9]

Also be on the lookout for articles published about teens. Every major news magazine has cover articles about teenagers. The Carnegie Council for Adolescent Development provides reports on teens. Books like Jane Pratt's *For Real: The Uncensored*

Truth About America's Teenagers (Hyperion, 1995) give insight into what teens are thinking, as well as Zollo's aforementioned book. Gallup publishes "YOUTHviews," a newsletter of the Gallup Youth Survey. Studies of teens are being conducted, and those results offer invaluable insight to librarians. Shell Oil Company collaborated with the U.S. Department of Education and Peter D. Hart Research Associates to inquire into the lives of one thousand high school students. Done in the wake of the Columbine tragedy, the survey asked teens about problems they face, how they felt about their education, their concerns for the future, and personal qualities they admire. For results of this survey see www.shell.us.com. Information such as this gives the reader an idea of the worries and thrills of teenagers and allows him to be more empathetic to them. Listservs that are youth- or YA-related can also be a good source of information. Many times subscribers will mention book or article titles that can help in becoming informed. The more a librarian can learn about teens, the better able she will be to predict their behavior and provide a collection of materials that will fly off the shelves and services that are fully utilized.

NOTES

1. Search Institute, 700 South Third Street, Minneapolis, MN, 55415; 1-800-888-7828; www.search-institute.org

2. Peter Scales, "A Responsive Ecology for Positive Adolescent Development," *The Clearing House* 69, no. 4 (1996): 226.

3. Thomas Hine, "The Rise and Decline of the Teenager," *American Heritage* 50, no. 5 (1999): 70.

4. Kimberly Kirkberger, "Are Teens Today That Different?" *Life* 22, no. 3 (1999): 48.

5. Teen Research Unlimited, 707 Skokie Boulevard, 7th Floor, Northbrook, IL 60062; (847) 564-3440; www.teenresearch.com

6. U.S. Department of Education. Office of Educational Research and Improvement. 1995. *Services and Resources for Children and Young Adults in Public Libraries.*

7. Margaret Littman, "Generation Stressed: Life on a Treadmill," *Teen Magazine* 43, no. 4 (1999): 78.

8. Lisa Wrenn, "How to Reconnect with Teens," Knight Ridder/Tribune Service, August 24, 1999: pk5757.

9. Erin Helmrich with Wendy Woltjer, "Teen Pop Culture: Are You Keeping Up?" *VOYA* (October 1999): 241.

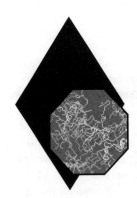

3

The YA Collection—Giving Them What They Want

Chapter 2 deals with who uses the YA section of the library. The next key element in a successful marketing equation is knowing the types of materials to include in the collection that will interest the teen patron. The simplest way to meet this challenge is to take heed of teen requests and follow up by purchasing those items. Teens can make their requests known in a variety of ways. An inexpensive way can be to set up a suggestion box. A dry erase board mounted on the wall or on an easel in the YA area can also be used as a forum where teens can speak informally. With both of these venues, be prepared to weed out the obscenities! Conducting a short survey, as mentioned later in this chapter, can be another way to find out what teens like to read. Don't forget to check the return carts or circulation records. Ordering materials similar to those continually checked out can be a successful way of targeting teens.

The idea of following patron demand has always made the most sense to someone interested in the marketing process. However, the idea of "giving people what they want" does not sit well with everyone in the library profession. Many librarians feel that offering popular materials (in the case of YA fiction, an example would be series paperbacks) appeals to the lowest taste of the public.[1] Others feel that materials such as comic books, graphic novels, or magazines do nothing to further the education of teens. However, it is important to remember that librarians in public libraries have no teaching responsibilities. Public libraries make information and recreation affordable to the general public through sharing. Placing value judgments on things such as series fiction or comic books can be considered a violation of the intellectual freedom that librarians profess to hold so dear.[2]

It is important to know the customer and provide a good dose of what he or she wants and expects the library to own, along with other items that can have appeal but may need pushing because patrons are not familiar with them or even know the library has them. Achieving this balance may be easier said than done. The easy part is buying the materials that young adults have requested and will fly off the shelves. Systematically reviewing the vast amount of exciting new materials (not to mention the backlists!) and finding things that will appeal to your target audience's varied tastes can be the more difficult task. Using what you know about the tastes of the young adults in your community is the starting point for looking at the materials. The next important step is finding items that are like the ones they ask for, but different enough to stretch their tastes and maybe lead them on to something else. This process needs to be monitored and refined. Often, some highly acclaimed book just bombs with young adults. Don't take this personally; just make sure that those items that are continually sitting on the shelf or circulating very little in a reasonable amount of time are removed. Efforts to merchandise may or may not help a title's appeal. If everything fails, use it as an opportunity to make room for another more marketable title.

Young adults will appreciate seeing things on the shelves that are of interest to them. They will know that they have been identified. Anyone who is serious about merchandising should understand this. The whole goal of merchandising is to make the collection enticing and exciting to teens so that they will want to check out handfuls of materials. This goal can best be accomplished with merchandising and display strategies that highlight an up-to-date collection that meets the public's needs and wants.

COLLECTION ISSUES

Many things may influence the type of collection a library can offer. A library's collection development policy may not allow for the inclusion of popular YA items such as comic books. This may cause some friction for the staff member who would like to utilize merchandising techniques in the library. It is up to you to change the attitudes of staff members in order to please young adults. It is a lonely job, but you are probably the only staff member that knows what teens are requesting and really believes that something needs to be done to fill the shelves with what they want. If you meet some resistance catering to the tastes of teens, do some homework. This requires good research skills and thinking about what your management will want to see. It may be that you talk to some teens, teachers, and parents and relay their views to the people who make the decisions in your library. Your library management may require you to write up a formal proposal citing articles you have researched or studies/surveys that you have conducted. If this is the case, gather as much supporting information as you can and assemble it into a concise report. Often, librarians will post queries on the listservs (i.e., PUBYAC, YALSA-BK, and YALSA-L) and ask their colleagues for suggestions on what to do in certain situations. This can be helpful because these people may have already done exactly what you wish to do. Their answers will provide varied ways of tackling the problem, and often they will share information on what worked or maybe what they should have done differently. Many times listserv discussions will mention new articles or books written in the YA publishing world that will help you state your case. Even if you just lurk, you can pick up valuable information on how other people make things work in their library.

You can also look to others in your community to help you make some changes. Libraries in neighboring communities may provide a service that you wish to initiate. In the case of adding graphic novels or comic books to your collection, ask a library close by for a copy of their collection development policy. See if the librarian will share usage statistics. When doing comparisons, make sure that you look to libraries of similar size or community demographics as your library. Statistics from a library that shares no commonalties with your library will mean nothing to your director and will be a waste of your time.

Work to change negative staff attitudes about young adults whenever you can. If you can change their views, they can help you make your case stronger. Make short presentations at staff meetings or staff in-service days. Have teens come in and give testimonials. Look to the community to provide experts on topics. For example, there may be teachers, other librarians, and education professionals from the local college or university or community groups that can help you win your case. Enlighten staff with research on how graphic novels can reach elusive older young adults. Reluctant readers who just read magazines or comic books may go on to read books later in life or even later in the school year when they have more time. The book *Serious About Series: Evaluations and Annotations of Teen Fiction in Paperback Series* by Silk Makowski (Lanham, MD: Scarecrow, 1998) takes the guesswork out of selecting the best series and can be helpful in making a case for adding them to a YA collection. Use the literature out there. *VOYA* has a monthly column dedicated to series paperbacks. Also, *What's So Scary About R. L. Stine?* by Patrick Jones (Scarecrow, 1998) sheds light on why Stine should be considered as a viable YA author. Hopefully your research done in library and education resources can provide you with enough information to develop a proposal to include materials that young adults request and bring a reconsideration of the collection development policy.

A librarian's own professional values may be put to the test. A personal distaste may need to be put aside in order to fulfill patrons' wants or needs. Also, some librarians just are not aware of teen tastes. This again stresses the importance of finding out teen likes and dislikes as mentioned in Chapter 2. For example, the skateboarders who congregate in the library's parking lot and use the handicapped access as their ramps may be a nuisance to staff. However, they would probably appreciate seeing *Warp* on the magazine rack. You will see few librarians at a wrestling match, yet *WWF Magazine* probably won't sit on the shelf for very long. Barnes & Noble held a focus group of boys aged eleven through fourteen and discovered that the one hardcover each boy had purchased in common was the autobiography of World Wrestling Federation's Mankind (aka Mick Foley).[3] The American Library Association (ALA) has added wrestling figures, which attract girls as well as boys, to their famous line of READ posters.

It may be that your collection defies the community's views on certain lifestyles and what materials are appropriate age-wise. Even though parents would like to think that teens are not sexually active, that may not be the case. Teens need information on options and agencies to turn to in the case of teen pregnancy or sexually transmitted diseases. Also, many teens silently struggle with questions about their sexuality. Despite many negative views on homosexuality in today's society, a library needs to be a place where teens can become informed and find materials (fiction and nonfiction) about others who are dealing with these issues or have resolved their identity.

Librarians may feel that when buying more popular titles, the professionalism of their job suffers. After all, aren't libraries bastions of knowledge and keepers of good literature? If we use the selection criteria of "Will it move?" aren't we missing a whole lot of acclaimed published works that may have touched someone? Ann Sparanese's chapter "R. L. Stine Meets Horatio Alger: Quality Versus Popularity in the Young Adult Collection" provides an excellent discussion on this age-old debate.[4] The bottom line is that it will be much easier to attract teens to your collection if they see more items that they have requested and that reflect their lives. You will still be able to find quality items that fit your collection mix and meet the varied tastes of your teens. These items can be the focus of your marketing and merchandising efforts.

A COOL COLLECTION

The findings from the DeWitt Wallace–Reader's Digest study, "Public Libraries as Partners in Youth Development," brought home what many librarians had in the back of their minds: Teens think that libraries are *not* cool.[5] A well-merchandised collection can go a long way to change that line of thinking. First and foremost, the YA collection needs to be separated and on its own. This ensures maximum exposure to teens. Literature in the business and library worlds supports this statement. Studies on teen products show that teens prefer things that are specifically for them, whether it is language, fashion, advertising, or brands.[6] Peter Zollo found that cool products must appeal specifically to teens, be relevant and desirable, and take advantage of teens' aspirations toward their next goal of achievement or accomplishment.[7] Elise Howard, head of the Young Readers program at Avon Books, also states that YA books need to get out of the children's section. "No self-respecting thirteen-year-old wants to walk past the *Goodnight Moon* plush toys or even *Animorphs* to find books. After reading a YA novel I'd given her, one girl told me, 'I love this book, but I'd never find it [in the YA section].' "[8] This just reiterates what many librarians with popular YA areas have put into practice. The YA collection should be as far away from the children's area as possible. The best place is near adult materials—magazines, videos, classic literature, even career materials. This provides a natural progression for the younger young adults into using adult works and accommodates the older teens who use the adult collection as well.

Teens in the DeWitt Wallace–Reader's Digest survey also stated that having a distinct place of their own in libraries would be advantageous. This would separate them from the many adult patrons and place them away from the noise and mess of younger children.[9] Several youths also wanted clearer arrangements of materials shelved together or color coded for age groups as well as paperback series shelved together.[10]

One of the most important things a library can do to show that they want to target teens is to offer them a collection of materials of their own. This project really takes no extra money, so it can be done in even the smallest library with the smallest budget. It may take some creative shifting of materials, but it could be as easy as pulling all YA-related materials out of the whole collection and shelving them together. Label the books with a "YA" spine sticker available from suppliers like Demco, design a sign, and you are in business. It is understandable that not every library can have a huge YA area or room with tables and chairs, and so forth, but every library needs to have a separate YA collection. If a library is really short on space and money, provide just a section of YA fiction or magazines. Teens can use the adult collection for reference and homework assistance, saving YA money for popular items. Some small libraries may have a spinner rack of YA paperbacks. This can be strategically placed next to a bulletin board or blank wall space that can house posters. While this is not ideal and may not seem like much, it still gives teens a collection to call their own.

YA budgets are usually smaller than their adult and juvenile counterparts. Work creatively and cooperatively with the selectors who choose adult and juvenile materials, as well as audio-visual works. Many items that fall into their categories cross over to YA appeal. Working together can stretch budget dollars and give you the opportunity to purchase other things. Merchandising efforts may seem futile for libraries with small collections and budgets. This is not true. When the shelves are not crowded, it is physically easier to browse among the books. There are more opportunities to display books on the ends of the shelves, face out rather than spine out. Hence, the number of materials is not as important as the mix of materials.[11] Libraries with large budgets need to understand this as well. Teens grow frustrated when library collections do not allow them to complete school projects and research. They want multiple copies of books needed for assignments or more copies of books they want.[12]

Teens are used to immediate gratification or quick answers to their questions via the Internet. No teen likes to hear that his request for a book is unfulfilled because copies are checked out. Often, after assignments are given, one teen comes to the library and checks out everything the library owns to complete the assignment. The practice of buying multiple copies of quality books on a topic can remedy this problem. One student cannot wipe out an entire shelf of books on abortion, and several students can be served. Working with the schools becomes necessary to procure required reading lists and topics of assignments requiring the use of nonfiction. Multiple copies of popular fiction or paperback series also help in immediately gratifying teens. It may be necessary to do the same with magazine subscriptions or any other type of material (CDs, etc.) that is frequently requested.

Before discussing the composition of YA collections, it is worthwhile to mention a contemporary movement in youth literature that has received some recent recognition. Eliza T. Dresang, associate professor of Information Studies at Florida State University, has given the name "radical change" to the fundamental departures from traditional literature in books.[13] Many books published today address the world of the "Net Generation." These people, born after 1977, have never known a time without computers and electronic media. Growing up using a computer and processing digitized information has resulted in different thought patterns. Net Generation brains have learned to process information in small bits and bytes. Books of the radical change movement allow the reader to peruse a book in a sequence that is logical to him, flipping back and forth in a non-linear pattern. This is similar to pointing and clicking with a mouse.

The most fitting books in this category are the increasingly popular non-fiction books published by Dorling Kindersley. The photograph-laden works allow the reader to browse bits of information on a different topic on each page. This approach to learning can make even the dullest subject more appealing and easier to digest than the black-and-white photographs and long, boring texts of books of yesteryear.

Radical change can also encompass works of fiction. In these works, words may no longer be organized in neat paragraphs with complete thoughts. They may instead reflect a character's way of thinking, as in Virginia Euwer Wolff's *True Believer*. Recently, more books have been written in free-flowing verse such as Karen Hesse's *Witness* and Sonya Sones's *What My Mother Doesn't Know*. Multiple perspectives can affect the way a story is told. Chapters may alternate offering the perspectives of different characters. In *Smack* by Melvin Burgess, every chapter offers a different character's point of view. The story is told through multiple perspectives. Radical change fiction can also be written in the form of diary entries or through letter writing, as in *The Perks of Being a Wallflower* by Stephen Chbosky.

While this introduction to radical change is brief, it is worthwhile to further research the topic in order to include these books in a YA collection. A librarian informed of this concept will offer a collection that has much more appeal and therefore is easier to merchandise than traditional linear formats. Substantial evidence exists that youth are likely to engage and stay engaged when they have digital resources such as the ones mentioned to access information. The interactivity of these resources connects them with the active learning of real life.[14]

AND THE SURVEY SAYS . . .

A survey conducted for *Publishers Weekly* in June of 1998 offers some encouraging news. The survey included a sample of one hundred teens aged twelve through seventeen and was conducted in shopping malls across the country and through telephone interviews. An overwhelming majority of teens surveyed think that reading is fun and makes them feel smarter than teens that don't pick up a book.[15]

A more recent survey conducted online by SmartGirl.com reinforces the *PW* findings. In the fall of 1999, SmartGirl.com and the Young Adult Library Services Association (YALSA), a division of ALA, joined together to encourage young people to consider the value and fun of reading. The survey was posted on the SmartGirl website from October 2 to October 25, 1999, in conjunction with the YALSA-sponsored Teen Read Week. Three thousand seventy-two teens (ages eleven through eighteen) from across the United States responded. The sample included 1,826 girls and 1,246 boys. Seventy-two percent of the respondents said that they like to read for pleasure when they have time; of that group 36 percent say they read constantly for their own satisfaction. When the teens are not reading books, they read magazines (two-thirds of respondents), the newspaper (59 percent), and even the back of a cereal box (48 percent)! As one might expect, more girls than boys, 50 percent to 32 percent, respectively, read most often for the fun of it. Eighty-one percent of girls would most likely read more if they had more time compared to only 62 percent of boys. Many teens were quoted as saying they like to read because it stretches their imagination and allows them to temporarily leave their current situation and takes them somewhere else. When asked why don't they read more or why don't they like to read, many cited a lack of time. Most said they were too busy with homework and extracurricular activities.[16]

When the teens were asked what kinds of characters they liked to read about, over 55 percent of the young adults (67 percent girls versus 36 percent boys) chose "people or characters like me" from a list. The second highest category of people teens like to read about were celebrities. Other popular choices were people or characters their age who have done a cool or amazing thing, characters from movies or television shows, and characters their age wrestling with tough issues (crime, drug abuse, and poverty). The survey also asked teens to mention which genres they preferred to read. Mystery, adventure, and horror stories were mentioned the most by teens while bio/autobiographies and factual books received the least mention. Table 1 provides the results of the survey question regarding genre preferences.[17]

Table 1. Most Popular Genres

Genre	Percent of Teens Mentioning
Mystery Stories	61
Adventure	57
Horror	56
True Stories	53
Fantasy	50
Science Fiction	36
Romance	36
Sports	33
Bio/autobiography	29
Factual books	20

Source: www.SmartGirl.com

Teens responded that they "sometimes" read about things they are passionate about. A sampling of their passions include aliens, romantic things about or between teenagers, animal rights, vegetarianism, the paranormal, and sports.

Valuable surveys such as SmartGirl.com allow librarians to better understand teen reading interests and habits. This allows for developing more effective strategies to raise or maintain teens' interest in reading. In addition, a less formal survey can be conducted in the YA section of any library. A quick survey can be developed in-house and can include questions such as "Do you read magazines, newspapers, comic books, and so forth?" "Do you prefer fiction or nonfiction?" "What types of fiction do you like best?" Have young adults check off favorites from a list of genres. Do the same for nonfiction. A short survey can give you localized information pertinent to your community. It will be easy to see what types of books to include in your collection. Another quick and easy way to see what teens in your area are reading can be within the structure of a contest or program. For example, a summer reading promotion may require teens to read books and enter their names for prize drawings. Design the entry slip to have a section to include the title of the book they read and have them circle a thumbs up or thumbs down symbol to share their like/dislike of the book. The portion of the slip that includes the participant's name can be detached and put in the entry box. The portion with the book title, after noted by you, can be displayed on an attractive bulletin board with the headline "Looking for a good read?" These reader recommendations not only offer a quick display, but also double as a reader's advisory mechanism. Teens are more likely to read something recommended by someone their own age than a book selected by the librarian.

Research has shown that teens prefer paperbacks to hardbacks. The aforementioned *PW* survey found that 79 percent of teens most often purchase paperbacks rather than hardcovers.[18] Likewise, David Gale, an executive editor at Simon & Schuster Books for Young Readers, states that teenagers don't like hardcover books because they remind them of schoolbooks. Paperbacks are easier to carry, and teens like the sophisticated look of adult trade paperbacks.[19] These two publisher perspectives may not be the steadfast rule for your own library. Tracking circulation records gives you a picture of what teens are checking out. If your budget is small, the majority of the money needs to go toward paperbacks, which are easier to merchandise anyway. Authors that are usually popular with your teen crowd can be purchased when they are released as hardcovers. The down side of this strategy is that you may have to wait on great literature, such as *Speak*, the first novel by Laurie Halse Anderson. Buying mostly low-cost paperbacks allows for multiple copies of a hot title.

Aside from asking teens what books they would like to see in the collection and reading reviews in journals, many librarians turn to award lists as aids in collection development. YALSA awards books yearly to lists such as Quick Picks for Reluctant Readers and Popular Paperbacks, which are chosen because of their appeal to teens. While YALSA's other award lists, Best Books for Young Adults, Outstanding Books for the College Bound, the Printz award, the ALEX awards (adult books for young adults), and Selected Films and Videos contain titles that have some appeal, the two aforementioned lists will have titles that are easiest to merchandise. All of these are easily accessible through YALSA's website at www.ala.org/yalsa

/booklists. Review sources also publish "best" lists. *VOYA* has a nonfiction honor roll, books in the middle (books to reach middle grades), and best of science fiction/ fantasy/horror lists. *Booklist* provides editor's choices and reprints ALA's best lists. Lists such as these offer recommended titles, chosen by librarians from all over the country.

FICTION

When people think of a YA collection, they are usually thinking about works of fiction. In a YA popular reading collection, fiction may outweigh nonfiction by as much as three to one.[20] Fiction titles make merchandising and display an easy job. Not all new teen releases are quickie biographies of the "crushes" or hot teen idols young adults read about in popular magazines or stars of their favorite television shows. YA books have become edgier and reflect teen lives today. Publishers are looking differently at a burgeoning $30-million youth market. Since teens make more purchasing decisions than teens of other eras did, publishers see them as powerhouses of opinions, culture, spending, and fashion. As a result new imprints have been created such as MTV books, Pocket Pulse, and Avon Tempest to provide teen products. Books are now published with adult-looking packaging, darker story lines, and flashy multi-media marketing.[21] Publishers are advertising their new books in magazines such as *Seventeen* and *Teen People*, and they are chatted up on teen Internet sites. This reiterates the need for the YA librarian to peruse YA magazines, culture, and websites.

The term *fiction* covers many different things. Fiction can include quality literature reviewed in journals and appearing on award lists, as well as the series paper-backs featuring teens either being bludgeoned by bloody knives or looking dreamily at each other in front of a locker backdrop. Most librarians love to purchase the quality literature and dream that young adults will stand in line to check them out. Reality is that teens would opt for the bloody, vampire cover. That is not an argument to cease buying quality YA literature. Young adults may not realize that some really good stuff is being published for them. This is where merchandising techniques can play a vital role. Creative displays or selecting a title as a suggestion for a book discussion group can draw attention to better books. Many students start reading classics as early as seventh grade. This cuts off the whole world of YA fiction. Teachers often label YA fiction as romance paperbacks or horror novels. Publishers spend a lot of time marketing to educators because teachers share a limited knowledge of the richness and depth of YA literature. Despite this, appreciation of YA titles among teachers is limited.[22] It then becomes the librarian's job to enlighten educators and turn them on to the compelling plots of YA fiction. Newer YA titles are more current and fast-moving than some of the old classics.

An absolute must of any YA fiction collection is the inclusion of YA paper-back series. While these titles may lack the traditional literary qualities of the books that make YALSA's Best Books for Young Adults list, their enormous popularity with teens cannot be disputed. Offering YA series lures teens into the YA area. Once there, your merchandising efforts can help them find other titles not in the series that interest them. Having series fiction also shows that you are there to serve young adults and to cater to their tastes. It is a good idea to join a series standing order plan with a distributor such as Book Wholesalers, Inc. A standing order plan allows you to chose series ahead of time. As each entry to the series is released, it will arrive at your library. Since you have preselected these series groups, there is no need to track down the next title and worry about gaps in the series. This can be a real time-saver and makes sense if you know young adults will want every Sweet Valley Senior Year title that is written.

Many of the teen paperback series reflect what teens are watching on television or at the movies. A TRU teenage marketing and lifestyle study shows that watching television is the number one teen leisure activity. Ninety-eight percent of teens in the study watch television for just over eleven hours per week.[23] Favorites such as *Dawson's Creek*, *Buffy the Vampire Slayer*, the *X-Files*, *Roswell*, and *Charmed* on the library shelves will again cater to YA tastes.

A YA fiction collection should include as many genres as possible, providing readers with the best in each category. The word *genre* is French for type or category, and so genres in literature are categories of writing that share common characteristics and patterns.[24] Genres include romance, science fiction, fantasy, horror/ thriller, mystery, adventure, humor, historical fiction, realistic fiction, sports, short-story collections, and multicultural literature.

Graphic novels are another type of fiction but appeal more to the older young adults. A graphic novel resembles a comic book in form and format. While this format is becoming more mainstream, the *Voice of Youth Advocates* can keep you updated with Katherine "Kat" Kan's column.

NONFICTION

Nonfiction has come a long way from the drab black-and-white line drawings and mostly boring text to bright photographs surrounded by snippets of information. Thanks to publishers such as Dorling Kindersley, YA nonfiction can add exciting dimensions to displays and merchandising. Many teen readers enjoy nonfiction topics in a leisurely non-academic setting. Well-written nonfiction, read at a person's own pace—be it biographies, sports stories, or "how to"—can provide a painless and stimulating supplement to classroom lectures and textbooks.[25] Other nonfiction, such as college guides and career planning resources, meets the needs of older young adults.

It is necessary to determine to what extent your library supports the school district's curriculum. This may guide you in your selection and set the parameters of your collection. Make sure the nonfiction is current and the information is presented in a manner that is easy to use. While nonfiction probably won't constitute a large part of the overall YA collection, the quality of titles recently published should not be overlooked. These newer titles appeal to teens' interests in areas such as sports, art, biography, and so forth. One of the newest trends in nonfiction for teens are self-help titles, which seem to appeal the most to girls. Books such as *Chicken Soup for the Teenage Soul*, *Taste Berries for Teens*, and titles that offer advice on such things as beauty, their bodies, and love seem to fly off the library shelves and are hot sellers in bookstores as well.

MAGAZINES/COMIC BOOKS

Any library collection serious about serving teens needs to include magazines. Zollo found that 76 percent of teens surveyed read magazines for pleasure.[26] Because of teen discretionary income, magazines are created just for them because advertising executives find them a lucrative market. Teens, especially girls, love magazines because of their currency. Fads in this month's *Seventeen* may be gone by the next issue. No better way exists to keep up with the fast-changing trends of teen culture. According to Zollo, teen girls rely more on magazines for the latest trends than on any other information source, including friends, peers, and other media outlets.[27] Magazines appeal to the short attention span of young adults. Likewise, it is easier to quickly browse a magazine on a tight schedule than read a whole novel. The cost per circulation of a magazine is much lower than that of a hardcover book. Also, magazines, when shelved face out, are a perfect merchandising tool. The covers are current, bright, and attention-grabbing.

The SmartGirl.com survey found that a majority of teens read magazines covering a variety of subjects such as fashion/beauty, music, computers, entertainment, sports, video games, news, and humor. Zollo's TRU teenage and marketing lifestyle study finds that *Seventeen* and *YM* are the strongest in the field, with *Teen* close behind.[28] For a good listing of popular YA magazines, review Patrick Jones's book *Connecting Young Adults and Libraries*, 2d edition (Neal-Schuman, 1998). The teen magazine market is booming, and many new titles are being created for them. Each new title will attempt to create its own market niche.

Comic books are very popular with teen readers and can be bought through subscriptions like magazines or, even better, through your local comic book store dealer. Comics, which attract boys, are inexpensive and have a high circulation. Comics suffer from negative comments and the myth that they cause juvenile delinquency. The bottom line is that librarians usually don't like them and come up with various reasons why to not include them in their collections. This is a huge mistake, as any twelve-year-old boy will gladly tell you.

AUDIO VISUAL

The only way to know what kinds of music to have in your collection is to ask the young adults. Music tastes vary widely, not just from state to state, but more realistically from neighborhood to neighborhood. Often teen library employees offer good suggestions and can give you an idea of what is popular. Zollo's survey found that after watching television, teens spend most of their leisure time listening to FM radio or listening to CDs and tapes.[29] Boys mentioned alternative music as their favorite radio format, followed closely by rap. Girls cited alternative music as their favorite, followed by R and B.[30]

MTV was the top cable channel of choice for both girls and boys. Watching MTV can give the librarian a clue as to what bands are out there, as well as trends in fashion and language. *Billboard* magazine is helpful in selection, as well as visiting music stores to see how they merchandise their titles. Music stores often give away promotional posters or cardboard displays if you just ask. These freebies can spice up the YA area in your library.

As a rule, most YA librarians don't buy videos specifically for the YA collection. It is important to make suggestions to the A/V librarian to include video/DVD titles that appeal to teens. An increase in movies made for teens has them spending more at the box office than before. Marketers have noted that teens are flocking to movie theaters and are attracting these fans with promotional tie-ins and cross promotions. It is very likely to find casts promoting lines of clothing popular with teens. Finding their favorite flicks on library shelves will make teens happy.

Another popular A/V item can be books on tape. How often has the library been inundated with requests for the books-on-tape version of a classic novel that just so happened to be on the summer reading list? This call usually comes the week before school is to start. A good way to help these circulate is to shelve them together with the actual books, *Cliffs Notes*, and the movie version, if available. This merchandising "package" can put smiles on the faces of students who have waited until the last week, after holding on to the list all summer. Mobile teens may prefer books-on-tape versions of popular fiction as well.

COLLECTION MAINTENANCE

Any merchandising efforts will be lost if the collection is in bad shape. No one will check out books in need of repair or that contain dated information. The same is true for torn-to-shreds magazines with all of the cute guys cut out. Weeding is important because it keeps the collection current, attractive, and responsive to the community's needs. Don't forget to remove books on celebrities whose popularity has faded. Keeping up with current movies, television shows, and music will help. Teen library staff members and those involved in your teen advisory board will probably love to look over that section of the collection and make recommendations as to who is hot and who is not. It also ensures the most productive use of space. This is especially important to YA librarians, who usually don't have much space to spare. Closely monitoring the collection and weeding as necessary will increase circulation. Weeding out the old stuff will make room for newer, flashier titles. Because a worn-out paperback has circulated over sixty times is not a valid reason to keep it. Reorder a new copy and two duplicates of it as well. Keeping a close eye on your collection also alerts you to materials that you can promote or use in ways you had not thought about.

Audio-visual items will need to be continually weeded as well. High usage and wear and tear can wreak havoc on CDs and videos. Patrons will often complain that the sound/video quality is bad, signaling the need for either a replacement or a deletion from the collection. Monitoring the A/V collection is also necessary to keep up on what has mysteriously left the building without being checked out. Obtain a computer printout of your holdings and check it against what is actually on the shelves. Most computer systems will allow you to track missing items over a certain amount of time before you delete them from the computer. Instead of brooding over missing items, expect that it will happen and replace them.

Maintaining an attractive collection is an on-going process, but is well worth the effort. Don't stop at weeding just the collection. That ripped-up or graffiti-ridden poster hanging crooked on the wall is not doing anything to help attract users. Sloppy, handmade signage, even if it is temporary for a special collection or event, has no place in a library serious about merchandising. Be aware of the whole picture. Look at the condition of the furniture and shelving. No one wants to sit on a filthy, ripped cushion. Maintain the furniture as you would the collection. Remove graffiti and clean, repair, or replace fixtures as needed. Even a rickety and squeaky paperback spinner can deter a teen from browsing. Shelving books face out on a shelf that is tilted or unsteady will not encourage young adults to further investigate titles. Who wants to pick up a book off the shelf and run the risk of causing an avalanche of falling display books? That would just solicit unwanted attention and result in dirty looks from library staff. Every time you enter the YA area, look at it with a critical eye. Is it screaming with old dirty books that have fallen over or are crammed on the shelves? Or is it clean and inviting with flashy books and exciting covers? Everyone should choose the latter.

NOTES

1. The Baltimore County Public Library's Blue Ribbon Committee, *Give 'Em What They Want!: Managing the Public's Library* (Chicago: American Library Association, 1992), 5.

2. Ibid.

3. Gayle Feldman, "Professional Wrestling vs. Harry Potter," *New York Times* (March 3, 2000), c15(N).

4. Mary Anne Nichols and C. Allen Nichols, *Young Adults and Public Libraries: A Handbook of Materials and Services* (Westport, CT: Greenwood Press, 1998).

5. Elaine Meyers, "The Coolness Factor: Libraries Listen to Youth," *American Libraries* (November 1999): 42.

6. "Teens, Products, and Brands," *Folio: The Magazine for Magazine Management* 28, no. 8 (July 1, 1999): 11.

7. Meyers, "The Coolness Factor," p. 45.

8. Elise Howard, "Making YA Cool for Teens," *Publishers Weekly* (June 1, 1998): 33.

9. Meyers, "The Coolness Factor," p. 44.

10. Ibid.

11. The Baltimore County Public Library's Blue Ribbon Committee, *Give 'Em What They Want*, p. 59.

12. Meyers, "The Coolness Factor," p. 44.

13. Eliza T. Dresang, *Radical Change: Books for Youth in a Digital Age* (New York: H. W. Wilson, 1999).

14. Ibid., 267.

15. Amanda Ferguson, "Reading Seen as Cool," *Publishers Weekly* (October 12, 1998): 30.

16. www.SmartGirl.com/results/trwreadingpref.html

17. Ibid.

18. Ferguson, "Reading Seen as Cool," p. 30.

19. David Gale, "What Teens Are Reading: A Publisher's Perspective," *Journal of Youth Services* (Fall 1999): 10.

20. Evie Wilson-Longbloom, *Hangin' Out at Rocky Creek* (Metuchen, NJ: Scarecrow Press, 1994), 106.

21. Clarissa Cruz, "No Kidding," *Entertainment Weekly* (October 15, 1999): 19.

22. Howard, "Making YA Cool," p. 33.

23. Peter Zollo, *Wise Up to Teens: Insights into Marketing and Advertising to Teenagers,* 2d ed. (Ithaca, NY: New Strategist Publications, Inc., 1999), 98.

24. Mary Arnold, "I Want Another Book Like . . . Young Adults and Genre Literature," in *Young Adults and Public Libraries*, edited by Mary Anne Nichols and C. Allen Nichols. (Westport, CT: Greenwood, 1998), 11.

25. Catherine Ritchie, "Where Do I Begin? Developing a Core Collection for Young Adults," in *Young Adults and Public Libraries: A Handbook of Materials and Services* (Westport, CT: Greenwood, 1998), 47.

26. Zollo, *Wise Up to Teens*, p. 98.

27. Ibid., 73.

28. Ibid., 74.

29. Ibid., 98.

30. Ibid., 70.

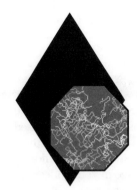

4

Merchandising Your YA Collection

O nce you have determined the unique nature of your teen patrons and realized their real needs, it is time to find a way to provide to them what they want from your library. What they want is not limited to what they ask for, but it also can be those efforts that attempt to fulfill their needs. This is where merchandising becomes important.

Merchandising is a part of the whole marketing process. It is basically concerned with the distribution or placement of items in your library in order to make the public more aware of your collection, with the ultimate goal of enticing patrons to borrow those materials. All aspects of marketing, including recognizing patron needs, promoting your services, and offering a good location in the community, bring patrons into the building, but it then becomes the job of the merchandise, the staff, and the building itself to make people want to check out materials. Merchandising involves "selling" library materials to customers by creating displays and using creative shelving and storage methods to catch the attention of the teen library patron. Its goal is to allow customers to see items they might not be familiar with and to check out items on impulse. Therefore, successful merchandising efforts allow YA browsers to choose something in addition to what they originally set out to find.

Why does merchandising play an important role in library services to young adults? YA reading tastes are as varied and diverse as the young adults themselves. Typically, teens do not ask for suggestions from library staff when looking for materials. A YALSA-sponsored program on teens and research skills at the 2000 ALA Annual Conference in Chicago reinforces this statement. A panel of teenagers present at the program admitted that they want help in finding information but rarely turn to a librarian to ask for it. When asked why, one teen responded, "I think it is a bit of pride. Teenagers think it's like being a little kid to go and ask a librarian."[1] If teens feel like little kids asking for help for important information needed to complete a school assignment, you can bet the chances of their asking for suggestions on pleasure reading are slim. The majority of teens accept suggestions on what to read, listen to, or watch from their friends and find materials themselves through browsing. It then becomes the job of the library collection to sell itself to YA patrons. A well-merchandised collection will aid young adults when browsing for materials and make it easier for them to find things to their liking. As discussed in Chapter 3, if you have done your home-work as librarian and figured out what the teens would like to see in your collection, much of your work is done. Learning the principles of merchandising in a library will allow you to use these materials in eye-catching displays in order to move them off the shelves and into the hands of young adults.

Business establishments are continually improving their merchandising techniques to sell their products for the maximum profit. Studies have shown that the longer someone browses in a store, the more items they will purchase. Therefore retailers set up their products and displays so that people can browse in a friendly atmosphere and feel comfortable spending time looking around the store. Libraries also need to be places where people can lose track of time, look at materials, and feel free to explore.

Ensuring that a library effectively merchandises its collection is not limited to providing thematic displays in the YA area. It also involves placing shelves and materials to attract attention. The first step in this process is having an ideal location for the whole YA section in a library. The best location for a YA section is away from the children's area of the library. Many libraries and even retail establishments are guilty of placing the YA section either inside or adjacent to the children's area. Teens do not like to associate themselves with younger children. Studies have shown that teens aspire to be older than their actual age. Part of the reason for this is because they can see the extra opportunities granted to older teens. Learning to drive or being able to date are major advantages as seen through the eyes of a thirteen-year-old. A TRU Teenage Marketing and Lifestyle study reported that twelve- and thirteen-year-olds wish they could skip most of their teen years and aspire to be age seventeen. Fourteen-, fifteen-, and sixteen-year-olds wish to be eighteen years old and seventeen- and eighteen-year-olds wish to be nineteen years old.[2] Therefore, even the best YA loca-tion, no matter how well merchandised, will be lost to teens if they have to walk through a maze of wall decorations from *Goodnight Moon* and *Mother Goose* and step over storyhour attendees, nametags and all, to find the hottest magazine.

A good location for the YA area is close to the entrance of the building. It should be easy to find upon entering the library. The YA section should be separate from all other collections in the library. Most librarians say they do not have enough money for a YA area. It takes no money at all (besides staff time) to pull all the YA books out of the adult and children's collections and shelve them together in one area. It may require some creative thinking and shifting, but every library needs to have a separate YA collection. If you are lucky to have a YA room, it would be best tucked away in a corner, allowing for privacy. However, it should not be so secluded that it is difficult for staff to monitor and supervise the area.

While it has been mentioned that the YA collection should not be next to the children's section, other areas of the library can be imposing as well. In his work

Why We Buy: The Science of Shopping, Paco Underhill reports on the studies that his firm conducts on the behaviors of shoppers. While his work centers on the retail trade, many of his findings can be applied to libraries. For example, in one study a store reported that the sales of aspirin products were lower than expected. After video observation of aspirin buyers, the firm discovered that most buyers of this type of product are senior citizens. This particular store placed the aspirin aisle next to the pop cooler frequented by teens. The senior citizens were uncomfortable being near the teens and hence avoided (consciously and subconsciously) buying aspirin in that store.[3] The point here is that if a patron or customer becomes uncomfortable because of the location of an item or items, he or she will not spend time to browse. Therefore, placing the YA room too close to the eyes and ears of the reference librarians, near the large-print section frequented by older patrons, or even next to the business collection can be a bad location. Keep in mind when planning library space the mix of patrons using the different collections in the library and how they all relate to each other in your community.

Many librarians tend to look upon their profession as a service-oriented one only. It is easy to forget that in order to ensure our ongoing success, we need to promote and sell our products and services. Merchandising your YA collection means taking an active daily role in making the collection one that teens will want to browse through and spend time within. Effective merchandisers are constantly moving things around, rearranging, restacking, reshelving, and refilling displays to keep the area and collection visually appealing.

Merchandising is not limited to inside the library building. It can include providing an information rack, posters, flyers, or booklists highlighting library information, services, and collections in places that are frequented by teens. Local teen hangouts, the YMCA, school media centers, and agencies serving youth are places where your information might reach teens who are unaware of your services. Displays in these varied locales can be a friendly reminder to those who already know about you. Again, this requires an active role in making sure that the supply of information packets are replenished or the posters and flyers are removed and changed as necessary. Some establishments may have a locked display case you can use to highlight a special collection or attraction of the library's that you would like to advertise. Keep your eye out for these special places as you are out and about in your community. Do not be ashamed to ask if you may use the space for a two-week to a month-long period. Those responsible for maintaining the space may be excited to have someone else take a load off their shoulders and fill the space for them. If you can tie in the library display to the atmosphere or nature of the store or hangout, it becomes much more memorable.

In the retail world, the easiest way to make a profit is to sell more items to the existing customer base. Shoppers enter an establishment usually with one item to purchase in mind. Good merchandising will make them pick up and purchase more than they can carry. This is why when you walk into an Old Navy store, an employee greets you and promptly offers you a canvas bag in which to place your intended purchases. Customers will likely purchase more items if they have something easy in which to carry them. If they become too bogged down with things to carry, their hands are not free to pick up and look at other items. The same idea can be applied to the library world. Libraries should be arranged in order to allow the teen coming in to find a book on a research topic to also want to check out several other things that may catch her eye. Many libraries are offering patrons bags or miniature shopping baskets in which to place materials intended for checkout. This leaves their arms free to look at other things without the worry of balancing everything in their spare hands. The bags should be placed throughout the library, not just at the entrance to the building. Remember, people are usually not expecting to check out so many items. Clever merchandising will make them pick up more than they intended. Having the bags/baskets readily available throughout the library is helpful to someone whose arms are full and encourages them to pick up more items as they go along. The bags or baskets are barcoded and are circulated along with the materials. It is the best answer for a browser who has found that she has hit the jackpot finding hot titles available that day.

Retail stores are interested in the statistic called "conversion rate." This measures how poorly or how well the entire enterprise is functioning where it counts most—in the store. It answers how well the store makes do with what it offers.[4] Libraries have traditionally used circulation statistics as a reflection of the service they provide. The circulation of materials is the most visible public library service and is the easiest to identify to interested members of the public and the government officials who determine budgets and funding. Successfully merchandising your YA collection will increase your YA circulation. This is important because often YA librarians manage a smaller budget than children's or adult services. It is quite common that YA services may not have its own budget but have to share that of the adult or children's services. Therefore, solid merchandising can resolve two important issues. One is to get books into the hands of YA browsers. The other is to give credence to YA services in your library and give you the ammunition you need to ask for a separate or larger YA budget. Solid merchandising can even be used to demonstrate the importance of adding a larger YA space within the library building.

The easiest way to track circulation of merchandised materials is to have your automated circulation system do it. You will be able to tell informally that more items are being circulated as you continually have to restock shelves and replenish display units. Check with your system's administrator and see if you can temporarily change the status of books you have chosen for a special display. Most systems will allow you to do this and then at the end of the display or certain time period, check the circulation of those titles. You should also be able to see how well other classifications, such as genres, paperbacks, series, or hardbacks are doing in circulation during any time period. Computer systems may have other bells and whistles that can keep track of how well your merchandising efforts are working. The book *Output Measures and More: Planning and Evaluating Public Library Services for Young Adults*, by Virginia Walter (ALA, 1995), is an excellent resource in guiding your efforts in evaluation. It has easy-to-use worksheets and explanations for use in the collection of data pertaining to YA services. Include all of the information you collect and your increased circulation statistics in your monthly, quarterly, biannual, or annual reports to bolster and improve the quality and quantity of YA services offered in your library. If you are not required to write such reports, do so anyway to help state your case to your supervisor, director, and the board of trustees. Any library official will appreciate the increase in the level of services and hence the best use of the public's money.

GETTING STARTED

Basically, merchandising efforts in any library can begin in three ways: through the use of shelving, the use of displays, and the use of signage. Future chapters in this book will cover these topics and offer ideas to maximize use of your collection. Each of these three ways may sound as if you may need extra money to get started; however, small things can be done first to start the process of better merchandising.

One of the first steps a YA librarian can make is to begin purchasing more popular titles in paperback. Paperbacks are easy to merchandise, especially with their more flashy front covers as compared to those on hardcover books. Having a smaller number of hardbacks versus paperbacks can free up some space for displays or creative shelving. Paperbacks also are usually what teens prefer to check out because they are easier and less conspicuous to carry. Since paperbacks are cheaper, multiple copies are able to be purchased. This is another key factor in merchandising. With multiple copies of a title you are able to shelve two or three together so that if someone grabs one, copies of the same hot title are available to others, and more importantly, the display is not emptied. In addition, purchasing multiple copies is necessary for any item in demand. Therefore, your budget should also permit you to buy multiple copies of audio-visual items and magazine subscriptions as well.

Another simple activity that will aid merchandising efforts is to thoroughly weed the collection on a continual basis. Chapter 3 discusses the benefits and reasons to be diligent in the weeding process. Keep in mind that in a well-merchandised collection any book is fair game for any mode of display. Unattractive, out-of-date books will stand out and beg for replacement or removal. Weeding does not have to take place once the books are on the shelves. Have the circulation staff keep their eyes out for books in disrepair or needing replacement that are returned. These books can be put aside and later checked for your approval to be removed. Have a way of noting titles that need replaced or subject areas that need strengthened because of heavy usage. Other staff or reference librarians may notice that certain materials needed for assignments are in high demand but never available. Keep a log or some way of keeping track of these items for ease in replacement.

Since teens are used to visual presentations, shelving books face out instead of spine out is crucial in merchandising. Chapter 7 will discuss special shelving units that allow for the better display of materials. Face out shelving can be used without the special purchase of furniture. Hopefully your YA collection does not crowd the shelving units completely. If so, teens are looking at a sea of unattractive book spines that do nothing to catch their attention. Shelve the books so that one half of the shelf has books spine out. Use the remaining shelf to display books standing face out. The tops of short shelving units or even window ledges are a creative use of space to highlight book covers. If your YA area does not allow for this, use the book covers on a bulletin board to highlight the titles.

A book's jacket is often the first interaction a reader will have with the book. After sizing up a book's cover, the teen will next look to the back cover or the blurb to find out more. Therefore it is important to note that face out display helps to sell the item to a YA browser. Publishers have struggled to make book jackets stand out on crowded shelves. Both aesthetic and marketing decisions go into creating an eye-catching jacket that the reader will connect with emotionally.[5] Over recent years, YA book covers have taken on a more adult or contemporary look. Some may be non-gender specific and picture unusual images, whereas in the past the cover depicted the character, his or her friend, or a pet.[6] Computers now allow for a better combination of elements on a book jacket, such as type, color, and imagery. Bold layouts and unique presentations help catch the reader's eye and make him or her want to pick up the item. As publishers spend millions of dollars on cover art and layout, it behooves the librarian to make use of this flashy marketing and show off the covers. It is a surefire way to increase the visibility of materials.

Merchandising can also mean taking a critical look at the YA area and collection. Posters and signs need to be laminated to ensure a longer life and offer a more professional look. Sloppy, handmade signs, as mentioned before, have no place in a library. The teens can maintain or design signs and bulletin boards to add appeal to the entire area. However, the same professional look applies to their signs as well.

If you are serious about merchandising, you may need to educate staff on its fundamentals. Be prepared for some resistance. Constant display and the shifting of materials can wreak havoc on staff who only like things found in correct Dewey Decimal order. Even though it is your responsibility to administer YA services to teens, other library staff are likely to help young adults find what they need. These staff members need to be aware of displays and shelving arrangements in order to provide quality services. Library staff whose job it is to shelve materials need to be informed as well. Do not forget staff whose job it is to search the library to fill items placed on hold or reserve. These are all important people who need to be persuaded of the reasons to merchandise. They may just see your efforts as prohibitive to the efficient completion of their job. Effective merchandising requires a trained and educated team effort that is constant and vigilant about providing a collection that will attract attention. Do not be surprised if staff in other departments take notice of your efforts and ask your advice to better merchandise their area!

NOTES

1. Rick Margolis and Andrea Glick, "Business As Usual? No Way: ALA's Annual Conference in Chicago Was the Most Exuberant Library Event in Ages," *School Library Journal* (August 2000): 16.

2. Peter Zollo, *Wise Up to Teens: Insights into Marketing and Advertising to Teenagers,* 2d ed. (Ithaca, NY: New Strategist Publications, Inc., 1999), 205.

3. Paco Underhill, *Why We Buy: The Science of Shopping* (New York: Simon & Schuster, 1999), 29.

4. Ibid., 36.

5. Nanette Stevenson, "Hipper, Brighter and Bolder," *Publishers Weekly* (February 17, 1997): 137.

6. Ibid., 140.

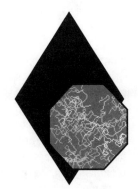

5

The Case for Display Shelving

When a "mega" book retailer opened a store in my neighborhood, people from the community crowded its aisles and spent quite a bit of time and money there. Despite its presence in the neighborhood for over five years, every parking space still remains occupied at all hours of the day and night. The community is so supportive of it, the other national "mega" bookstore chain has recently built a two-story store less than a mile down the road from its direct competitor. Once again, finding a parking space at this new bookstore can be nearly impossible. From a librarian's point of view, one wonders what all the excitement is about. After all, don't libraries essentially offer the same materials—only at no cost? Isn't the public library's staff more qualified to answer literary queries—again at no cost to the customer? Even more troublesome from the YA librarian's perspective can be the answer to the question of why teens are so attracted to a retail bookstore, but often will not be caught being seen in a library.

After spending some time in retail book establishments, one realizes that bookstores are popular for many more reasons than just being a place to sip a cappuccino while glancing through a magazine. It is about marketing and merchandising. Retail establishments do it best, while libraries fall far behind. Economic good times have made consumers more market savvy and bookstores have learned to cater to them. More important than the extended hours and fancy coffee drinks, bookstores make reading and books downright exciting. Your eye usually catches colorful and exciting window displays before the front door is cracked an inch. Then right inside the door, in the vestibule, are usually displays of bargain books to grab your attention. Once inside the bookstore, you will find display after display of books with gleaming covers in a well-lit area begging for your attention. Creativity reigns and materials are merchandised in ways that make even a hard-to-impress teen stand up and take notice.

Walk into a library and you will not likely experience the same merchandising euphoria. If the library is well lighted at all, it most likely highlights a sea of crowded book spines sitting on shelves in straight rows. Exciting and colorful covers are usually drowned out or downplayed in the sea of book spines and information. Usually the most exciting section of the library is the children's section. One has to wonder why this is the case. Toddlers and preschoolers are certainly not the only ones who appreciate bright colors and shapes. YA librarians need to take lessons from bookstores and other retail establishments in order to better merchandise material for teens. Better merchandising can not only make a librarian's job more fun and exciting, it can show teens that the library is much more than a place to borrow a book or *Cliffs Notes* for a required reading assignment. There are obvious differences between libraries and bookstores, and it is not implied that one establishment is superior to the other. A bookseller's bottom line is inventory turnover and financial gain, while libraries want to maintain well-rounded collections that are used by their communities and meet the communities' needs. However, libraries should still be able to use some of the same tactics and techniques of visual merchandising that bookstores employ to draw customers into their stores and increase their sales. Using these techniques in a library setting will not only increase exposure to the YA collection, but also increase circulation of its materials.

Before any discussion of the advantages of displaying books in a library can begin, it is necessary to understand the thought processes someone goes through, both consciously and subconsciously, when deciding which items appeal most to him or her. People who work in retail establishments study consumer behavior with great interest and intensity, since it significantly affects how or what people will purchase. Anything that can be done to help people along in their thought processes and decision-making can increase sales, or in a library's case, increase exposure and circulation of materials or fill someone's basic informational needs.

As a consumer makes decisions on choosing items to purchase, he or she becomes involved in three important cognitive processes. A consumer must interpret relevant information in his environment to acquire knowledge that has a personal meaning to him. Secondly, consumers must integrate this knowledge to evaluate what they are looking at and what actions may be taken in order to choose among alternatives. Lastly, the consumer must retrieve what he knows from his memory to use in the integration and interpretation process.[1]

In order to interpret any piece of information, a person must be exposed to information and become involved in two other cognitive processes. The process of attention governs how someone selects what information to interpret and what information to ignore. Comprehension refers to how people determine subjective meanings of information and thus create personal knowledge of it.[2] These cognitive processes all affect consumer behavior. The American Marketing Association defines consumer behavior as the "dynamic interaction of affect and cognition, behavior and the environment, by which human beings conduct the exchange aspects of their lives."[3] In other words, consumer behavior involves the thoughts and feelings people experience and the actions they perform in the consumption process.

It may appear that the use of the common meaning of the word *consumer* cannot be compared to the use of the term *library patron*. The word "consumer" is usually referred to in the retail world, while most libraries refer to people who use their services as patrons. Some libraries have changed their terminology and now refer to patrons as customers. The word *consumer* implies a material substance being used up or consumed. Library materials are technically consumed; they are returned by one person and recycled for use by others. This writer agrees with Charles Emery's argument that a library is an example of a service organization that is at least partly oriented to the marketing of material goods, books, journals, and so forth.[4] Consumers in a retail establishment participate in the acts of buying and selling that include an exchange of resources involving money or something of value. A library patron can experience a process similar to a retail consumer. While the terminology differs, the process by which a benefit (information, self-improvement, recreation) is provided to a consumer (or library patron) in return for the expenditure of something of value (his/her time, tax levy moneys) remains the same.[5] A retail shopper in a brick and mortar bookstore must go to the store when it is open during his free time. He or she must process all of the information and influences within the store in order to choose an item to purchase. A library patron experiences the same process. Emery states:

> Though in one case an individual may be called a "consumer" and in the other a "reader," the difference is purely semantic. In each of these cases, an individual receives some form of stimulus about a product, commodity, or service, to which he or she is predisposed to respond in a particular way, and arrives at that response through a decision making process that is essentially the same for both cases.[6]

Emery further states that libraries have characteristics of service organizations that offer and guarantee intangible but very real benefits. Libraries also perform roles similar to those of a commercial organization that is dedicated to the marketing and dissemination of consumable products.[7]

Realizing these similarities with commercial establishments, libraries must understand consumer behavior and thought processes and finally put to rest the theory that they cannot learn and borrow techniques from the commercial world. Visiting bookstores, video stores, or any other retail establishment in a community is an appropriate beginning for any librarian interested in merchandising a YA collection. People, including teens, are spending more time in bookstores, purchasing books and other items. A previously mentioned *Publishers Weekly* 1998 survey found that teens surveyed spend 10 percent of their disposable income on books. Seventy-two percent of the fifteen- to seventeen-year-old book buyers said that they spent their own money rather than money from their parents on their last book purchase.[8] The survey showed that most teens make their book purchases at bookstore chains. Seventy-six percent of all teen book buyers purchased a book at a chain bookstore within three months prior to being surveyed, with Barnes & Noble and Waldenbooks mentioned most frequently followed by B. Dalton and Borders as the places of purchase.[9] These statistics again imply that teens are affected by the visual display techniques found in retail establishments. Libraries need to try merchandising to draw teens to the library for materials.

Visual merchandising in libraries can be done in two general ways. Libraries can adopt face-front shelving techniques that bookstores use to highlight items. Chapter 7 will discuss special shelving units and fixtures that maximize bookstore-style display techniques. The other way that libraries can maximize visual merchandising is through the use of displays, which can be thematic in nature. Chapter 6 will discuss how to assemble a good display that will grab a young adult's attention and entice him or her to check items out.

Whichever merchandising method, face-front shelving or thematic displays, is chosen, the goals are the same. Display methods can "sell" an item by showing it off through promotion. They can be a way of introducing new materials. A display can encourage someone to enter a library or to pause and look at something that has been highlighted. Display methods can also promote and enhance a library's visual image. All of these lead to the bigger goal of raising interest in the YA collection and increasing circulation.

Why make such a fuss over displaying materials? Several researchers have conducted studies to test the effect that displays have on circulation. These studies support the fact that books displayed circulate significantly more than books left on the regular shelves.

Herbert Goldhor, a prominent library educator and public librarian, conducted two separate studies, one in Illinois and one in Jamaica. In his first study, Goldhor wanted to note the effects on circulation in a public library of putting a group of selected adult titles in a prime location, off of and away from the regular shelves. He hypothesized that adults borrow books from the public library primarily as a result of browsing. When selected titles are collected and placed in a prime location, they will circulate significantly more than when they are scattered on the shelves of an open stack collection.[10] The study was conducted at the Champaign Public Library and the Urbana Free Library in Illinois. Goldhor chose from each library one hundred ten titles (fifty-five fiction and fifty-five nonfiction). The titles were the same in each library for the sake of consistency. In phase I, he observed the circulation data of the titles for six months when left in their regular places in the general collection. He found the circulation of the selected titles in each library were very similar. This proved that the two libraries were comparable before the experimental variable was introduced.[11] In the second six-month period, the selected titles were placed in a prime location (near the circulation desk) in only one of the libraries, the Champaign Public Library. A sign above the display rack read "Good Books You May Have Missed." During this Phase II, when the circulation data of the titles at the two libraries were collected, it showed that the experimental library's (the Champaign Public) circulation was far greater than in the first six months or in that of the control library (Urbana Free). As a follow-up to Phase II, borrowers at each library were asked the following four questions:

1. Did you borrow the book for yourself?

2. How much of the book did you read?

3. How did you happen to select the book to read?

4. Did the book do for you what you wanted it to do?[12]

An analysis of the responses to these questions was used to shed light upon the reader's method of selection of the book he or she borrowed. The result of the analysis was that browsing was more often used to select books at the experimental library, where books were on display, than in the control library, where books were on the regular shelf.[13]

Goldhor conducted a second study at the Kingston and St. Andrew Parish Library of the Jamaica Library Service. In the second study, he selected specific adult biographies that had not circulated as much as the rest of the collection. A three-month pretest and a three-month test period was used. The biographies were divided into three groups:

- Group A was placed in a display near the checkout desk with a sign above it that read "Good Books You May Have Missed,"

- Group B was left on the regular shelves, but was listed on an annotated booklist,

- Group C was a control group of books left on the shelf with no special attention.

The results of this study again found that the books placed on display circulated more frequently than the books in either of the other two groups.[14]

Another researcher, Sharon L. Baker, further studied the effect of displays on an increase in the use of books. Baker's research dug more deeply and studied the factors thought to cause the increase in circulation. Baker, reviewing previous studies, thought that a display's ability to increase use may be linked to two possible factors. First, placing books in a prime location increases their visibility and accessibility and makes them more likely to be noticed and ultimately chosen by browsers. Second, displays are thought to help narrow a reader's choice by guiding him or her to a small collection of titles.[15]

Baker conducted her study in two small Illinois public libraries: the Mahomet Township Public Library and the Monticello Public Library. Using a three-month pretest period, she observed the use of fiction books left in their regular places on the shelves. During the three-month test period, the books were randomly divided into three groups to test the effects of location or physical accessibility. Seventy-five books were placed spine out on a book cart in a prime location near the circulation desk. They could be readily seen by all patrons entering the library. Seventy-five books were placed in a non-prime display location (behind the stacks) where they were not easily visible. The rest of the books in the study acted as a control group and remained on the regular shelves.

During the test period, a second experiment was conducted to see what effect professional recommendations had on selection. Thirty-eight books were randomly selected from each prime and non-prime display location, as were seventy-five from the regular fiction shelves. Each was marked with a red dot. A large sign was placed at each location to inform patrons that books with red dots were recommended.

During the second three-month test period, the variables of location and recommendation were reversed. In other words, books that were in the prime display locations were moved to the non-prime display locations and vice versa. In addition, books with no recommendation during the first test period were marked "recommended" and vice versa.[16]

The data collected in the study showed that books on the prime display circulated substantially more than those in the non-prime display and those on the regular shelf. In addition, during the second test period, the books that had been switched to a more visible location circulated more than when they had been in a less visible area. The same happened for books that had been in a prime location during the first test period. The circulation data for those books during the second test period was not as high. Because the reversal of the experimental treatments was associated with a reversal of circulation trends, it can be said that the changes in circulation were associated with the display location.[17]

Interviews were conducted of patrons who checked out titles in both the control and experimental groups during the first test period to determine why they had selected certain titles. Data from the interviews confirmed that browsers are the primary users of displays. While many respondents said they were browsing, significantly more browsers checked out books from a prime display than did non-browsers. Of the browsers who checked out books from a prime display, 85 percent said they did so because the book caught their attention, as opposed to 40 percent of browsers who selected from a non-prime book display and 9 percent of those who selected a book from the regular shelves.[18]

As for the second experiment on recommended books, Baker found that recommended books circulated more than their non-recommended counterparts. This was true in the first test period and also with the reversal in the second test period. The interview data showed that slightly more than half of those who selected a recommended book said they did so because it was recommended. However, there was no significant difference between the number of browsers choosing recommended books and the number choosing non-recommended books.[19] Different experimental results were found at the two libraries. Data collected from the interviews seemed to support the theory that collection size was a factor in determining why recommended books circulated significantly more than non-recommended books at one library but not the other.[20] The inconclusiveness of this second experiment gives reason to believe that narrowing the selection of books, such as labeling them "recommended," may work better in larger libraries with bigger collections. However, it is important to note the finding that display books placed in high traffic areas, where they catch the attention of browsers, will circulate more than those books not displayed in prime areas and those found on the regular shelves.

The results of these studies certainly gives credence to having displays in any library. Baker noted that in her study the use of displays did not increase the circulation of the fiction collection as a whole. The average circulation of the fiction titles that were not in a display decreased in both libraries.[21] However, if a YA librarian were to make a conscious effort to regularly plan and implement displays at certain intervals, YA circulation should increase. After all, different materials will be highlighted at different times. Any type of display method can offer the opportunity to bring attention to items that, while they appeal to young adults, have been neglected. Many of the materials that show up on award lists are of excellent quality, but often are not the first choice of a young adult over many of the more popular mass market items. While quality items should not be excluded from collections, it is worth an effort to try to gain exposure to these items through some type of display. The popular materials, such as magazine and series fiction, are often what draw young adults to the collection and stamp it as their own. Once there, the use of savvy merchandising efforts can entice them to check out these other items they may have never known were available.

Displays can broaden YAs' interests and introduce them to different authors, artists, and genres. Rather than seeing parts of the collection go unnoticed and waste away on the shelves, displays expose them. It is better to use the library's money to get the books that might not normally circulate out in front to grab people's attention. More importantly, displays highlight a library's collection, its biggest and most visible service aspect. They entice teens to use the collection, which is one of a library's major goals.

FACE-FRONT SHELVING

The easiest way to merchandise a collection can be to utilize more face-front shelving. Often this can be accomplished with little or no purchases of extra specialty fixtures or furniture. Books can be displayed standing up face front at the ends or on top of existing shelving units. Window ledges also come in handy for this purpose. Staring at bright, interesting covers of materials is certainly preferable to craning the neck sideways and squinting to read the titles on a thin spine of a book. Spines have no exciting illustrations, photographs, or print, and one looks very similar to another, with just their color to distinguish between them.

Sarah P. Long conducted a study on the use of face front book display in a public library. The purpose of the study was to look at the method of face front book display to discover if these books circulated significantly more than those books displayed spine out. The research was conducted at a branch of the Durham County Public Library in North Carolina. Long chose books at least four months old from the adult current fiction section and used two random samples of fifty books to be the control and experimental groups. Long used a pretest as well as a test period in the study. The control group was displayed spine out only during the test period. The experimental group was displayed face front only during the test period. Both groups were randomly displayed face front during the pretest period, according to usual library practice. At the completion of the study, it was found that displays did increase circulation for the books included in the experimental group. It was concluded that the face front display method does have an effect on library patrons by gaining their attention, narrowing their choices, and causing them to select certain titles.[22]

Long also concluded that the method of display, and not just the display itself, can significantly increase the circulation of books.[23]

While Long's study centered solely on books, YA librarians should not forget that audio titles need face front exposure as well. A B. Dalton prototype store on Staten Island in New York City uses what it believes are the three most effective in-store approaches for boosting audio sales:

- a bestseller display at the entrance combines hardcover book and audio titles,

- a sign that heralds the audiobook section is visible throughout the store, and

- in the audio section, best sellers and other carefully selected titles are stocked face out.[24]

A Barnes & Noble buyer also found that titles displayed face out sold the most.[25] In addition, Borders is also creating more mixed displays, placing audiobooks with books in many areas of its stores.[26] Libraries should follow this advice. Merchandising audiotapes can be advantageous to those young adults reading below their level. Audiotapes of popular books can provide young adults access to the same titles that their friends are enjoying and broaden the options of what they can enjoy. Highlighting audiotapes of books on reading lists can be popular, especially in summer when August rolls around and many students have left summer reading assignments to the last minute. Audiotapes can also draw attention to other titles by popular authors.

BROWSING

The concept of browsing is covered fairly well in the library literature. Browsers are patrons who directly approach the shelves to look for something they want, rather than using a computer catalog to look up a particular item. They are usually not looking for anything specific, but rather something that will pique their interest. While the number of browsers varies from library to library, researchers agree that browsers form a substantial portion of a library's clientele. In order to understand browsers, it is important to return to the concept of how consumers process information. A sound knowledge of how people perceive things is essential when communicating anything to a target audience.

A person processing information goes through a series of activities by which stimuli are perceived, transformed into information, and stored. This series of activities includes exposure, attention, interpretation, and memory.[27] These processes can occur simultaneously and interact with one another. Both perception and memory are extremely selective. Of all of the massive amounts of information available, someone can be exposed to only a limited amount. Of all the information to which someone is exposed, only a small percentage is passed on to the central processing of the brain for interpretation.[28]

Exposure

Exposure occurs when a stimulus is placed within a person's relevant environment. Most of the stimuli someone is exposed to are self-selected. A person will deliberately pick out something perceived to help him or her achieve one goal and avoid others.[29]

Attention

Attention occurs when a stimulus activates one or more sensory receptor nerves and the resulting sensations go to the brain for processing.[30] Certain things can affect attention:

1. Size—larger things are more likely to be noticed than smaller ones.

2. Color and movement—bright colors are noticed more, as well as moving objects versus stationary ones.

3. Position—objects near the center of something are more noticeable than those on the edges.

4. Isolation—people tend to notice white space on signs more.

5. Format—simple presentations receive more attention than complex ones.

6. Information quantity—if there is information overload or too much information, all of it cannot be processed.[31]

Interpretation

Interpretation is the assignment of meaning and expectations to sensations.

Memory

Memory is how information is retained, both long and short term.

FACTORS THAT INFLUENCE BORROWING DECISIONS

While a person's information processing can affect how decisions are made, other factors come into play when dealing with unplanned purchases. An impulse purchase is a purchase made that is different from those the consumer planned to make prior to entering the establishment.[32] In libraries this type of borrowing is usually made when browsing or when merchandising efforts grab someone's attention.

Influences that can cause alternate evaluation and modify intended purchases include displays, layout of the building and materials, and staff. The atmosphere of the establishment also plays a role. Factors such as lighting, fixtures, floor coverings, colors, sounds, smells, and presentation of merchandise can enhance or deteriorate someone's experience.[33] It is important to make sure the physical environment interacts with the characteristics of the individuals using it. Consider other factors as ambient conditions (temperature, air quality, noise, music, and color), physical conditions (layout, furnishings, color, and space), social conditions (customer characteristics), and symbols (signs, displays, and decor style).[34]

Department stores are especially adept at this. One can immediately tell when coming upon the teen department. Televisions extend from the ceiling playing MTV or music videos, neon lights burn brightly, the colors are brighter and flashier, and merchandise hangs from the ceiling and the walls. Even the mannequins look a little funkier. Sears recently used life-sized Christina Aguilera cut-outs for a back-to-school promotion. All of this excitement happens in stores without a huge sign saying "Young Adult Area." Libraries need to follow suit and make sure their YA areas appeal to teens. The young adults themselves can guide librarians in the type of decor they prefer. Some changes can be done on a low-cost basis. *VOYA* has a column on "Young Adult Spaces of Your Dreams" that highlights YA spaces in libraries around the country. These columns can offer recommendations for librarians needing assistance. Any type of excitement in a YA area will aid browsing efforts because young adults will spend more time in a place where they feel comfortable and feel like they belong.

What other techniques can be used to aid YA browsing efforts in a library? Sharon L. Baker addressed the issue of browsers and libraries. Baker felt that patrons who are browsing can easily suffer from information overload or become overwhelmed by the large number of choices available to them. This may lead to a patron subconsciously or consciously using some sort of strategy to help him limit his selection. After examining previous studies on the effects of library displays, as well as the work of consumer researchers, she concluded that libraries should use the strategy of "exposure" used in consumer research. This strategy exposes a large number of consumers (patrons) to a smaller set of items and significantly increases consumer choice from this smaller group. Two exposure techniques that libraries can use are book displays and booklists. Baker's research found that both displays and booklists can successfully capture the attention of the potential user and require little effort from him. Displays will work if placed in highly accessible and easily visible places. Booklists are a successful technique when they are distributed widely and in a manner requiring little patron effort to find them.[35] The use of booklists will be discussed further in Chapter 8.

Baker found that the processing of information by consumers can be negatively affected by time constraints. Those whose time is limited cannot process information as effectively as those with more time.[36] Techniques such as displays can help those patrons pressed for time. In today's world, many people suffer from time constraints and overloaded schedules. Young adults seem to stand out in this category. Anything that can speed up the selection process for them is useful. Teens are accustomed to quick responses via instant chat and the Internet. Why wouldn't an already highlighted display of books appeal to them?

In addition, teens are most likely not to ask anyone for help in finding material, but rather will try to find something appealing on their own. Don Gallo reported in *American Libraries* on how young adults find out about new books. The information, while dated, is summarized on Table 2:[37]

Table 2. Where Teens Turn for Reading Advice

Source	Grades 7–9	Grades 10–12
Friend's Suggestions	42%	38%
Browsing in Store	28%	31%
Browsing in Library	27%	18%
Teacher's Suggestion	8%	11%
Parent's Suggestion	8%	10%
Store Display	7%	8%
Advertising	6%	9%
Sibling's Suggestion	8%	8%
Bookclub Catalog	7%	3%
Library Display	5%	5%
Librarian's Suggestion	4%	2%
School List	6%	2%

In a more recent *Publishers Weekly* survey it was found that a friend's recommendations and a book's front or back cover are key factors in deciding what to purchase. Nearly four out of ten or 39 percent of teenagers said the book they bought last was recommended by a friend. A surprising number, 77 percent of younger and 57 percent of older teens, said their parents have some influence over what they purchase.[38] Other influences on teen book purchases were the author, a movie, a teacher, a magazine article, a television show, an online/ad listing, and a radio program.[39] Only 15 percent of teens mentioned a librarian as an influence.[40]

Thus, it can be stated that teens will be more likely to choose recommended books if the recommendation comes from their peers. A librarian-recommended title usually will not gather too much excitement. Any type of material can use a recommendation. A librarian can have teens complete cards on those items they liked or disliked. The file can be kept handy or the cards can be kept with the material so other teens have easy access to the recommendations. Brightly colored slips of paper that stick above the top of the item can say "recommended." Below, the teens can write their thoughts about what they liked or disliked. It does not have to be a long statement. A rating system, similar to the one used in *VOYA*, can be used. Even simpler would be the use of a star method or just a thumbs up and thumbs down symbol. If keeping slips of paper with the items is not desirable, have teens post slips of paper on a bulletin board, wall, or other empty space. A dry erase board also serves well as a sounding board for their thoughts. Allow teens to be creative and develop their own rating system. Computer savvy teens could probably design a database or a link to the library's website to use as a way of compiling recommendations on different items in the collection.

WHAT ARE GOOD BOOKS TO DISPLAY?

Now that an understanding as to why books should be displayed face front on a shelf or highlighted in a display has been established, the next question to tackle is what makes an eye-catching display item. Materials chosen for inclusion in a thematic display are obvious choices. They fall into a certain subject category that meets the goal of the display. Do not be afraid to mix fiction and nonfiction titles, as well as other types of materials, such as audio, video, DVDs or CD-ROMs. An example of a display highlighting adventure books could include fiction titles by Will Hobbs as well as nonfiction such as *The* Endurance: *Shackleton's Legendary Antarctic Expedition* by Caroline Armstrong. This technique introduces different types of materials to teens and may lead them to other types of things they might not normally check out. Displays are also an opportunity to highlight items that may need gentle pushing.

If it is possible, display hardbacks and paperbacks together also. Paperbacks usually come in two formats. Mass-market paperbacks are produced for a mass audience. They have a standard size, usually 4 by 6¾ inches, and are easy to display because of their popularity. Trade paperbacks can be produced in formats comparable to hardbound books. They can be shelved similar to hardbacks. Keep in mind that trade paperbacks can buckle if displayed standing up.[41]

When looking for eye-catching items to shelve face front at the ends of or on top of shelves, window ledges, and so forth, consider examining their front covers. Why are front covers so important? It is the first thing a person sees. It is what lures the eyes to examine a book. A cover can make or break a book. A boring, unattractive cover can doom a book to sit on a shelf, no matter how many displays or book talks a librarian does to create excitement for it. Publishers have begun to take note of this. Traditional illustrated book jackets have started to disappear. Beverly Horowitz, editor in chief of Random House Children's Books, states, "They're much more inventive—not just a 'moody girl looking out the window.' We're using much of the same special effects that adult books use: high gloss covers, computer collage, *film noir* style."[42] Andrew Smith, vice president of marketing at Random House, has stated that his company has focused on making sure that the "look and packaging" of teen books is on target. Hardcover sales for his company have risen, and they hope to experiment more with slicker looking packaging for hardcover books.[43] *Rolling Stone* magazine has been known to raise a few eyebrows with its cover art. Those eyebrow-raising issues are usually the first to be stolen from the library because of their appeal.

Many a reference librarian has heard patrons say, "I don't remember the title, but it had a red cover." A preservation and cataloging librarian at the New England School of Law in Boston had developed a website, now defunct, to search for books by the color of their binding.[44] While a search tool may not be practical in all cases, it still emphasizes the point that many people remember books by something other than a compelling plot.

Librarian Ed Sullivan felt strongly enough about ugly book covers on YA books while he served on YALSA's Best Books for Young Adults Committee that he conducted two experiments with young adults in Staten Island, New York. He wondered how young adults felt about covers and if they affected their judgment of a book. In his first experiment, twenty-one young adults—the majority of them between the ages of twelve and fifteen—evaluated hardcover first editions of fiction titles by their cover art only. Participants rated the books on five points from "most appealing," meaning the cover is so good it makes me want to read the book, to "least appealing," meaning an awful cover that completely turns me off the book. The teens wrote explanations for covers that earned the highest and lowest ratings. They offered details as to why they felt something was most or least appealing.[45]

Many of the reasons for the least appealing covers were similar. Teens disliked covers that were "too weird or abstract." Teens were looking for the cover to tell them something about the book and became frustrated when it did not. Color also plays an important role in cover art. The wrong color combination or lack of color on a cover can be distracting, unappealing, and dull. The covers that were most appealing were intriguing ones whose pictures made the young adults surveyed want to read the story to find out what it was about. A mysterious quality about the cover art caught their attention. For example, one cover showed a girl half-hidden behind a curtain and made the teen want to find out what happens to her. All of the survey participants agreed that a good or bad cover often determines whether they choose to read a book or not. While not scientific, the survey indicates that young adults look closely at the cover to give them clues as to what the story is about. Readers feel misled and disappointed when their expectations about a cover is not met.[46]

In a different study, Sullivan asked teens to look at hardcover jackets and paperback covers of the same fifteen YA novels and decide which of the two was most appealing. Participants filled out a checklist and then elaborated on some of the titles they thought were more appealing. Twenty-four young adults, the majority ranging in age between twelve and fifteen years (mostly from the Richmondtown Branch of the New York Public Library on Staten Island) participated. Again, the teens evaluated the books by cover art only.[47]

The covers chosen as appealing offered an explanation of the book's contents. Teens preferred covers with a realistic look and an action being portrayed. Color, or its absence, again was something that teens looked at during evaluation.[48] Covers that had a mysterious look about them, making the reader want to read and find out what will happen, again had appeal.

A surprising outcome of the survey was that hardcover jacket designs were often preferred over the paperback version, even though paperbacks are usually the preferred format for young adults. In summary, teens liked the covers that gave them an idea of what the story was about. The use of color, as well as the presence of an action or an emotion, was again stated as important when determining appeal. More importantly, a cover that provokes emotions such as fright, humor, or sadness intrigues the reader enough to want to pick it up.[49]

Also keep in mind that any book on display should be clean-looking without any evidence of disrepair. Sometimes all it takes to make something look newer is a new crystal jacket on the cover. Obvious things like broken bindings, graffiti-ridden text, or ripped pages indicate the item should be replaced or discarded. Anything outdated or unattractive (for example, those items with covers of teens with big hair from the 1980s) will not help merchandise the collection.

FICTION CLASSIFICATION

Another way to highlight certain parts of a collection and make it easier to browse is to shelve genres together. This can help the teen who finds himself/herself hooked on mysteries and who will read nothing else at the moment. It is especially helpful also when teens come in with the assignment to read a historical fiction title. Most people find it hard to search among the other fiction titles to choose a historical fiction one. A popular genre classification already in most libraries is science fiction. It does not have to stop there. Many library suppliers offer genre spine labels to help with classification. For example, Demco (www.demco.com) offers subject classification labels in a 500-per-roll dispenser box. Often this purchase will not add an expense to the YA budget, but rather it will come out of the library's general supply budget that all departments use. Some libraries find these labels useful because some genre books are interfiled together with the rest of the fiction, and it causes them to "stick out" from the rest of the fiction.

Sharon L. Baker conducted a study to determine if fiction classified into genres helped browsers who are subject to information overload. Baker felt that two methods, physically separating the fiction into categories and using spine labels on books that were interfiled with the regular fiction collection, should increase use. Three libraries in the Davidson County Public Library System in North Carolina participated in the study.[50]

Data showed that when experimental books were labeled and physically separated from the general fiction, their circulation increased. However, circulation of the control books, which remained unlabeled in their normal locations on the regular fiction shelves, did not.[51] In the two larger libraries, a substantial portion of library users admitted to being overwhelmed by the large number of books to choose from. Classification made selection at all libraries quicker and easier and enabled patrons to become familiar with other novelists in a particular genre.[52]

Data also found that simply marking the spines of regular fiction titles with classed category labels increased circulation because it guided browsers to the type of novel desired.[53] The last idea the study explored was whether the use of less popular fiction would increase when books were placed in a genre category. Significant increases occurred in the number of books that circulated under the categories. This proved that fiction classification appears to narrow a patron's selection within a genre category. At the same time, the patron's reliance on known authors decreases and his use of books by other authors within a genre is broadened.[54]

Baker concluded in this study that users do not need extra selection guidance unless the browsing collection grows too large. Libraries with very small collections do not need to classify their fiction. While most YA collections are not large, using techniques such as genre labels may still be helpful to teens. The fact that teens usually do not ask anyone for help and their sometimes lack of knowledge of library lingo (for example, the difference between a science fiction and a fantasy) may warrant any technique that makes it easier for them to find what they need. A YA collection may not have enough titles of a certain genre to make physically separating them from the rest of the collection practical. Using spine labels may be a way to make those genres stick out from the rest of the fiction. Instead of premade, purchased labels, some libraries use self-adhesive dots of different colors to signify different genre categories. While this may appear to be a cost-cutting idea, it may be difficult for the teen to remember which color of dot indicates which genre. Too often librarians think that patrons understand their little shortcuts or shelving techniques. Using something that is labeled with the genre name, with a corresponding graphic is far easier to understand. Remember, **a goal of any merchandising effort is to make items easily accessible in order to gain exposure to the collection.**

The type of material that is best separated from the rest of the fiction or paperback collection, no matter what the size of the collection, are series books. This is especially important in series with different authors. No one likes to hunt through titles and authors to find the next entry in a series. Depending on a series' popularity, it may take no merchandising effort at all to move it off the shelves. Simply shelving all the books together or in numerical order, spine out, may do the trick. Usually no browsing is done with series fiction because young adults come in knowing that they want the next book. It is important to make sure that series fiction is cataloged in the computer by series name and that the number of the book within the series is also entered. Too often patrons come in looking for the next book, but have no idea what the title of it is. Cataloging books in this way is helpful in this instance.

READER'S INTEREST CATEGORIZATION

The Dewey Decimal or Library of Congress classification systems can be difficult for teens to understand. Think about it; it is not normal for a person to correlate a subject heading with a set of numbers. While librarians have had courses of study to explain the rationale and gain an understanding of these systems, teen patrons are left in the dark wondering what the number 133, for example, has to do with the subject of witchcraft. According to their thinking, shouldn't witchcraft be under the number 666? It can also be confusing when doing a report on a subject such as rainforests. Materials on rainforest destruction are found under the Dewey Decimal number 344; while animals and plants of the rainforest are found in 574. Many bookstores use easily understandable reader interest categories that place nonfiction items in separate, well-marked sections organized by broad subjects.[55]

These categories are used in lieu of the call numbers assigned in the classification systems. Librarians have discovered, through trial and error, that collections of up to 30,000 items can be successfully handled in this way.[56] It is therefore most useful for any small- to medium-sized collection, but is especially appropriate for paperbacks, audio-visual (books-on-tape, CDs, videos, DVDs, CD-ROMs, etc.), and bookmobile collections.

This arrangement can make the collection more attractive and easier to use. This, in turn, can foster a greater sense of independence and self-worth in patrons because they can more easily choose materials without help. For example, all biographies would be shelved under the reader interest category "Biography" instead of having biographies of musicians shelved in the Dewey classification with the "history of music" or Bill Gates biographies under the "business" section. This would definitely make it easier for a teen to browse through and choose items for a report.

Again, while all of these techniques take time, they will prove to be well worth any effort. The key to displaying items is to really believe that the enthusiastic effort put forth will enhance the library and its image. The most obvious place to begin to gather ideas is to visit bookstores and retail outlets in the local community. Take notes or even pictures, if permitted, and observe how items are displayed to create enthusiasm and excitement. While all of these observations may not be practical in a library setting, ideas can be adapted to make a library a more exciting and inviting place for teens.

NOTES

1. J. Paul Peter and Jerry Olson. *Consumer Behavior and Marketing Strategy*, 5th ed. (Boston: McGraw Hill, 1999), 45.

2. Ibid.

3. Ibid., 6.

4. Charles Emery, *Buyers and Borrowers: The Application of Consumer Theory to the Study of Library Use* (New York: The Haworth Press, 1993), 16.

5. Ibid., 17.

6. Ibid., 20.

7. Ibid., 24.

8. Amanda Ferguson, "Reading Seen as Cool," *Publishers Weekly* (October 12, 1998): 30.

9. Ibid., 31.

10. Herbert Goldhor, "The Effect of Prime Display Location on a Public Library Circulation of Selected Adult Titles," *The Library Quarterly* 42, no. 4 (October 1972): 371.

11. Ibid., 374.

12. Ibid., 380.

13. Ibid., 387.

14. Herbert Goldhor, "Experimental Effects on the Choice of Books Borrowed by Public Library Adult Patrons," *Library Quarterly* 51, no. 3 (1981): 253-268.

15. Sharon L. Baker, "The Display Phenomenon: An Exploration into Factors Causing the Increased Circulation of Displayed Books," *Library Quarterly* 56, no. 3 (1986): 238.

16. Ibid., 240.

17. Ibid., 246.

18. Ibid., 248.

19. Ibid., 249.

20. Ibid., 253.

21. Ibid., 255.

22. Sarah P. Long, "The Effect of Face-Front Book Display in a Public Library," *North Carolina Libraries* 45, no. 3 (Fall 1987): 152.

23. Ibid., 153.

24. Matt Kopka, "Show and Sell," *Publishers Weekly* 242, no. 14 (April 3, 1995): 27–29.

25. Ibid.

26. Ibid.

27. Del Hawkins, Roger J. Best, and Kenneth Corey, *Consumer Behavior: Implications for Marketing Strategy*, 6th ed. (Chicago: Richard D. Irwin, 1995), 237.

28. Ibid., 238.

29. Ibid., 239.

30. Ibid., 240.

31. Ibid., 242–245.

32. Ibid., 498.

33. Ibid., 503.

34. Ibid., 504.

35. Sharon L. Baker, "Overload, Browsers, and Selections," *Library and Information Science Research* 8 (October 1986): 315–329.

36. Ibid., 324.

37. Don Gallo, "Ask Your Librarian! Four Surveys Reveal Where Young People Turn for Reading Advice," *American Libraries* (November 1985): 736.

38. Ferguson, "Reading Seen As Cool," 31.

39. Ibid., 30.

40. Ibid., 30.

41. Robert D. Hale, Allen Marshall, and Ginger Curwen, *A Manual on Bookselling: How to Open and Run a Bookstore*, 4th ed. (New York: Harmony Books, 1987), 193.

42. Clarissa Cruz, "No Kidding," *Entertainment Weekly* (October 15, 1999): 19.

43. Shannon Maughan, "Growing Pains: The Success and Challenges of Reaching Teen Readers," *Publishers Weekly* (October 23, 2000).

44. Walter Minkel, "Judging a Book By Its Color," *School Library Journal* 46, no. 9 (September 2000): 42.

45. Ed Sullivan, "Judging Books By Their Covers: A Cover Art Experience," *VOYA* (August 1998): 180–181.

46. Ibid., 182.

47. Ed Sullivan, "Judging Books By Their Covers Part II: Hardcover vs. Paperback," *VOYA* (October 2000): 244.

48. Ibid.

49. Ibid., 247.

50. Sharon L. Baker, "Will Fiction Classification Schemes Increase Use?" *RQ* 27 (Spring 1988): 366–368.

51. Ibid., 369.

52. Ibid., 372.

53. Ibid.

54. Ibid., 374.

55. Sharon L. Baker, *The Responsive Public Library Collection: How to Develop and Market It* (Englewood, CO: Libraries Unlimited, 1993), 272.

56. Ibid., 274.

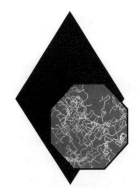

6

Techniques of Display

The significant value of displays in both bookstores and libraries has been established. Now it is important to know elements that make up an effective display. Before this discussion can begin, one must realize that libraries may not experience a smooth transition when incorporating merchandising activities into their overall plan of service. Bookstores obviously have an advantage over libraries in the merchandising process. Retail establishments have large budgets to support extravagant marketing activities year round, while libraries must learn to be creative in finding money and materials for the same purposes. Bookstores also keep a large inventory of popular titles in stock and can easily create displays using a number of copies of the same book. Libraries are not as fortunate and must limit their acquisitions to just one or two copies, depending on a title's popularity, making a special display of one title virtually impossible.[1] In addition, bookstores are specially designed to allow for adequate display areas and ease of traffic flow. Most libraries, on the other hand, must contend with little or no space in which to house the regular shelves of materials, let alone special areas for display. Many times, library floor space is taken up by office and desk space.[2] Libraries need not despair, these disadvantages can be overcome. No matter how small or large a library's budget or available floor space, this chapter will highlight many low-cost, creative techniques that can be utilized to make a library's collection more marketable.

Perhaps the biggest arguments against planning and executing any type of merchandising effort are meager budgets and no space. This chapter will attempt to give the YA librarian a plan for creating attractive displays using most of what is already on hand or what can be borrowed or begged. Thinking "out of the box" will allow for the use of interior walls, ceilings, tabletops, bookcases, window ledges, or unused corners. It does not matter if a library is antiquated or if a budget is small, many displays can skillfully use second-hand materials that can be recycled.

VISUAL MERCHANDISING

In much of the literature on the displaying of materials, one will encounter the words *visual merchandising*. What is visual merchandising? It can be defined as any visual presentation that sells merchandise or promotes a product or idea.[3] Therefore, any type of display promoting library materials falls under the guise of visual merchandising. The use of book displays in libraries can accomplish three main goals:

1. Expose patrons to items they have never heard of but would like to use.

2. Remind patrons of authors or titles they have heard about and would like to borrow.

3. Trigger patron recognition of latent needs that they have not previously acted upon.[4]

In the age of instant entertainment and sound bytes, displays can create excitement about the library by attracting attention and reflecting the interests of young adults.

Terminology borrowed from the business world can be used when discussing displays. Deliberate displays appropriately placed in a library can be referred to as point of purchase (POP) displays. POP advertising can be defined as any merchandising device, sign, or advertisement used inside or outside a retail store (or in our case a library) to provide information about products or services available there, with the purpose of influencing and motivating favorable buying decisions among shoppers or passersby.[5] A POP display in a library is usually thematic in nature and is creatively designed to catch a young adult's attention. Displays in libraries can take on two meanings. For example, a display can be a collection of objects and books in a glass exhibit case. When the merchandising concept is added, the objective of the display is not just visibility. The other type of display attracts attention to a certain part of the collection and brings about an action, such as a teen checking out and taking home items from the display.[6]

Successful POP displays in retail outlets are usually set up near the checkout counter in order to maximize opportunities for last-minute impulse purchases. To parallel this opportunistic location, libraries often display materials near the circulation desk to give patrons standing in line something to browse while waiting to check items out.

Supermarket retailers especially love to take advantage of these front-end displays since they represent a multibillion dollar opportunity. More than half of all magazine sales and more than one third of all candy sales take place there.[7] Chapter 5 mentioned impulse purchases, which play a role in POP design. It is a major element in customer satisfaction with the overall shopping experience. Sixty percent of consumers buy gum or mints and 56 percent buy candy at checkout stands once a month.[8] Front-end displays have been so successful that retailers have added more space and more merchandise. Along with candy, gum, and mints, consumers can now find soft drinks, batteries, film, cosmetics, razors, and magazines. The increase in sales has caused supermarket front-end displays to expand to eight or more shelves and thirty to forty feet of linear space.[9]

As noted, the impact of front-end displays on sales is tremendous. This is especially so when accompanied by an advertisement.[10] While libraries do not advertise, as most name brand products do, highlighting new materials with displays should become a common practice. This can be done in library newsletters, through websites, flyers, or bookmarks, as well as highlighting these materials when visiting schools or hosting a library program.

While POP displays gain the most exposure near the circulation desk or front end of the library near the entrance and exit, other places can be used and be just as successful. These locations will be discussed later in this chapter.

Another term can be borrowed from the retail merchandising environment when talking about library displays. Retailers have found that cross-merchandising or cross-promoting can increase customer awareness of products. If you are an observant shopper, you may have noticed health-related books or magazines in the aisle that houses vitamins and dietary supplements. Parenting materials often can be found adjacent to the baby formula and diaper aisle. You are likely to find an item like a chip clip (a gadget that keeps chips fresh by clamping and sealing the bag closed) in the snack aisle, as opposed to the kitchen gadget aisle.

The concept of cross-merchandising can be used in a library setting to expose young adults to different types of materials. For example, teens are usually attracted to the audio-visual section in a library. For many teens, this may be the only section of the library they visit on a regular basis. Having a display of YA titles (music-related or not) in the audio section can expose these "audio-visual only" teens to different kinds of materials. A display of classic literature titles on audio can be placed in the classic book section. Classics that have been made into movies such as *The Scarlet Letter* and *Lord of the Flies* should also be included. Just mix the videos/DVDs right in with the audio titles. The classic book titles can be on display in the audio/video section of the library as well. The point is to avoid thinking that certain materials cannot be displayed outside of where they are normally housed. The goal is to expose young adults to other types of materials. The teens that go to the audio section already prefer that format. Why not try to get them to appreciate books and magazines as well?

When creating displays, think about expanding them by including all types of materials. If the theme allows, all formats should be considered. A music-related display could include *Rolling Stone* magazine, fiction titles about teens and music, biographies of musicians and teens' favorite groups, popular music selections on CD and cassette, and video titles on music groups. It may be hard to find much exciting fiction on teens and music, so let the other formats add depth to the whole display. A display appealing to teens obtaining their driver's license should include books on car maintenance, buying a car, racing videos, CDs and cassettes to play in a car, and fiction titles such as *The Beetle and Me* by Karen Romano Young.

In addition to including different formats in a display, also include materials at different levels. Adult books can be mixed in with related YA titles in a display. If other departmental staff is planning a display in which YA titles can be included, such as sports or poetry, do not hesitate to bring the titles to his or her attention.

Sometimes sharing upcoming display ideas with other staff members or within the context of a staff meeting can solicit titles from other staff, as well as help with idea generation. Do not forget to put out a call for staff to clean out attics and closets to help gather props to go along with the display's theme. (See Chapter 10 for some suggestions.)

BEFORE YOU BEGIN

Before an active merchandising program can begin, some organizational tactics should be employed. It is a good idea to keep a calendar listing of all displays. This can be kept in the same daily calendar/planner that is used to document all other YA activities, such as programs, library tours, school visits, appearances at community events, and so on. Plan displays just as you do these other programs. Thinking ahead will allow you to tie in displays with future programs or events. Some libraries require programs and events to be planned three to four months in advance. This allows time for proper promotion and event planning. Other libraries are not as rigid in their scheduling and are able to plan, produce, promote, and conduct a successful event in just two weeks. The advantage to planning displays ahead is that it allows you to gather enough materials to keep the display full for the time period in which it will be on display. It also allows you time to carefully design the artwork and signage while collecting and assembling the props that will accompany the library materials. If props need to be borrowed from staff members or local businesses, notice can be given to those individuals who offered to provide them.

Keeping a calendar of displays is also a good idea so that displays are not repeated too often. The calendar can include the theme, as well as the titles displayed. The same books may fall into several themes, but using the same old book will bore, not excite young adults. Using the same prop too often can also be boring.

Along with the calendar, it makes sense to develop an idea/resource file. This too can be added to the calendar. Sometimes a great idea for a winter display will come to you in the heat of the summer. A magazine picture you just happen to be browsing can set the mind racing with all sorts of display ideas that you will not be able to execute right at that moment. Where will ideas come from? Think of what is happening in the lives of the young adults you serve. What trends are hot? Again, by keeping up with teen culture, these questions are easily answered. Chapter 10 offers examples of actual displays that will allow the busy librarian to get started. Coordinate displays with what is going on around your particular community. Try to stay flexible with what is happening around you. For example, if the local high school football team is heading to the playoffs, it may be a good time to highlight sports-related books. Sometimes little advance notice will not allow for proper planning, but a display may be worth the extra effort. *Chase's Calendar of Events* offers many ideas about unique events, anniversaries, or birthdays celebrated throughout the year around the globe. Some of these never-before-heard-of celebrations are just wacky enough to incorporate into a library display. (See Chapter 10 for some suggestions.)

YA-related listservs can also be helpful in idea generation, as well as keeping current with YA library literature.

Before choosing a theme, another necessary point in proper planning is to take a critical look at the YA area of the library. What kind of space is available for display? Locations of displays will be discussed later in this chapter, but it is too important not to mention in the beginning stages of display development. Do not be afraid to move things around to make room for displays. Creating excitement through constant change is key to successful merchandising. Look at the location of past displays. Were they in visible places? Measure possible areas for displays to see if ample room exists to house the intended display. Does enough room exist to put up a poster? A location may dictate how large accompanying signage will be. The decision must be made as to the type of display. Will the display fill a window case or a glass cube and therefore be the type that will draw attention to an event and contain items that young adults cannot touch? Or will it be a display that showcases materials available for circulation? Look at the area that needs to be filled. Is it an entire slat wall with an accompanying bulletin board or a small area, such as a window ledge or endcap? These areas need to be assessed and the determination needs to be made as to how many different materials will be included in the display.

Whatever topic or theme is chosen, make sure that the library owns enough materials centered around the theme in order to keep the display full throughout the life of the display. The purpose of the display is to entice teens to check items out. As young adults choose items from the display, it will need to be refilled on a regular basis. Holding back some of the materials and not using them all at the beginning can help. Make sure that the theme is broad enough to allow for the inclusion of many items and formats as refills. It is probably a good idea to have a core list of fifteen to twenty items. A great idea for a display may seem exciting, like teens featured in westerns, but finding enough materials in your library to keep the display filled will be a challenge.

Many display planners find that drawing a preliminary sketch of a display can be helpful. This can be a rough drawing or outline of how everything will look once it is in its place. It can also be a more formal sketch drawn to scale using graph paper. Formal or informal, these sketches map out lettering, signage, furniture and fixture arrangement, and prop placement, as well as where items destined for circulation will go.

The next step in creating a display is to pool all necessary materials together. These will include art materials, background fabrics or papers to add excitement and color, posters, fixtures for mounting books, any props, and so forth. Once these have been gathered, signage lettering and illustration can be decided upon and produced. Make sure that lettering will fit into the intended space. Once this has been accomplished, the display can be assembled. Once everything is in place, take a photograph of the display to keep with the preliminary sketch for your files. This will be beneficial when assembling other displays or remembering past features.

It is important to think ahead and plan where the display materials will be stored when they are not in use. Library materials intended for circulation will obviously be reshelved in their correct places in the collection. However, storage must be found for things such as fabric, papers, props, stencils and art materials, posters, and illustrations. Posters and illustrations, if reusable, are best stored flat. Library suppliers sell storage boxes for posters and other display items. Filing cabinets work well for most display items. Fabrics can be refolded and hung over wire hangers in a coat closet. The more carefully items are stored, the more likely they will be able to be reused or recycled in the future. Library storage and office space are usually scarce, and often finding places to put things requires more creativity than other aspects of the job. Keep all of this in mind, as merchandising efforts become serious and the accumulation of "stuff" becomes necessary. If possible, try to keep all display materials in one general area so when looking for ideas or searching for things, items are at the fingertips.

How long should a display remain? Karen Litt warns that even the best displays lose effectiveness if they are left up too long.[11] Some bookstores change displays in windows as often as once a week because their clientele visit the store that often. Others find that twice a month is sufficient. Sometimes a display topic may dictate how long a display will stand. For example, a display highlighting Banned Books Week may just run a week or two in September. A display encouraging teens to vote for their favorite title to have with them if stranded on a desert island may be present for four weeks during October in honor of Teen Read Week. A good rule of thumb is to plan to keep a general display up for a time period of three to four weeks, especially if a library's regular loan period is two weeks. Smaller displays, such as those on endcaps, should be changed more frequently. Those in glass cubes or windows should be changed more often also, for example, every two weeks. If materials circulate for two weeks, patrons are likely to revisit the library when the items are due, if not before. Some teens are regulars in the library every day after school. These teens will become bored looking at the same display day after day for two weeks, so changing things around every week may be necessary. While this may be labor intensive, concentrate on full-blown displays for special events, but make smaller displays or interactive games, contests, and bulletin boards more prominent. Smaller-scaled displays may just include a poster or a sign and no theme—just new books to fill in during the in-between times.

If all items in a display are taken out, and it becomes sparse and empty before the scheduled time to disassemble it, take it down anyway. Nothing looks worse than having a display with great signage and props, but no materials. If someone comes back to the library to find the display missing but wants a book that was featured, hand him/her a booklist that highlights all of the items in the previous display. If a booklist does not accompany displays, make sure a list of materials included is available to yourself and to all staff so that any requests can be handled.

At the end of a display's usefulness, it will need to be disassembled. Props, posters, and illustrations can be stored together in a box labeled with the theme or stored separately in boxes including all topics. This will depend on the storage space in the library. Boxes with each theme will require more room for storage. Whichever way is used, make sure to post a list of materials included in the box on the lid so that it is easily viewed and does not have to be opened to figure out its contents. It is preferable to break down displays and store fabrics together, posters together, and so on, as opposed to storing thematic units together. Materials will be easier to find and can be used in other displays, not just limited to one topic. This saves storage space, and the photographs of the displays can be stored and filed by topic to help you remember the placement of items.

To review, the important steps to follow in maintaining effective displays are:

1. Keep a calendar listing of displays.

2. Develop an idea or resource file to help with idea generation.

3. Look at areas in the library to find possible locations for the display (window cases, slat wall, endcaps, bulletin boards, glass cubes). Measure the intended area.

4. Pick a theme for a particular display and find props to enhance visual effectiveness.

5. Make a sketch of what the display will look like. Gather materials needed to make signs, illustrations, mounting materials, plus items to be included in the display.

6. Choose a title. Create signage and lettering.

7. Assemble display.

8. Take a photograph of completed display and keep for records.

9. Decide how long display will remain.

10. Watch as materials fly into the hands of teens.

11. Plan next display.

12. Disassemble display and store reusable items.

PRINCIPLES OF DISPLAY

Certain layouts or shapes of design can illustrate what is pleasing to the eye through the attractive use of space. These creative arrangements convey visual messages to the young adult looking at the display.

Balance

Balance requires that the visual weight of a display be evenly distributed.[12] It is as if a person visually draws an imaginary line down through the middle of a display or sign and expects to see equal amounts on either side. If this does not happen, the viewer feels a need to rearrange things to make it so. Balance can be symmetrical or asymmetrical. The easiest to achieve, symmetrical balance requires the left half of the design to be a mirror image of the right side.[13] In other words, the same shapes or items are repeated in the same positions on either side of the imaginary central line. The negative side of symmetrical balance is that it can become dull and boring. Asymmetrical balance is achieved when elements are place anywhere, so long as they balance each other visually.[14] This type of balance is less formal. While each half is different, the whole arrangement is harmonious. It can be more interesting as it creates more imaginative, often shocking effects.[15] An element of asymmetrical balance can mean placing a large item close to the center of a display that is balanced by a smaller item placed toward the edge.

Emphasis

Emphasis requires that some elements stand out from the rest. These elements can have a border around them, be in a different color, or be made bigger, brighter, or bolder.[16] Often these highlighted elements become a focal point to which the eye is drawn.

Simplicity

The display design should accomplish its purpose as directly as possible.[17] An example of simplicity would be thinking about adding an illustration to a sign heavy with text. While one illustration will break up the monotony of text, two or three would become distracting.

Variety

Variety is the opposite of simplicity. An eye-catching display should include the greatest possible variety of shapes and sizes, colors and textures.[18]

Unity

Unity is also known as consistency or harmony. All of the elements of a design work together effectively toward a common goal.[19] In other words, all of the elements look as if they belong together and not as if they were thrown together by chance. Through proper planning unity can be achieved by placing things in close proximity or in groupings.

Shapes of Design

Designers of periodicals or advertisements use certain layouts that can be used in library display design. Alan Heath, author of *Off the Wall: The Art of Book Display*, suggests that one of seven formal layouts can be used to help structure ideas and enable the display viewer to get the point quickly.

Clothesline. In this design shape, photographs or drawings in combination with text and headlines all share a common top margin. The different bottoms may end at various distances from the top. This can relieve the boredom of having the top be in a straight line.

Townscape. Related to the clothesline, the elements in a townscape share a common bottom. It can again include text and illustrations or book jackets with irregular top margins, resembling a city's skyline.

Pinwheel. This layout format is popular with teen magazines. It contains four or more pictures or elements revolving around a central imaginary point similar to a pinwheel. This positioning creates visual motion, causing the eye to sweep around the circle continuously.

Dominant Element. A dominant element in a display can be in the form of a large poster or illustration. This element is noticeably larger than everything else found in the layout.

Mosaic. A mosaic layout usually contains many small elements around a larger one. All elements fit like a puzzle and share an inner margin. Outer margins are not shared. This layout can be found in art galleries where paintings are grouped together as units with the same margins between each frame.

Isolated Element. An isolated element draws attention to itself by being related but worthy of special attention. It must be far enough away from the rest of the display but connected to it somehow, usually by a narrow line or border.

Sketch. The sketch normally evolves around an imaginary triangle or other shape. It combines collage, drawings, or other art forms in irregular shapes.[20]

Techniques/Arrangements

When arranging items for display, it is important to ensure they are as accessible as possible. Try to stand materials up, and never lay them flat. To create a sense of movement, arrange items in triangles. Use boxes to elevate the smaller items and place larger things in front of the boxes.[21] Remember to make sure that the items are not placed in a tower-like or domino-like fashion so that pulling out one item may cause the whole display to topple. Different heights and surface angles attract the eye.[22] To add dimension to displays, think in terms of spatial orientation. Avoid arranging merchandise in a straight line. Think in terms of foreground, middle ground, and background.[23] Display shelving, among regular shelving, can be arranged to show a sense of movement also. Display shelving can be moved out of line with regular shelving to differentiate the two. Colorful paper placed behind the display shelving also can make it more appealing.[24]

COMPONENTS OF DISPLAY

Color

Color can be the single most important element in drawing attention to your display.[25] Color is what teens will see first and can affect the way they feel or react. Often color is recognized before a person interprets such things as a form or shape.[26] Teens are attracted to bright colors. Remember, the brighter the color, the greater its capacity to attract a person's attention.[27] Colors can suggest moods and meanings:

- Yellow signifies relaxation, optimism, and expectancy. It is usually happy and bright.

- Orange is agreeable and friendly.

- Red is powerful, sexy, exciting, stimulating, loving, and assertive.

- Pink is sweet and pretty.

- Green signifies growth.

- Blue, the favorite of most people, is cool, calm, and comfortable.

- Purple is regal and aloof.

- Black is sophisticated, mysterious, and often associated with death.

- White offers hope and innocence.[28]

In addition, people of certain ages and social groups respond differently to color. For example, young children and non-sophisticates respond to bright, sharp colors such as yellow, red, green, blue, shocking pink, and turquoise. Casual, outgoing, fun-loving people who are high spirited are drawn to warm colors such as red, orange, yellow, and pink. These colors are considered more aggressive.[29]

Anyone who was around in the 1970s surely remembers the colors of gold, brown, and avocado green. In the nineties, mauve and hunter green were found in lobbies everywhere. Decor colors change with the times, just as colors in the fashion world. Just when your closet is filled with bright jewel tones that are the rage, fashion designers announce the new clothes line dominant in pastels. The Color Association of the United States (CAUS), America's oldest forecasting organization, foresees shades of pinks, green and blue turquoises, oranges and corals, lilacs and lavenders, sky blues that resemble gray, and yellowed greens to impact the giftware industry in years early in the 2000s.[30] The beginning of the new millennium will also move in a glittering, electrically colored direction that leaves the bareness of nineties minimalism behind.[31]

When working with teens, predicting color can be easy. Just be in tune to their clothes, shoes, makeup, and "fun" items they buy with their discretionary income. When planning displays, take clues from what is around them, especially in the stores they frequent and in the popular magazines they read.

Lighting

Lighting is very important to any display. An unused corner may seem an ideal place to set up a display but probably has little or no direct lighting. An area must be well lit to attract attention and allow teens to browse without squinting to read text and titles. Darkened corners can be lightened with inexpensive track lighting or portable battery-operated lights. Window display cases and window ledges require strong spotlights to attract attention. Keep an eye out for burned-out bulbs, especially in display cases. These are often forgotten or ignored. Inexpensive Christmas tree lights can add unexpected attention to a display. String them around a window frame, and set up a display on the window ledge or space below. These lights can also be used as a border for a poster or sign. Different color light bulbs in spotlights can also attract attention. Try placing a strobe light in a window display to give it a funky feeling. Lighting should not only be functional, but should definitely add instant pizzazz.

Signage

Any type of display will need a sign explaining its topic or theme. Signage and illustration can enhance a display and make it more memorable and attractive. All displays need a title or a headline, preferably with a subject and a verb. They should also be short and to the point.[32] Make sure that the title or headline is not dull or boring. Would you rather pick up an item from a display entitled "Test Materials for College" or something from "Is that Your Final Answer?" borrowing from the popular television show, *Who Wants to Be a Millionaire?* Spend some time when thinking of a title. A weak one will lessen the impact of the display. Use techniques such as alliteration and, by all means, borrow from current trends.

No matter what your artistic abilities are, signs should never be sloppy. Signs should look professional, even if they are homemade.[33] Some people like to use stencils to create uniform lettering. This is fine, but the signs can lose effect if the lettering is colored in with magic marker or cut out with uneven edges. If this technique is used, make sure the letters come out neatly. Ellison or other die-cut machines make lettering easy to do. The one way to create professional lettering that most libraries will have access to is using a computer and a laser printer or a high quality ink-jet printer. Decorative papers can be used to attract attention. Suppliers such as Highsmith, Demco, and Gaylord sell paper whose color does not fade as time goes by. Faded paper and yellowed tape will give any display a shop-worn look. A computer can give you attractive and different typefaces, while the printer prints out even colored ink. Letters can then be cut out and mounted on pieces of cardboard or foam core. Make sure good quality paper is used in the printer. When mounting letters, use double-sided tape, glue stick, or white glue. These adhere the best and dry clear. Artistic teens may like to make your signs; however, the same professional look and feel should apply to their signs as well. Depending on the theme, a small portable chalkboard may even do the trick. Instead of using preprinted signs on windows or glass partitions, use window sign kits that are available from library suppliers. Static cling letters come in bright colors to attract teens' attention. The letters are reusable and cling to a window using no adhesive.

When arranging lettering or text on signs, certain elements should be considered. Remember that the eye needs a certain amount of free space in order to read text comfortably. Some lettering styles can be so fancy and decorative that they can be hard to decipher. Crowded text or hard-to-read lettering are useless because reading them requires too much effort, which means they will most likely be ignored. Empty space on a sign is not a bad thing; it gives the eye a place to rest. If letters are cut out and pasting them in a straight line is worrisome, letters can be staggered.

Signs in libraries do more than just state display titles and headlines. For example, signs are used to help people locate sections of the library. These often use library terms such as "circulation desk," which the average patron may call the "checkout desk." Make sure signs use terms teens will understand. Most libraries use signs that read "Young Adult Area" or "YA Area," while teens do not refer to themselves with those terms. Some libraries have changed to "Teen Center" or "Teen Area." Signs announcing programs, displays, or events should be posted perpendicular to traffic flow, as opposed to parallel. Teens will face signs perpendicular to them, while signs posted parallel to them will require them to look to the side. Signs posted on doors, such as the front entrance, should only contain two to four words, since people will spend about 1.5 seconds in front of them, and that is all they have time to read.[34] Think in terms of road signs that contain large lettering and the perfect color and contrast.[35]

Rules for contests or summer reading programs are often posted but usually contain too much text. These rules should be worded as succinctly and concisely as possible, as teens will not spend time poring over each sentence. Also caution against placing signs on any blank wall or space just because it is available. Walk around with an open mind and think about what a person will be doing at each location or where his/her eyes will focus. Will he/she be walking through quickly or standing still, as in a line at the checkout?[36]

Avoid placing a sign too high up on a wall. Keep in mind who will read it, how he/she will approach it, and if he/she will be able to see it. If something can be approached from all sides, make a multi-faceted sign so it can be viewed from all sides. The same idea applies to posters and signs hanging in windows. People outside will be able to read a one-sided sign, while patrons inside the building will face a blank poster.

Signs can be in the form of shelf talkers. These small signs can be as small as or smaller than index cards. Book reviews can be photocopied, cut out, and placed in a metal stand on a shelf next to the items. These metal stands are similar to those found in restaurants highlighting daily specials or drinks. Often teens are confused as to whether display items can be checked out. A small sign reading "All display items can be checked out" can be made and placed among the displays. Other little blurbs, such as "Pick me" and "No, pick me" captions, can be cut out in odd shapes and placed next to materials indicating the same thing.

Signs not posted on a surface such as a wall will need to be sturdy, as they will probably get knocked around. They will also need to be self-supportive. This type of sign will need to be mounted on heavy cardboard or foam core. Sign supports can be made for both lightweight and heavier materials. A lightweight sign support is made by cutting an isosceles triangle from a sheet of cardboard and then folding it down the middle. The triangle should be at least two-thirds as tall as the sign. One half of the triangle is then glued to the back of the sign, and the other half is extended at a ninety-degree angle.[37] For a heavier sign, a support can be made by folding a strip of cardboard into a wedge and gluing it to the back of the sign. When observed from the side, the wedge takes the form of a right triangle. The longest side of the triangle should be at least two-thirds the height of the sign.[38] Acrylic sign supports can also be purchased from library supply companies.

A self-supporting sign board can be made by folding a rectangular piece of heavy cardboard into three equal widths. The rectangle can then be folded up into a triangular column. The edges are taped together to make the sign sturdy. A tab or flap can be left at the one end that can be folded into the signboard and taped internally.[39] In addition, two pieces of heavy paper can be glued together, around the top and sides, leaving the bottom and middle free of glue. This creates a sleeve that can be placed over a free-standing metal bookend.

Many signs and displays are enhanced using graphics and illustrations. Unless your artistic talents are of high caliber, clip art and graphics found on electronic publishing programs will suffice. Outlines of images can be enlarged using a large roll of craft paper. First find a clip art of an image that is drawn using simple lines. Photocopy this picture and place it on a transparency. Use an overhead projector to project the image onto a large sheet of paper that has been taped to a wall. The size of the projected image will depend on the distance of the projector form the wall. Trace the outline of the image onto the paper. Take the picture down from the wall to add finishing touches, and then cut it out.[40]

Display makers with little artistic talent may find that using photographs from old calendars or magazines in displays can add a professional look. Keep in mind, however, that items of this type fall under copyright law and should be used with the proper discretion.

Display Locations

The most obvious place to display YA books is in the teen section. However, location is not limited to this area of the library. It has already been suggested to place displays targeted at young adults in other popular areas of the library, such as the audio-visual section. Teens also use adult nonfiction for research, so that area too may be a place to try something different. Popular locations are also near the front entrance and the checkout desk. Libraries usually have enclosed display cases throughout the building. Make sure that YA displays are highlighted periodically in these areas, regardless of where the YA section is located. These types of displays will help to gain exposure. The only place that should be avoided, if possible, would be the children's area.

Regardless of which collection the YA display is adjacent to, there are some spatial arguments to be taken under consideration. Retailers have noticed that crowding displays has an adverse affect on the sales of items. Videotape of a busy entrance showed that a rack featuring men's ties was too close to the door. People who were looking at ties were bumped or brushed from behind as others tried to enter through the door. People did not like being bumped from behind and thus abandoned their search for a tie.[41] It therefore becomes necessary to make sure that there is enough room to navigate a display and the area surrounding it. Placing a display too close to the copy machine or a bathroom that many people use may inhibit browsing efforts. The same rule can apply to areas too near the checkout desk. Patrons will be standing in line and could possibly block with their bodies another's view of a display. Teens will be less likely to browse titles and say "excuse me" in order to pick something from the display. Along the same lines, aisles need to be wide enough for people to browse and still allow for someone to pass behind them.

A popular place for displays in a library can be in the lobby or foyer as people enter the building. While this may seem like an ideal location, one consumer researcher has discovered otherwise. As patrons walk through doors, a transition zone is needed. People are coming in from the parking lot, walking at a pretty fast pace. As they enter the building, their pace slows, their eyes are adjusting to the indoor lighting, and their senses are responding to the new sounds and smells. The patron needs about ten feet to adjust to lighting and size things up. Therefore, anything placed directly inside a door may well be lost to patrons. Often signs on entrance/exit doors are ignored because people are not looking for a sign but rather a handle or push/pull sign. Their main goal at that point is to get in the door, not read what is on it.[42] This concept hit home in my own library. Tax time (January–April) was tremendously busy, like in many libraries, and the library provided free tax forms to patrons. To aid in self-service for patrons, tax forms were placed directly inside the front door, so people could walk in, take the forms they needed, and go on their merry way. In theory, this was an ideal location, since the reference/circulation staff, who were already doing a million other things, would not be over-burdened with tax form queries. However, day after day, patron after patron entered the building, walked past the tax forms without a glance, and proceeded to the checkout/reference desk to ask where the tax forms were located. After the staff pointed out the location, the patron invariably said, "Oh, I walked right past them!"

Consumer research also has revealed that as people enter buildings, they have a tendency to drift toward the right. This is probably tied into the side of the road on which we drive. Therefore, layouts should be designed in accordance with where people walk or where they look. Placing a display to the right of a door, after a proper transition zone, takes into consideration people's habits of movement.[43] Ends of aisles are excellent places for displays because teens will approach them face forward versus walking forward down an aisle and having to look unnaturally from side to side.[44]

A common problem of display placement is that there is just not any room in the library to add anything else. Creative thinking and the rearrangement of things can solve this dilemma. Even an ironing board can be covered and used as a flat surface. In fact, it does not hurt to move furniture around in order to draw attention to a display. The rearrangement itself will draw attention because something will be different.[45]

Displays can be set up on shelf tops, tables, windowsills, even floors—almost anywhere. Any flat surface that is visible to patrons can be a good spot for a display, but the best areas are within normal traffic patterns.[46] Materials can be displayed on shelves that are between 36 and 60 inches from the floor.[47] The middle shelves are at eye level and are the best ones to use for display. Books can be moved to the top and bottom shelves to make space for display in the middle.[48] As this tactic becomes successful, more books will be checked out, leaving more space on the shelves for display.

The ends of aisles offer display opportunities. Using fixtures and stands described in Chapter 7, these highly visible areas should be taken advantage of as much as possible. Be careful, though, that these areas provide adequate space for teens to browse and others to walk past them.

Many libraries have support posts or columns. These can be decorated according to a display's theme and books can be placed around the bottom. Given the right amount of creative attention, these columns can be naturally eye-catching because they reach all the way up to the ceiling.

Speaking of ceilings, too many people miss the opportunity to fully utilize this possible display space. Most any sign or item can be hung from a ceiling. Dentists have taken advantage of this opportunity. Many place calming pictures on the ceiling so that when a patient is laying in the dental chair undergoing dental procedures, which can at times be stressful, the eyes have something pleasant on which to focus. Book jackets can be hung from the ceiling using fishing line, which hangs almost invisibly. Signs are not the only things easily hung from the ceiling. Many toy suppliers sell inflatable items that can be adapted for any theme. Disc jockeys hand these props out at bar mitzvahs and teen dances. An inflatable electric guitar in hot pink hanging from the ceiling can do wonders to perk up a display for the Grammy awards. Remember, when hanging anything from the ceiling, it needs to be two-sided. Also be aware if the library uses motion sensors for nighttime security. Items hung too close to these sensors can set off alarms.

If your teen area does not have a bulletin board, things can be adapted. Purchase a sturdy easel and make signs on posterboard for display. Materials can then be placed around the easel. This allows the display to be moved wherever there is room.

Window ledges can offer another opportunity. The window itself gives you a place to post a sign, while the ledge houses the materials. Windows are a natural place for people to look because they are used to looking outside. Anything put on a window will need to be two-sided. While the side facing the outside does not have to advertise the display inside, it can announce upcoming programs or events.

The important thing to remember is to place a display where teens will spot it—in areas of the library that they use the most. Also, make sure that enough room is available around the display, so everyone can navigate around it and reach the items in it. Then let the imagination run wild.

Props and Other Materials Used in Display

An important component that can make a display more memorable and eye-catching is the inclusion of props. A prop is any item in a display other than merchandise. Props are meant to complement and enhance a display but not upstage it or provide too much clutter.[49] Props can be found everywhere you look. Do not make the mistake of thinking that props must be handmade by someone who has an artistic flair. Always consider using real, three-dimensional objects in displays. If something must be made, ask local art students to lend their creative talents. Local merchants may lend merchandise to be used in a display. If this is the case, put a small sign near the borrowed or donated item to acknowledge the merchant or store. Bookstores, movie theaters, card shops, music stores, and video stores should definitely be on the list of places to beg and borrow. Oversize cardboard cutouts, posters, and other promotional items are just a few of the things that merchants might be willing to part with. Even fast food restaurants and grocery stores sponsor promotions that include extraordinary materials that can be incorporated into a library display. Publishers can provide posters and book jackets. Book jackets can be placed on dummy books and placed in enclosed window displays without taking the real book out of circulation for any time. Also consider asking fellow staff members to lend prop items. Surprising things can turn up in attics, basements, and garages. Also ask teens for items. Teens who have collectibles may be willing to showcase their collection in an enclosed display case or lend something for display. Remember when borrowing props that anything can happen to them. Someone's heirloom may be a great addition, but taking the chance that something might happen to it may not be worth its inclusion. Items placed in window displays will be exposed to extreme heat or cold, which can ruin things. Garage sales, flea markets, and closeout stores can be treasure troves for inexpensive prop items.

Everyday, ordinary items can turn a display into something really special. A small foldable beach chair can enhance a summer reading display and also provide an alternative place on which to display materials. A blowup kiddie pool or an old television can be a flat surface on which to display materials while also fitting into themes. Props hung from the ceiling can be especially attention grabbing. Items that you really do not want handled can be hung out of people's reach, while still being effective display items. For example a hockey stick or any type of sports equipment would probably look great in a sports display. These items would also be tempting for any teen to pick up and use with a wad of crumpled paper as a puck or a ball in a high spirited imaginary game right in the YA area. While in some libraries this behavior may be considered acceptable fun, other libraries would consider these actions as grounds of banishment from the building. Hanging items such as these from the ceiling can provide the visual but remove the temptation.

A prop such as a battery-operated clock as the focal point of a display can be especially eye-catching because usually everyone looks to see what time it is.[50] Possible themes to go with the prop could be "time travel," "time for a good book," or even "No time to read? Check out these short stories and magazines."

Some libraries own a mannequin that is used for display purposes. While the use of one may seem repetitious, it can actually be quite comical for patrons to see where the mannequin will turn up next or what new outrageous way it will be dressed. A mannequin can fit into an empty chair with related books settled around it on the floor. Dress shops or clothing stores going out of business usually liquidate all items and fixtures at the time of closing. A store may be willing to donate a mannequin or charge only a small fee for it.

Props do not have to be large-scale in order to be effective. Even small items, such as artificial grass or snow, silk flowers, metallic tinsel, or ribbon, can help a display. Props can also be recycled and reused in different settings. Avoid using the same prop in the same way several months or displays in a row. Keeping good records in a calendar of displays will prevent this from happening. Variety and creativity are important, especially when working with teens. Storage of props that are not borrowed can be another problem. Ideally all props should be stored in the same location for ease in finding things and reusing them.

Other materials used when creating displays should be kept in the same place also. Fabrics, while not a prop per se, can add color and flash. Fabrics can add a festive flair while hiding stands, fixtures, or tables on which a display is placed. Fabric can be draped over book holders and fixtures so that materials placed on the fabric have an unseen support. Fabric can be purchased inexpensively by the yard at local fabric stores. Purchase at least one-and-one-half yards of each fabric.[51] Seasonal fabrics can be purchased after the season ends in preparation for the next year. Fabrics such as gold lamé can be versatile and used across many themes. The color can be used with a glittery effect and also be attractive in a futuristic theme. The reverse of this fabric is usually plain black in color, which again can be very versatile. Fabrics can also be used as background for bulletin boards. If budgets are tight, forget buying seasonal fabrics and just stick to basic colors that can be used in different ways. When buying fabric, purchase types such as lamé, soft wool, or jersey that drape nicely and do not require special care or ironing.

Foam core can be another invaluable material for displays. It is lightweight, easy to paint, and easy to cut for creating sturdy shapes. Items can be glued or stapled to it as well.[52] Decorative screens can be used as a background as well as for hiding structural deformities. Baskets, barrels, and boxes can also be used. Wallpaper can also serve as a background.

As you become more display savvy, it may be advantageous to create a display toolbox. Such a toolbox would keep all necessary items at the fingertips for easy assembly. This would include things necessary to assemble a display. Some items to include are a utility knife, pins, a hot glue gun, scissors, white glue, rubber cement, thumbtacks, a tape measure, a ruler, a stapler, erasers, tape, and fishing line. When using fishing line to hang items from a ceiling, for instance, it appears invisible from a distance, as opposed to yarn or kite string, which are easily visible. A paper clip can be unfolded to resemble a hook and the fishing line attached to it by a knot. The other end of the paper clip can then be hung from the ceiling tile as a support.

The tips and techniques included in this chapter are meant to serve as a starting point for display novices. Several books on this subject have been published, and these should be reviewed as well. Many offer themes or ideas for display as well as instructions on how to make props. While these are not related specifically to teens, ideas may be adapted. When creating displays, keep an open mind and avoid the trap of thinking that you do not have the time, talent, or room in the library to market materials. A little imagination, creative thinking, and preparedness will lead to fun and exciting displays.

NOTES

1. Julie C. Doepken, "The Use of Display as a Merchandising Tool in Bookstores and Its Implications for Public Libraries" (Master's paper, University of North Carolina at Chapel Hill, 1994), 33.

2. Ibid., 34.

3. Karen Litt, "Visual Merchandising of Books," *Unabashed Librarian* 60 (1986): 3.

4. Sharon L. Baker, *The Responsive Public Library Collection: How to Develop and Market It* (Englewood, CO: Libraries Unlimited, 1993), 263.

5. Ben Menin and Arthur E. Benning, *The Power of Point of Purchase Advertising* (New York: Amacon, 1992), 3.

6. Kenneth G. Sivulich, "Merchandising Your Library," *Public Libraries* 28 (March/April 1989), 99.

7. Barry Janoff, "Show and Sell—Retailers Re-design Point of Purchase Displays," *Progressive Grocer* 79, no. 4 (April 2000): 107.

8. Ibid.

9. Ibid.

10. Del Hawkins, *Consumer Behavior: Implications for Marketing Strategy* 6th ed. (Chicago: Richard D. Irwin, 1995), 501.

11. Litt, "Visual Merchandising," 4.

12. Mark Schaeffer, *Library Displays Handbook* (New York: H. W. Wilson Co., 1991), 15.

13. Ibid.

14. Ibid., 16.

15. Ruth Laszlo, *Display Design: An Introduction to Window Display, Point-of-Purchase, Posters, Signs and Signage, Sales Environments, and Exhibit Displays* (Englewood Cliffs, NJ: Prentice Hall, 1983), 40.

16. Schaeffer, *Library Displays*, 16.

17. Ibid.

18. Ibid., 18.

19. Ibid., 19.

20. Alan Heath, *Off the Wall: The Art of Book Display* (Littleton, CO: Libraries Unlimited, 1987), 10–11.

21. Chris Rippel, "Displays Help Browsers Select Books." *Unabashed Librarian* 106 (1998): 25.

22. Sylvie Green, "Merchandising Techniques and Libraries." *School Library Journal* 28 no. 1 (1981): 37.

23. Litt, "Visual Merchandising," 4.

24. Rippel, *Displays Help*, 25.

25. Litt, "Visual Merchandising," 4.

26. Margaret Walch, "New Colors for a New Age," *Gifts and Decorative Accessories* 101, no. 3 (March 2000): 52.

27. Ibid.

28. Martin Pegler, *Visual Merchandising and Display* (New York: Fairchild Publications, 1983), 29.

29. Ibid., 30.

30. Walch, *New Colors*, 52.

31. Ibid.

32. Heath, *Off the Wall*, 9.

33. Litt, "Visual Merchandising," 3.

34. Paco Underhill, *Why We Buy: The Science of Shopping* (New York: Simon & Schuster, 1999), 64.

35. Ibid.

36. Ibid., 63.

37. Schaeffer, *Library Displays*, 104.

38. Ibid., 105.

39. Heath, *Off the Wall*, 19.

40. Wendy Barteluk, *Library Displays on a Shoestring: Three Dimensional Techniques for Promoting Library Services* (Metuchen, NJ: Scarecrow Press, 1993), 59.

41. Underhill, *Why We Buy*, 18.

42. Ibid., 46–47.

43. Ibid., 76.

44. Ibid., 79.

45. Barteluk, *Library Displays*, 4.

46. Sivulich, "Merchandising Your Library," 99.

47. Ibid.

48. Lesley J. Farmer, "Displays for Libraries that Don't Have Room for Displays," *The Book Report* (January/February 1991): 17.

49. Robert Colborne, *Visual Merchandising: The Business of Merchandise Presentation* (Albany, NY: Delmar Publishers, 1996), 109.

50. Barteluk, *Library Displays*, 67.

51. Susan E. Cozzens, "Goddesses of Library Display Unveil Their Secrets," *Today's Librarian* (December 2000), 23.

52. Colborne, "Visual Merchandising," 114.

7

Fixtures for
Merchandising

Some display techniques can be executed using furnishings that the library currently owns, such as tables and countertops, as well as various building features, including window ledges. Even traditional shelving can be adapted to make the collection more attractive. As previously mentioned, the ends of shelves can be used as areas for the face front display materials. The collection also may be able to be shifted, leaving shelves at eye-level free of spine out books and making room for more face front display. The chapter on display techniques also mentioned some creative props, such as an ironing board or other "everyday" objects, that can be used as the base fixture for a display.

This chapter will discuss fixtures and furnishings that are specifically structured to enhance merchandising efforts and create a browsing atmosphere similar to that found in bookstores and other retail outlets. Some of these fixtures can be purchased rather inexpensively, others may require more of a budgetary commitment. While these furnishings are available through vendors of library products and supplies, some of the fixtures can be made by or purchased through local craftspeople. Others can be acquired by contacting local merchants who no longer have a need for a particular piece.

In the following pages, pieces of furniture and fixtures will be discussed and their potential uses will be explained. A selected list of vendors of these products will also be given. The fixtures and furnishings mentioned in-depth in this chapter, however, are pertinent only to the merchandising aspects and the display of the YA collection. It is important to mention that other furnishings in the YA area can make the atmosphere of the library more exciting to teens. While an in-depth discussion of YA spaces is beyond the initial scope of this book, it is important to gain a general understanding of what constitutes an ideal YA section of a library. If a YA section is nonexistent or planned without the input of teens or without their lifestyles in mind, any attempt to merchandise the collection may be lost. As a result, teens will notice that little was done to specifically target "their" space to their lifestyles.

Despite the increasing population and demographic studies of teenagers, it has been said that public libraries give more space to restrooms than to young adults.[1] Indeed, there seems to be a vast disparity in the way libraries treat space dedicated to teens. Some libraries have separate rooms for teens filled with computers, couches, easy chairs, study carrels, tables, and appropriate signage. Others can only offer a magazine rack or shelving range. Either of these options is a far cry from the teen sections found (or more likely not found) in libraries ten years ago. Despite space constraints, the biggest mistake a library can make is to fail to have a separate YA collection or space designated especially for teens. Teens who offered their opinions in the DeWitt Wallace Reader's Digest Fund's Initiative, "Public Libraries as Partners in Youth Development," mentioned that having a "distinct area of our own" was an advantage. Teens frequently mentioned not going to libraries because of "too many adults," "not enough people my age," and being bothered by "too much mess and noise from younger children."[2] It is understood that libraries in large cities or those with enviable budgets can offer spaces and collections of which many smaller libraries can only dream. But libraries with little space and smaller budgets can make their spaces more appealing to teens. All it takes is creativity and the willingness to take a leadership role in teen advocacy to show library administrators that a section of the population needs more services directed at them.

When dreaming of ideal YA spaces, it is often thought that a separate room is necessary. This is not always the case nor is it very probable in most libraries. Before the idea is given up completely, existing space should be looked at creatively. Shelving can be rearranged to create a sort of enclosed space for teens—imagine an office cubicle. This is especially easy to do when one wall already exists to serve as a boundary. With a wall and shelves as boundaries, a coffee table and comfortable chairs can be placed in the center. Office dividers can also be purchased to create a "room" or type of boundary.[3] Furnishings found in YA areas, such as comfortable chairs and coffee tables, do not have to be purchased from library furniture vendors. In fact, many of these vendors do not make chairs comfortable enough for a young adult's tastes anyway. Instead, shop at garage sales, estate sales, or second-hand stores for furniture in good condition. Make sure though, that tables are sturdy enough because odds are teens will sit on them too. Bookstores offer comfortable easy chairs and places to relax. Teens will tell you what types of furniture they would like. Take clues from their bedrooms, which is where they spend most of their at-home time. A book by Adrienne Salinger, *In My Room: Teenagers in Their Bedrooms* (San Francisco, CA: Chronicle Books, 1995) highlights forty teens and their bedrooms. For a more recent look, check out teen magazines aimed at girls. These magazines offer articles and photographs depicting teens and their bedrooms. Their room decor defines who they are or would like to be. Also, do not be afraid to go with the current trends. Butterfly chairs (inexpensive chairs sort of shaped like butterflies), blow up chairs, floor pillows, or bean bags may be uncomfortable for a librarian but are great for young bodies that stretch and fidget. Think creatively; even booths purchased from a restaurant going out of business may be the right furniture. For even more ideas, check out the previously mentioned *VOYA* columns "Young Adult Spaces of Your Dreams."

In libraries where absolutely no space exists for even a chair, just shelving ranges, displays, or a small bulletin board can suffice. In fact, a bulletin board does not even have to exist to display a poster appealing to teens. A wall or window can be sufficient. Colorful milk crates, purchased cheaply through discount stores, can offer a break from the often institutional-looking library shelving. In areas where no comfortable seating exists, it is especially important to provide eye-catching displays, interactive bulletin boards, or contests to show that teens are wanted there. Whatever room or space you design, make sure teens have input and then put their ideas into action. Put to use all of the ideas suggested in Chapters 5 and 6 on merchandising and display techniques. A steel support column may be considered by some as an eye sore, while other libraries use it as an opportunity for a magnetic poetry board. Contact music or video stores to see if they will give you a cardboard cut-out of popular movie stars or music groups. Even small items can be a surprise to teens who think that the library is a boring place and not for them.

FIXTURES FOR MERCHANDISING AND DISPLAYING THE YA COLLECTION

When shopping for fixtures or furnishings specifically designed to merchandise the YA collection, it is important to remember that the best ones make it easy to show off titles in a display. Many pieces of this type of furniture are free standing and designed to make titles more attractive, appealing, and more importantly, available to patrons. The design of any fixture should be as simple as possible. When a basic fixture becomes too elaborate, it can dominate the display and detract from its appeal.[4] While many of the merchandising and display fixtures can be expensive, it is important to remember that these purchases do not have to come from just the YA budget. Some of the fixtures' expense can be shared between departments so that every department can take turns using them. Their success in displaying the collection can be used as an argument to purchase additional pieces. Also tap into community volunteer agencies or Friends of the Library groups who may be willing to offset costs with their monetary donations.

The following factors are things to think about and look for when selecting any type of fixture for merchandising:

- Does it have good craftsmanship and durability? Look at the bottom and back for clues as to how it is made. How long will it last?

- What is its function or purpose?

- Will it be moved from place to place? Does it need casters?

- Are its shelves adjustable?

- Can more than one category of materials use it?

- What type of finish will it have?

- Does it require special signage?

- What are its dimensions?

- Is it better to buy from store fixture manufacturers or from a distributor or wholesaler? Will the latter end up charging more because of a mark-up for handling the transaction?

- Have you considered used fixtures? It may be possible to buy them from a bookseller as he/she replaces old fixtures. Also, *American Bookseller* and *Publishers Weekly* advertise used pieces in almost every issue.

- If you cannot see the equipment before you make a purchase, ask for the names of places in your area that use fixtures made by the company you are considering.[5]

Fixtures for Shelving

Literature Racks. Magazines and pamphlets/brochures can be shelved face front in the same type of display system. Fixtures that are wall-mounted typically have cascading pockets that magazines or pamphlets can drop down into. The structure can be made of acrylic so that the pockets are clear, thus showing off the front covers (see Illustration 1). Others are made of wood and many only show off the top third of a magazine. Some wood-framed models do have a clear front, thus showing off the whole cover (see Illustration 2). The number of pockets per row varies as well as the size of each pocket. These can be a good way to showcase a YA magazine collection that is not too large. The pockets can house other materials in addition to magazines. Bibliographies, pathfinders, and flyers announcing upcoming events are just a few ideas of what can be displayed. Some pockets are large enough to hold newspapers. A disadvantage to this type of wall mounted display is that it does not allow for the storage of more than a few back issues of magazines. Often YA magazines are so popular that even back issues are checked out most of the time, so this may or may not be a problem.

Literature racks also come in tabletop and free-standing models (see Illustration 3). Some of the floor stands are two-sided for a maximum display of titles. Others can be attached to an end of a shelving range or placed against a wall (see Illustration 4). Both tabletop and floor fixtures are available in three- or four-sided models that revolve, allowing for viewing from all sides. Other models can be made of wire. Free-standing displays often come with wheels, making them mobile.

Illustration 1.
Acrylic Magazine Rack;
**photograph provided courtesy
of Displays 2 Go**

Illustration 2. *Economy Wall Mounted Displayers*; **photograph
provided courtesy of Gaylord®**

Illustration 3. *Rotating Countertop Literature Holder*; photograph provided courtesy of Displays 2 Go

Illustration 4.
Periodical Module; photograph provided courtesy of Library Display Shelving

Other types of periodical shelving are free-standing shelving units that have slanted shelves for face out display (see Illustration 5). The shelves have a lip so that the magazines do not slide off. Some models come with room for storage of back issues, located underneath the shelves. The shelves lift up and storage is underneath. One type that is made this way also fits at the end of a shelving range, thus maximizing the use of space. The type of periodical shelving just described tends to be the best way to shelve magazines face front. The covers of teen magazines are trendy, loud, and fun. These catch the eyes of teens right away. Some libraries file teen magazines in boxes, spine out. This method not only hides the cover, but does nothing to advance merchandising efforts.

Slatwall. This is becoming more popular in libraries as people realize its merchandising value. Slatwall is made of wood and is usually covered in Formica or other similar covering. It can come in a variety of wood-colored finishes (for example light, medium, or dark oak or cherry). Slatwall is made in sheets with horizontal four-inch boards fastened from top to bottom, in a horizontal slat configuration. The boards alternate one in and one out, creating a ridge to fasten small hanging figures. Slatwall provides endless horizontal fixture arrangements. Vertical fixture arrangements are restricted by the four-inch board width.[6]

Merchandising materials using slatwall can take a variety of forms. It can be purchased in a variety of sizes of panels to cover a wall or a portion of a wall. The panel can be mounted securely to an existing wall using the wall studs. Special panels can be purchased to fit the ends of a shelving range as well (see Illustration 6). These too can be mounted in the same manner.

Slatwall can also be purchased in free-standing or adjoining frames or panels. A panel can be purchased as a single unit and held up by support feet. Frames can be purchased in multiple numbers and attached with adjustable hinges to combine them into a screen or divider. These modular units allow you to customize the type of furnishings to suit the collection's needs. Using a number of these panels can be a way to create a YA area if a separate room does not exist. While this would not be the same as having a four-walled room, it can still section off the YA space from the rest of the library. These panels are double-sided with slatwall and can be combined with panels covered in fabric, which can display signs and posters using Velcro® or pushpins. A spinning tower that can hold paperbacks or videos can also be part of the configuration. This arrangement creates a versatile display environment.

Free-standing pieces of furniture for book displays also contain sections of slatwall. These can be an alternative to filling a large area with a slatwall configuration. These units come in a variety of shapes and sizes. Some can be triangular in shape, while others take the shape of a cube. Another popular display shape is an A-frame (see Illustration 7). Many models have casters that allow them to be moved around to better fit a library's needs, while others spin around for viewing on all sides. These slatwall furnishings often contain sections of regular shelving to alternate the display technique (see Illustration 8). Others can come with a storage section inside the cube. One of the slatwall sides acts as a hidden door to the storage space.

Illustration 5.
Hinged Display (Magazine) Shelf;
photograph provided courtesy of
Texwood

Illustration 6.
End-of-Range Display Panel;
photograph provided courtesy
of Gaylord®

Illustration 7.
*Brodart Classic Double-Faced
 A-Frame Slatwall Displayer;*
photograph provided courtesy
of Brodart

Illustration 8.
*Gaylord® Baldwin
Kiosk;* photograph
provided courtesy
of Gaylord®

The success of merchandising with slatwall depends on the usage of different kinds of accessories made especially for this type of configuration. Books and other materials are displayed on slatwall using special shelves (both flat and angled), easels, baskets, or pockets. These accessories fit into the grooves of the slatwall. They can be made of clear acrylic or wire. The accessories can be moved and matched to allow any display to be customized to fit the type of material being presented. CDs, audiocassettes, videos, paperbacks, hardbacks, magazines, and newspapers can be shelved using slatwall. Using slatwall and its accessories can make displays more creative by altering the style and format as each display changes.

Grid Merchandising. An inexpensive alternative to merchandising with slatwall is to use grid wall panels. Grid paneling uses criss-crossing wires to create a mesh or grid-like look (see Illustration 9). Shelves (angled or straight) can be hung with brackets from the grid panels to display merchandise. Other accessories include different sizes of wire baskets, as well as acrylic pieces. Grid shelving also comes in free-standing units on wheels for mobility or in cubes that can interlock together to make a display.

Illustration 9.
Grid Wall Panel;
**photograph provided
courtesy of Highsmith**

Inserts for Pre-Existing Shelving. Special inserts can be purchased to turn existing flat shelving into display shelving. Inserts shaped in a zigzag formation create pockets or slots that allow books to be displayed face front (see Illustration 10). These can be attached to shelves in a variety of ways. Zigzag shelves are also sold as an accessory for slatwall. These inserts can be made of acrylic or metal.

Illustration 10. *Back-Slant and Zigzag Shelf Inserts*; **photograph provided courtesy of Demco**

Other shelving accessories that aid browsing efforts are special shelves that are slanted. These shelves have a back-slanted feature that holds materials at an angle so patrons may be encouraged to browse. Special free-standing furniture units for all types of media can be purchased that contain slanted shelves. This type of slanted shelving is most commonly used for periodicals.

Endcap or End-of-Range Shelving. A common complaint in libraries is that there just is not enough space for displays or extra shelving. Endcap or end-of-range furnishings can help to solve this problem. These compact fixtures fit neatly against the end panels of shelving ranges (see Illustrations 11 and 12). The shelves are adjustable and depending on the model, materials can be shelved face front or spine out. Many fixtures are made of wood and come in a variety of finishes.

Free-standing fixtures are not the only pieces that can be attached to end-of-range shelving. Wire or acrylic displays can be hung from the same place as well. Metal, U-shaped rods adjust to the shelving widths and hold the displayer in place. These displayers only hold a few items per displayer. Other options include tiered displayers that have open pockets. These can hold more items and attach to the end panel in the same manner. Other tower displayers resembling a paperback spinner can also be purchased. A compact table can also be used at the ends of a range for a unique display area. No matter which model is chosen, ends of existing shelving

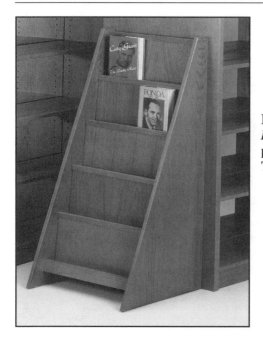

Illustration 11.
End-of-Range Display and Shelving;
photograph provided courtesy of
Texwood

Illustration 12.
*End-of-Range Space-Saver
Displayer*; photograph
provided courtesy of
Brodart

ranges make good use of space and are ideal for thematic or seasonal displays without taking up too much extra room. This can be a popular area because patrons will be facing the display as they are walking toward a shelving range. A poster or sign accompanying the display can be attached to the end panel above the display.

Bookstore Shelving. A common phrase one might hear when merchandising library materials is the term "bookstore shelving." Bookstore shelving is typically ideal in height at 60 inches or below with an open top. Popular heights are either 42 inches or 60 inches. This type of shelving usually contains slanted, adjustable shelves that showcase materials both face front and spine out (see Illustration 13). Signs can be fitted atop the shelves to help browsers quickly find their desired subject matter. Bookstore shelving is made with the browser's needs in mind. It offers ease in searching for titles. A modular starter unit can be purchased and act as a free-standing display, or add-on units can be added to create rows. This modular system allows for great flexibility when designing shelving ranges.

Spinners/Multimedia Shelving. Spinner racks are commonly used to shelve many types of materials, including paperbacks, books, videos, CDs, and DVDs. These racks are made of rotating towers that allow quick access to all titles (see Illustration 14). The molded plastic tiers have special edges that keep the materials in place as the tower rotates. Racks can come with a wooden frame or a steel stand with molded plastic tiers. Many have signs that attach to the top of the rack. Racks are found in almost every library because they normally can house a large number of titles for compact storage. While spinner racks make searching for titles easy, materials are typically shelved spine out within each tier. The only covers that are then showcased belong to those materials that happen to be shelved in the last slot on the end. This can be a major disadvantage in displaying YA items.

There are also spinner racks resembling greeting card racks found in specialty gift stores. These allow for face-front shelving of materials and are more desirable for merchandising purposes. Many in this latter category are made with a metal frame and wire grid pockets. While some models revolve, others come as a single stand-alone unit, such as an A-frame design, and are able to be moved around.

Fixtures for Displaying

Exhibit Cases and Panels. Exhibit panels can provide a backdrop for any display. Tri-folded models (smaller scale models are used for things such as science fair presentations) are flexibly hinged together and can be stored flat (see Illustration 15). The tabletop/countertop displays are portable and come with the option of carrying cases. These can come in handy in spaces where no bulletin board exists. The panel can then become a bulletin board and materials can be displayed around or in front of it. The stable, floor-sized models are ideal for larger exhibits (such as artwork made by teens) and allow patrons to walk around them. Creative placement of this type can also serve as a room divider of sorts, blocking off the YA area as well as providing display space. Both types can be double-sided and covered with a fabric surface compatible with Velcro® products or a tackboard surface used with pushpins, staples, or thumbtacks.

Illustration 13. *Bookstore Shelving;* photograph provided courtesy of Texwood

Illustration 14.
Mar-Line Quad Rotor Stand;
**photograph provided courtesy
of Gressco**

Exhibit cases can be used for displays that contain valuable or rare items that patrons will not be able to handle or check out. Cases such as these are ideal when displaying a patron's or staff member's collectibles. My former library has a display case built into the side of the building so that one side of it can be viewed from the parking lot and the other can be viewed from inside the building. A popular display was a teen's Pez® collection, which contained over eighty Pez® dispensers. Some exhibit cases can be flat and rectangular-shaped with a glass top resembling a tabletop. Others are free-standing, tall, and upright (up to six feet) with adjustable shelves, resembling a trophy case (see Illustration 16). Still other models are counter cases with glass rear doors, resembling what is found in jewelry or department stores, while others of this type are tall and cylindrical shaped. Many types of exhibit cases have four glass sides so that materials can be viewed from all sides, while others allow for three-sided viewing and have a wood or laminate back wall. These cases can be locked and usually have a light fixture inside to highlight what is being displayed. Wall-mounted models, as well as small countertop cases big enough to hold one item eight to eighteen inches tall, are also available. Those with wooden or aluminum bases come in a variety of finishes and colors. As fingerprints are likely to appear on the cases, the glass should be cleaned often with a cleaner made especially for this type of product to present a sparkling view and prevent streaks.

Illustration 15.
Display Exhibit Divider System; photograph provided courtesy of Gaylord®

Illustration 16.
Lighted Display Case; photograph provided courtesy of Brodart

Glass or Acrylic Cubes. Acrylic cubes, similar to exhibit cases, allow for the displaying of items that patrons cannot handle or check out. These five-sided cubes come in different sizes, attach to a base, and can sit on any flat surface, such as a table or desk. Floor models that are attached to legs, similar to a table, are also available. Cubes offer an unobstructed view from all sides. Some suppliers (especially those who sell to retail outlets) sell models that can be purchased without a base, therefore using any flat surface underneath, as the base. These then cannot be securely locked. Display cubes can easily be moved around the library. Large models can hold any number of props and glitzy items, while materials for circulation can be displayed on top of or outside of the cube. Depending on the size of the cube, these displays will be smaller and require less space. They should be changed quite often. It is important to remember that as with display cases, the Plexiglas should be cleaned with an appropriate cleaner that does not leave streaks.

Wooden Cubes. Wooden cubes can be used in any display to create height and the feeling of movement (see Illustration 17). While this type of display fixture is available in a variety of finishes, a local handyman or lumberyard can be contacted for inexpensive construction. Even a high school student in a wood-working or carpentry class can construct these for a library. Libraries might even ask a local school to make the construction a shop project. The cube can be made of plywood and then painted with a high gloss enamel for a bright appearance. Cubes of different sizes can be used anywhere—from on a table to on the floor. Wendy Barteluk, in her book *Library Displays on a Shoestring*, suggests using cubes with dimensions as small as 2 by 2 by 3 inches or as large as 2 by 2 by 4 feet.[7] Smaller materials can be displayed on top of the cubes with larger or oversize materials surrounding them. Materials can be displayed inside the cube as well, leaving the opening in front. The cubes can also be covered in bright fabric to further add to the color and visual appeal of the display.

Unconventional Fixtures. Not all fixtures in displays need to be purchased from suppliers. Simple items such as large baskets found at local craft stores can be the perfect thing to hold uncataloged comic books. Teens can just browse through them as they wish. Milk crates now come in many colors and can be used just like wooden cubes and even covered in fabric. Sturdy boxes may also do the trick. These too can be purchased cheaply at local stores. Creative librarians are always searching for ways to use things for which someone else no longer has a need. The best part about these items is that they are free. Perhaps the most unconventional fixtures are wooden spools that wire comes on. A local electric supply company donated these to a library in North Carolina. These can be painted and decorated or just left plain. When stacked three or four high, these spools can hold many materials and provide for an attractive display area.[8] To highlight a nature theme, the creative librarian might even use tree stumps as fixtures. These could be used in the same manner as wooden cubes. Raid a woodpile and make sure that sap has not seeped from the stump. As long as the stump is cut level at both ends, it can have many potential uses.

Always be on the lookout for stores that are closing or are replacing fixtures. Again, think broadly—bookstores are not the only ones with fixtures. Even places such as specialty gift shops may want to get rid of old card racks, which could creatively house paperbacks or some other library item.

Illustration 17. *Modular Display Cubes*; **photograph provided courtesy of Demco**

Bulletin Boards. While it is not always necessary to have a bulletin board in the YA area, it may be a good place to post announcements for upcoming programs and events. It can also become a site that displays can be built around. The bulletin board can show off the theme and signage for the display, with the materials presented underneath it. Many bulletin boards sold today are covered in cork, which can sometimes be replaced. Gone are the days when cork only came in a drab brown/sand color. Cork boards are now produced in more attractive colors that draw much needed attention. Others are covered in colorful long-lasting fabric. Boards can also be a combination of cork and dry erase. While most people think of bulletin boards mounted on a wall, if not enough wall space exists, think about a mobile one. If a budget is too tight, an easel can be used to hold signs or posterboard made into a sign for display purposes. Some bulletin boards can be attached to the ends of a shelving range to save wall space, while other smaller versions are placed on a pedestal.

Instead of covering a wall with cork, consider a cork strip. These strips are 1 to 3 inches wide cork pieces trimmed in aluminum and mounted to a wall. The top edge of a sign, poster, or flyer can then be attached to the strip using staples, pushpins, or thumbtacks, while the bottom edge of the paper hangs free. Bulletin boards can also be purchased with accompanying slatwall pieces. A fabric or magnetic board is flanked by a section of slatwall on both sides. The middle section can hold signs, posters, and announcements (see Illustration 18). This information center concept is an attractive way to distribute information. Bulletin boards/information centers do not only have to highlight just the collection. They can be a great place to highlight local school information. Obtain a color picture of the school's mascot, and show articles highlighting local teens from that school who are in the news (whether it be for sports, academics, or volunteer efforts) as an on-going display. It is a wonderful way to foster pride in the community.

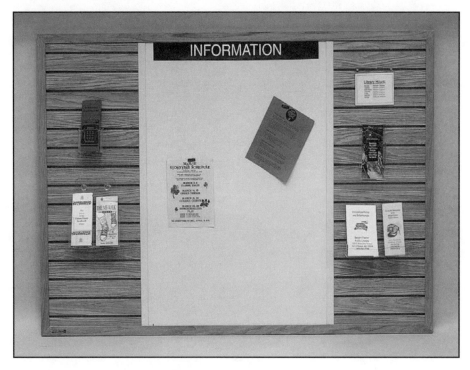

Illustration 18. *Information Center with Slatwall*; **photograph provided courtesy of Highsmith**

Signs. It has already been mentioned that when creating any type of sign for display purposes, the lettering and graphics need to look professional. Manufacturers sell a variety of products that allow signs to be displayed in a professional-looking manner.

Sign holders are typically made of acrylic and allow a ready-made sign to be displayed (see Illustrations 19 and 20). The holder can give a sign printed on quality paper or card stock long life by protecting it from the elements. The paper is inserted

Illustration 19.
Double-Sided Tent Sign Holder; photograph provided courtesy of Literature Display Products

Illustration 20.
Three-Sided Sign Holder; photograph provided courtesy of Literature Display Products

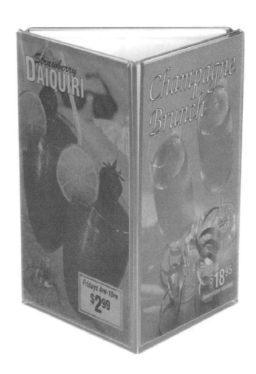

between the front and back covers from an opening on the side, front, or bottom. Sign holders are available in a variety of sizes. One of the smallest being a table tent size (4 or 5 inches high) that can be placed next to books shelved face front. These signs can be used to encourage teens to check out display books or just read "New Book" to draw attention to recent acquisitions. For some reason patrons are hesitant to check out display books, thinking that they are not for circulation. Signs such as these can help ease patrons' concerns in this situation. Student reviews of display books can also be placed in the table tents. Larger models (8½ by 11 inches or larger) range from a slanted or concave front for easier viewing, to a simple, straight, head-on view. These holders are free standing and can be placed on any flat surface that holds a display. They are perfect for use during contests, since the rules can be printed out and placed in the holder, which can in turn be placed next to an entry box.

Some designs of sign holders can be mounted on windows, walls, or ends of shelving ranges. Others are made specifically to slide into the grooves of slatwall shelving. By sliding the sign into the space between the acrylic back and front, these holders provide an easy way to have signs appear more professional. The acrylic holder prevents the sign from being torn and the edges from curling, thus preventing it from becoming shop worn.

Floor sign holders have a pedestal design and can stand up to 36 inches high. These frames can display signs and posters in a horizontal or vertical fashion. Some models include a shelf on the bottom to hold literature and pamphlets. As an example, these can be used to display a poster on an upcoming college information program and offer brochures on financial aid questions and answers beneath it. Other options for posters include acrylic tabletop models very similar to the afore-mentioned acrylic sign holders and easy to insert plastic holders or frames that snap together and can be mounted or hung from the ceiling. Instead of a four-sided frame, top and bottom grips stabilize the poster. Ceiling models also come in three-sided and four-sided displays.

Demco offers a SIGN-EEZ® system that allows signs and posters to be hung from the ceiling. These can be replaced without using a ladder but using instead a special pole to grab a metal ceiling grid and beam. Two magnets clamp the bottom of the poster and stabilize it as it hangs. Wall-mounted and ceiling-hung options usually come with the hardware for installation.

Many manufacturers offer label holders designed to fit on individual shelves. This allows smaller portions of a YA collection to be highlighted. Since the labels are blank and come in a variety of widths, they can be customized to fill the need of any collection. Movable label holders clip onto the shelf, gripping the top and bottom. Other models are self-adhesive, while still others are magnetic. Permanent shelf label holders mount with screws or double-sided tape. While many lay flat against the shelf, models that are angled upward or downward are made for shelves that are hard to see, such as those on the very top or bottom. Shelf labels can be made that say "All display books may be checked out" or "Check me out today." Shelf labels can also be attached to a book support/divider that can act as a bookend as well.

Labels can also be fitted into premade frames that fit onto the ends of shelving ranges or on the top of spinner racks. The models that attach to the ends of shelves range from those mounted flat so that someone has to be facing it to read it clearly to those that are fastened so that they extend into the walkway. The latter are double-sided and allow someone to read them clearly while walking in-between a range of shelves. The frames hold signs that are engraved or ones that can be made on a printer. Not all have to be mounted; some styles come with a pedestal to sit on top of a short shelf. Both the frames and holders are reusable and allow for the signs to be changed.

Shelf talkers are similar to shelf labels. Shelf talkers are wider and sit on the shelves as opposed to laying flat on the bottom edge of a shelf. Shelf talkers are similar to acrylic table tents and can highlight new arrivals or special collections. Teen comments on books can be placed inside the frame of a shelf talker. Less expensive sign clip holders can also be purchased. A sign made from card stock can be slipped into the clip holder and displayed on a flat surface.

Book Easels and Stands. Book easels allow books to be displayed face front on a shelf or within a display. Often when books are displayed standing up face front on the shelves, they are susceptible to falling over. Three or four books shelved this way next to each other often fall like dominoes, creating a shelving mess. Book easels allow for the whole book to be supported and cradled. Some models are made of wire covered in plastic, others are molded acrylic, while still others can be chrome plated or of an elegant brass finish (see Illustrations 21 and 22). These easels can be placed in

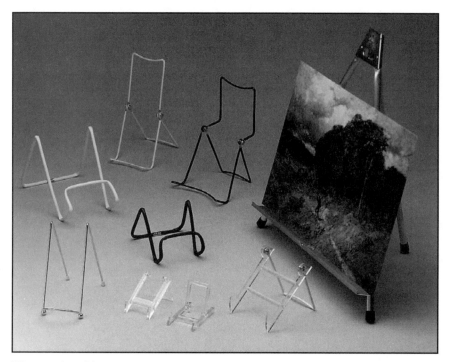

Illustration 21. *Gibson Easels*; **photograph provided courtesy of Highsmith**

a display under draped fabric offering a book support without the frame being visible. Easels can be two or three tiered to support two or three books at a time. A metal book display support is also available. It clips onto most shelving to allow face-front shelving within a stack. The front also has room for an identification label. For those in a pinch, short metal bookstands can be used as a support for books as well. Just open the pages midway through a book and slip the book on top of the bookstand that extends upward. Mark Schaeffer, in his book *Library Displays Handbook*, explains how to make book stands using a wire coat hanger.

Illustration 22. *Acrylic Easels*; **photograph provided courtesy of Highsmith**

Countertop Display Units. Countertop displayers are available for those libraries who have ample space on counters, tables, or the tops of low shelves (see Illustration 23). These can be made of clear acrylic, wire, plastic, sturdy corrugated fiberboard, or wood. Some versions have sloped backs for easy viewing. These displayers are also available with multiple tiers to display many items at different levels. This type of fixture can be a good way to draw attention to small parts of the collection when floor and shelf space are very limited. Carousels or models that revolve and have many pockets for magazines, paperbacks, videos, and other media are also available for countertop storage.

Illustration 23. *Tabletop Displayers*; **photograph provided courtesy of Brodart**

Stand Alone Display Units. Many of the fixtures mentioned in this chapter are somewhat common to libraries. Many of the shelving configurations and display items are what patrons typically expect from a library. The fixtures that will be discussed in this section, however, are more typical of retail outlets. They are designed with one purpose: to merchandise and draw attention to the collection. These fixtures are not commonly found in libraries. However, as more and more libraries recognize the importance of merchandising, they have become more popular. Because of their expense, only those libraries who truly believe that merchandising belongs in their plan of service have made the necessary adjustments to their budgets for the inclusion of these furnishings. It is important to keep in mind that if a YA budget will not allow for the purchase of this type of furniture, the cost can be shared with another library department. The piece of furniture can then be rotated from department to department as displays come and go.

When glancing through catalogs, terms such as "gondola" and "island" are used to describe fixtures for merchandising. An island unit is a display or exhibit designed to be viewed from all sides.[9] These units stand alone in the display area. A gondola is island shelving, open on two sides (see Illustration 24). These are often supplied with a gondola topper or a sign that can be seen from both sides.[10] These types of display furnishings are typically made of sturdy wood and come in a variety of finishes. Many models combine small sections of slatwall with shelving that allows face front or spine out display. The top of the unit can also be used for display (see Illustration 25). It can hold risers that allow for variety in the display. This type of fixture can come in a variety of shapes, such as round, oval, cube, and even octagonal (see

Illustration 26). Other types of display furniture include multilevel displays that have a solid core in the middle, surrounded by levels of shelving open on all sides. Double-sided display tables can be purchased that contain wells in which to display materials and have the added feature of a double-sided cork display area. Signs and other promotional information can be posted in that area.

Illustration 24. *Brodart-Crafted Book Gondola*; **photograph provided courtesy of Brodart**

Illustration 25.
Best Seller Table, Riser, and Step Pedestals; photograph provided courtesy of Demco

Illustration 26.
Octagonal Display Table; photograph provided courtesy of Highsmith

A-frame display racks are shaped like the capital letter "A." They are double-sided and usually contain adjustable shelves. The shelves have a slight slope for easier face front display. Another book displayer has a triad frame that is compact, yet interesting enough to catch a patron's eye (see Illustration 27). An inexpensive alternative to wooden display furniture is a floor display book rack made of corrugated fiberboard offered by Highsmith. These come in bright colors and have a removable header that can hold a sign. These book racks are tiered to display a number of titles. While the price of these fiberboard fixtures may be right, it is important to remember that these types will not last as long as furnishings made of sturdier materials.

Illustration 27.
Triad Book Displayer;
**photograph provided
courtesy of Gressco**

* * *

This chapter has presented a myriad of possibilities available for librarians wanting to physically merchandise materials within the library. Readers should not, however, limit themselves to the ideas presented in this book. Visiting other libraries and retail outlets, browsing through catalogs, and talking to exhibitors at trade shows and conferences at the state and national level will help in forming a plan to make merchandising a top priority in any library. Examine the environment and limitations present in your library and move on from there. Take this aspect of merchandising very seriously to maximize the advantage of exposing the collection to teens inside the building.

LIST OF VENDORS

Adirondack Direct
31-01 Vernon Blvd.
Long Island City, New York 11106
(718) 204-4500
800-221-2444
www.adirondackdirect.com

Beemak Plastics, Inc.
185545 Susana Road
Rancho Dominguez, California
   90221-5620
800-421-4393
www.beemak.com

Brodart Company Library Supplies
   and Furnishings
100 North Rd
PO Box 300
McElhatten, Pennsylvania 17748
(570) 769-3265
888-820-4377
www.brodart.com

Chicago One Stop/Browser Display
210 S. Des Plaines Suite 309
Chicago, Illinois 60611-5573
(312) 822-0822
800-822-4410

Clear Solutions
P. O. Box 2460
West Brattleboro,Vermont 05303
800-257-4550
www.clearsolutionsdisplays.com
   /index.html

Color Optic Literature Display Systems
2311 Thomas Street
Hollywood, Florida 33020
800-789-6707

Demco, Inc.
Box 7488
Madison, Wisconsin 53707-7488
(608) 241-1201
800-356-1200
www.demco.com

Display Fixtures Company
PO Box 7245
Charlotte, North Carolina 28241
(704) 588-0880
800-737-0880
www.displayfixtures.com

Display Warehouse
8820 Kenamar Drive
San Diego, California 92121
800-842-5501
www.displaywarehouse.com

Displays 2 Go by Plasticrafts
55 Broad Common Road
Bristol, Rhode Island 02809
800-572-2194
www.displays2go.com

Fasteners for Retail
225 Alpha Park
Cleveland, Ohio 44143
800-422-2547
www.ffr.com

Gaylord Bros.
PO Box 4901
Syracuse, New York 13221-4901
(315) 457-5070
800-448-6160
www.gaylord.com

Gressco, Ltd.
328 Moravian Valley Road
PO Box 339
Waunakee, Wisconsin 53597
(608) 849-6300
800-345-3480
www.gressco.com

Highsmith, Inc.
W 5527 Hwy. 106
PO Box 800
Fort Atkinson, Wisconsin 53538
(920) 563-9571
800-558-2110
www.highsmith.com

Library Display Design Systems
PO Box 8143
Berlin, Connecticut 06037
(860) 828-6089

Library Display Shelving
173 W Ohio Avenue
Lake Helen, Florida 32744
(904) 228-0436
800-762-6209
www.librarydisplayshelving.com

Literature Display Products
PO Box 501790
Indianapolis, IN 46250-6790
800-669-4399

M. F. Blouin Merchandising Solutions
710 Main Street
PO Box 10
Rollinsford, New Hampshire
    03869-0010
800-394-1632
www.mfblouin.com

Siegel Display Products
PO Box 95
Minneapolis, Minnesota 55440
(612) 340-9235
www.siegeldisplay.com

Specialty Store Services
6115 Monroe Court
Morton Grove, Illinois 60053
888-779-2425
www.specstoreserv.com

Texwood Furniture
1352 W 2nd Street
Taylor, Texas 76574-0431
(512) 352-3000
888-878-0000
www.texwood.com

Vernon Library Supplies, Inc.
2851 Cole Ct.
Norcross, Georgia 30071-2100
(770) 446-1128
800-878-0253
www.vernlib.com

NOTES

1. Anthony Bernier, "On My Mind: Young Adult Spaces," *American Libraries* 29, no. 9 (October 1998): 52.

2. Elaine Meyers, "The Coolness Factor: Libraries Listen to Youth," *American Libraries* 30, no. 10 (November 1999): 44.

3. Renee Vaillencourt, "Couch Central," *School Library Journal* 44, no. 7 (July 1998): 41.

4. Ken White and Frank White, "Elements of Effective Bookstore Design," in *Manual on Bookselling: Practical Advice for the Bookstore Professional*, 5th ed. (Tarrytown, NY: American Booksellers Association, 1996), 148.

5. Ibid., 148–150.

6. Robert Colborne, *Visual Merchandising: The Business of Merchandise Presentation* (Albany, NY: Delmar Publishers, 1996), 324.

7. Wendy Barteluk, *Library Displays on a Shoestring: Three Dimensional Techniques for Promoting Library Services* (Metuchen, NJ: Scarecrow, 1993), 6.

8. Barbara Cashwell, "Merchandising the Collection from a Small Branch Perspective," *North Carolina Libraries* 43, no. 1 (Spring 1985): 46.

9. Ruth Laszlo, *Display Design: An Introduction to Window Display, Point-of-Purchase, Posters, Signs and Signage, Sales Environments, and Exhibit Displays* (Englewood Cliffs, NJ: Prentice Hall, 1983), 161.

10. Ibid., 160.

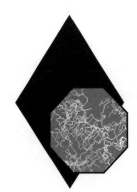

8

Promoting the YA Collection: Other Ideas

Placing eye-catching displays throughout the YA area and beyond is not the only way to promote the YA collection in order to increase its use. Many other common practices, most often found in young adult librarian job descriptions, work to increase a teen's awareness of how the library collection meets his or her needs. This chapter will discuss these practices, as well as ways to promote a YA collection using services such as book-lists, library websites, and library tours, just to name a few. Many of the ideas that will be mentioned can be effective promotion techniques when used both inside the library, as well as outside of the library.

PROMOTION

The key to creating a greater awareness of the YA collection is to constantly be aware of activity in the library and to take advantage of the "busy" times to draw attention to new titles. The beginning or ending of a program can provide an opportunity to introduce materials. The content of the material may or may not complement the program theme. It will not matter, as long as the item is "good enough" to talk about. A captive audience is already present for the program; it only makes sense to use this time to highlight materials, programs, and services that the library is offering. These mini-presentations do not have to take up a great deal of time, so a long-winded booktalk for each item is not necessary. All that is needed is a short introduction, an annotation, for instance, to grab the attention of patrons. Incorporate this technique in programs before introducing the speaker or while thanking everyone for attending the program at the end, but before they bolt for the exit door. When setting up a room for any type of program, always include a display table for materials. This can be done informally without props, and so on. The table can be covered in some type of fabric and the items placed on top. A small sign can be designed and printed from the computer that says "Check out these new books!" Many library meeting rooms have countertops or deep window sills and displaying materials there works just as well. Hopefully this impromptu display can be located by the entrance/exit to the room and not hidden in the back corner of the program area.

The content of the program may dictate what types of materials to display. A craft program may allow for the display of craft-related materials and also provide a time to mention certain fiction titles whose main teen characters may have hobbies. Do not always use the obvious, but branch out and broaden the topic to fit what is found in the collection. For example, a college information night provides the obvious time to display college testing books, college catalogs, and video tours of college and university campuses. Also think about including a few fiction titles about teens dealing with college experiences such as *Getting In* by James Finn Boylan (Warner, 1998), *Battle Dress* by Amy Efaw (HarperCollins, 2000), and *Plebe* by Hank Turowski (Paradigm Press, 1994, 1998). Do not forget the fine nonfiction title *College Reading Lists*, 3d edition, by Don Estell (Arco/Thomson Learning, 2000), which provides reading lists for colleges and universities around the country, as well as sample essay questions that have appeared on college entrance applications. Along the same lines, a sports-related program can provide opportunities to display and talk about magazines such as *Sports Illustrated* and *BMX Biking*, fiction titles such as *Players* by Joyce Sweeney (Winslow Press, 2000) and *Night Hoops* by Carl Dueker (Houghton Mifflin, 2000), and nonfiction such as Lance Armstrong's biography, *It's Not About the Bike: My Journey Back to Life* (Putnam, 2000). And do not forget those great snowboarding videos.

Also include a mini-display when advertising for programs. Just displaying the flyer inside the library is nice and can be sufficient advertising. Blowing up the flyer to a larger size and displaying it creatively, with related materials, can advertise and promote the event even better. Mounting the enlarged flyer on a bulletin board or wall, surrounded by book jackets, can be effective as well. For those very special programs such as author visits and those whose speakers are being paid, these mini-displays should not only be advertised in the library but outside as well, such as in schools or community centers.

Another idea is to take the time to introduce new materials as part of teen advisory board meetings. Again, the captive audience is present and, since they have a vested interest through their membership in the library and its services, they will appreciate the sharing. Ideally teens will check out the new materials and read, listen to, or view them to create reviews or recommendations. These can be displayed in a folder, database, on a bulletin board, or highlighted in a newsletter or on the library's website. Even if the reviews are not actually published anywhere, the teens will still be able to tell their friends about the materials they have checked out. This word-of-mouth advertising from teens can do more for the collection than just the librarian making recommendations.

Hosting a book discussion group can create awareness of the collection. For each book read and discussed, create a list of related materials to give participants. This provides them with additional items to read on their own time. Or take time within the actual book discussion meeting to talk about related materials using the same short presentation technique previously mentioned. Again, broaden the topic, highlighting all types of formats.

The idea of using teen reviews to increase awareness of the YA collection can be expanded upon. The teen advisory board, teen book discussion group, or just interested teens may be willing to create commercials or testimonials for new materials. These commercials can be videotaped by library staff or the teens themselves. This project not only involves the teens in library services, but also provides an avenue for them to show off their creative side. The video commercials can be played in the YA area. An even better place for the videos to be seen is at the schools in the library's service area. Hopefully the library and the school have developed a strong enough relationship so that the school would be willing to incorporate a project like this into its video announcements. The project can also be a joint effort between the school and the library, using the school's technology. The school library media specialist may be willing to highlight the video commercials in the media center if the video cannot be shown as part of the school's video announcements. This can become a sophisticated program and can even be offered to teachers who would like supplemental reading materials for certain units. Also, local cable television access may be willing to show these type of commercials.

If videotaping commercials seems too ambitious, have teens write reviews for materials that can be published in the school's newspaper. In the SmartGirl.com Teen Read Week survey, 47 percent of the teens responded "school papers or newsletters" to the question "Which of the following do you read?"[1] Fifty-nine percent responded "newspapers" to the same question. Therefore, publishing student reviews or submitting booklists of recommended reading to the local newspapers can be advantageous to a library. Local homeschooling groups often have newsletters that circulate throughout their group. The same reviews and recommended reading booklists can be submitted to these groups as well.

Teens can also be photographed with their favorite materials from the YA collection. The photos can be enlarged and displayed in the teen area a la ALA's popular READ posters. The "star" teen can explain why he or she likes the item, and this explanation can be displayed along with the picture. This idea can be used for special promotions such as National Library Week or Teen Read Week. This gallery of sorts not only involves the teens, but offers their recommendations (which is what their friends want anyway, as opposed to the librarian's recommendation) and provides another way to highlight the YA collection. Be sure to follow the library's policy on photographing patrons and displaying them for public viewing. Because of confidentiality, a parent or legal guardian's signature may need to be obtained before any photograph can be displayed.

CONTESTS

Contests are a form of programming that are fun to develop and a great way to reach teens, especially those who do not attend library events, but do use the collection. A contest placed in the YA area will easily attract teens who visit there—especially if it is creatively developed and the prizes appeal to them. Contests are a nice way to include teens who would never attend an actual planned YA program. In my former library, I was able to attract older teens (tenth through twelfth graders) with this type of passive programming. This hard-to-reach age group rarely ever attended any other type of programming. Teens can enter to win anytime they visit the library, so the conflict of planning a program at a specific time to meet their busy schedules is eliminated. It is something teens can do on their own, often anonymously. In other words, their friends are not actually witnessing them taking part in a library function (which may be taboo in their peer group). A library staff member does not have to be present, a meeting room does not have to be secured, and a speaker and refreshments are not even required. The YA librarian can create the contest and the accompanying visual materials, display it, and monitor the entry box for the duration of the contest.

Designing a contest usually just requires a visual image of some type. It may mean rummaging through old magazines for pictures of celebrities and creating something eye-catching on a posterboard. A popular contest with the teens I have worked with had them identifying television celebrities and the shows in which they performed. The pictures of the celebrities were displayed on a posterboard that had been shaped to represent a television. An answer sheet was designed on a computer, and copies were made from the photocopier. Some contests may just require an answer sheet and a sign telling participants what to do. Contests, just as displays, should not be left up too long. A week, two at the maximum, should be sufficient to avoid having a display that has worn out its welcome. Once the contest is finished, the librarian must disassemble it and determine the winner.

Contests can drum up excitement about certain materials in the YA collection more so than a display. Contests often do not take up much space, so those libraries with limited space can still provide an exciting contest for teens. Because of the small space requirement, contests can also be used effectively by those providing YA services in a bookmobile setting. Certain contests can accompany a display of materials to add even more punch. The following list offers examples of such contests:

1. Create a bookmark contest. Have teens choose a favorite book from the collection and create a bookmark for it. Winning entries can be run off in multiples on heavy card stock using a photocopier. Teens can also enter their bookmark on disk using desktop publishing. The library's graphic arts department or the librarian can then make enough to allow teens to keep while having some to distribute to others.

2. Teen Poetry Contest. A great way to kick off National Poetry Month, which is held during the month of April, or Bad Poetry Day, which is celebrated on August 18th, is to host a poetry event. It provides a creative outlet through which teens can express themselves. Of course,

poetry books from the teen collection will need to be showcased. Selections written by teens are best displayed here, such as collections from Naomi Shihab Nye. In the past few years, many fiction titles have been written in verse, one of the first being *Make Lemonade* (Henry Holt, 1993) by Virginia Euwer Wolff, who completed a sequel to that book entitled *True Believer* (Antheneum, 2001) and has promised to complete the last installment of the trilogy. Other titles include the Newbery Award winner *Out of the Dust* by Karen Hesse (Scholastic, 1997), anything by author Mel Glenn, and *Stop Pretending: What Happened When My Sister Went Crazy* by Sonya Sones (HarperCollins, 1999). These titles could enhance the display. This contest can culminate with the teens presenting their poetry during a program. The poems can be assembled and made into a booklet for participants and a copy for the YA collection itself.

3. Ugly Book Contest. If you are tired of looking at ugly covers of YA novels, have teens design new covers for them. Protect their new creations with new crystal jackets and place them on display.

4. Pick the Oscar® winners. The Oscars® usually are held in March, but the nominations are announced about a month prior. Using a computer, develop an Oscar® ballot for teens to choose their favorites in the major categories. Make sure your entry date is before the actual date of the telecast. The teen whose ballot choice closely matches the actual winners can win movie tickets or video store gift certificates. A display of books made into movies can accompany this contest.

5. Pick the Grammy® winners. This can be run much like the Oscar® contest. Prizes can include gift certificates to a music store. A display of materials (audio, video, and print) can easily accompany this contest.

6. Misheard Lyrics. A pen and paper contest can be created using misheard lyrics, which are also called *mondegreens*. The most common misheard lyric comes from a song entitled "Purple Haze" by Jimi Hendrix. The phrase "Excuse me while I kiss this guy" sounds very close to what is sung in the song, but is not quite correct. Collections of mondegreens are available in both print and off the Web. The following sources can be used for this contest:

Edwards, Gavin. " *'Scuse Me While I Kiss This Guy" and Other Misheard Lyrics*. Fireside, 1995.

———. *He's Got the Whole World in His Pants and More Misheard Lyrics*. Simon & Schuster, 1996.

———. *When a Man Loves a Walnut: And Even More Misheard Lyrics*. Simon & Schuster, 1997.

————. *Deck the Halls with Buddy Holly: And Other Misheard Christmas Lyrics*. Harper Perennial, 1998.

The Archive of Misheard Lyrics. www.kissthisguy.com

Using these examples, create a contest where teens have to match the misheard lyric to the song title from which it came. This contest also can be accompanied by a display of music titles (fiction and nonfiction) and recordings.

7. Scavenger Hunts. Scavenger hunts can be devised where teens must use resources found in the library to answer certain questions. More popular versions allow students to answer scavenger hunt questions using only the library's website and the links it provides. These can be completed on-line using any available computer, such as the student's home computer, school computers, or those provided by the library. If an on-line version is not developed, the participants can answer the questions on a handout, which can also be used as the entry form.

TOURS

Often different groups request a tour of the library and an explanation of its services. These groups can be made up of teens, such as those involved in special activities, for example, the Scouts, or those enrolled in a special class and required to complete a project that demands the use of the library and its resources. Parents of homeschooled teens or just the homeschooled teens themselves also can benefit from a library tour. When presenting a tour, while highlighting reference sources and electronic databases is important, do not overlook the materials that teens use for pleasure, such as audio, video, magazines, comic books, graphic novels, and paperbacks. While these may not be directly related to the reason for their visit, the opportunity to show off the entire YA collection should be used. If time allows between the booking of the tour and the actual tour date, plan to have a contest and display ready for their enjoyment and bring attention to it during their visit.

Tours consisting of adults who work with teens provide another opportunity to show off the YA collection. Groups of teachers, media specialists, church youth ministers, parents, and the staff of community agencies can all gain in learning about what the library has to offer. If you do a good job introducing them to your collection and services, they will be able to tell the youth that they deal with every day about you. Thus, you will be able to reach many more teens who would not normally think of the library as a place to go for answers. While this type of group may also be interested in reference sources, it is also beneficial for them to see the other recreational items a library provides as outlets for teens. Someone working in a crisis agency for teens may be interested in the nonfiction works on subjects such as rape or abusive relationships. This person should also be shown quality fiction titles, such as the Printz

Honor Award winner *Speak* by Laurie Halse Anderson (Farrar, Straus & Giroux, 1999) and *Dreamland* by Sarah Dessen (Viking, 2000). Both of these works deal with these difficult subjects and have tremendous appeal to teens.

BULLETIN BOARDS

Bulletin boards, though briefly mentioned before, can be a part of a display. For example, a bulletin board can show off the theme of a display as well as provide space for visual props. The materials for display and circulation can then be placed nearby. While this technique shows off the actual items for display, this is not always necessary. A large bulletin board can highlight a collection displaying only book jackets. Bulletin board presentations require artwork and creativity. Clever themes can vary and allow you to bring attention to certain parts of the collection. The word "Read" can be made by fashioning old magazines covers to create the letters and bring attention to the magazine collection. Also, a bulletin board with a mystery or Clue® theme can draw attention to the YA mystery novels.

The chapter that discusses fixtures mentions different types of bulletin boards, such as those that can be hung from an end panel of a shelving range. Bulletin boards as parts of a section of slatwall offer the best of both worlds. The slatwall and its shelving accessories can display actual materials face front, while the complementing bulletin board creatively shows off the theme. It is also a good idea to install a bulletin board in between shelving ranges to break up the monotonous look of a wall of shelving.

The design of the bulletin board follows many of the same guidelines that apply to the design of a point of purchase display. Plain bulletin boards made of brown pressed board are often unattractive and institutional looking. They now come in more attractive colors. The easiest way to make a bulletin board more exciting is to add a colorful background over the entire board. Backgrounds can be in the form of newspaper (the comics are especially colorful), an old sheet that has been dyed, wallpaper, wrapping paper, an old tablecloth, material remnants, or poster/craft paper.[2]

Several library suppliers, such as Highsmith, offer brightly colored fadeless paper for bulletin boards. This is especially helpful when the bulletin board receives direct light. When choosing any type of background, remember that cloth is more durable. The key to an attractive bulletin board is to cover the entire background using one piece of material, cut to the size of the bulletin board. Avoid using many smaller pieces to cover it because these will have to be stapled together. These staples will stick out like a sore thumb. Whenever a bulletin board changes, a fresh background should be used for the next one to keep the displays varied.

A border could also be used to finish the edges and form a boundary for the area. A border also draws the viewer's eye to the display.[3] The easiest borders to use are those that are commercially produced. However, avoid those that are too elementary for teen tastes. Just as with display signage, any lettering produced for a bulletin board theme should look professionally done. Use a computer and laser printer or stencils to create the right effect. As with displays, it is a good idea to take a photograph or make a sketch of the bulletin board to be included with all of the pieces when it is placed in storage. Many resources are available to teachers and librarians that offer actual bulletin board ideas, suggestions of titles, themes, and visuals that can be adapted into different library areas (see Table 3 for some suggestions). Be sure when designing any type of bulletin board for the YA section that it does not look too juvenile by depicting teens who look too young or by having a border that someone would find in an elementary school.

Table 3. Resources for Bulletin Board Ideas and Themes

Gomberg, Karen Cornell. *More Books Appeal: Keep Young Teenagers in the Library.* McFarland, 1990. Written for librarians to support them in developing interest in reading for pleasure. Includes contests and active games, bulletin board activities, fun with booklists, and reading activities.

Kostrowski, Karen, and Linda Wiley. *Eye Catchers: Library Bulletin Board Ideas, Innovations and Instructions for the Non-Artist.* Library Learning Resources, Inc., 1992. Provides some good, very simple, one-dimensional ideas. Reproduction permission granted for individual library use.

Sivak, Patricia, and Mary Anne Passatore. *Bulletin Bored? Or Bulletin Boards!* Scarecrow, 1998. Lists ideas in chronological order following the school year calendar.

Skaggs, Gayle. *On Display: 25 Themes to Promote Reading.* McFarland, 1999. Includes 25 themes that can be used almost any time of the year with a few more that are seasonal in nature.

BOOKTALKING

Booktalking provides a unique way to highlight and deliver information about materials in the YA collection. What is a booktalk? A booktalk is a presentation designed to persuade an audience to read a book or books. A booktalk is *not* a book review or literary criticism.[4] Properly done, booktalks allow teens to learn about books in a fun, nonthreatening, emotion-filled, and relaxed atmosphere. The main objective of a booktalk is to increase awareness and use of materials.

While developing an individual style for booktalking presentations takes time and practice, it is well worth the librarian's effort to incorporate booktalking as an integral part of his or her service plan. Booktalking is a wonderful public relations tool to create a greater awareness of a library's service to the schools in its community. As a staff member of a public library, it allows you the opportunity to build a working relationship with the local school, its faculty, and students. Booktalking in classrooms will allow you to reach a large group of teens who probably do not use the library and may never step foot in it. It also provides a proactive avenue for promoting the YA collection, instead of staying inside the library hoping the teens will come to see you.

Approaches to booktalks and information on how to get started booktalking can be found in several sources (see Table 4). Joni Richards Bodart is the author of many valuable booktalking resources. Practical information can be found in Patrick Jones's resource, *Connecting Young Adults and Public Libraries*, 2d edition (Neal-Schuman, 1998) as well. Renee Vaillancourt's *Bare Bones Young Adult Services: Tips for Public Library Generalists* (ALA, 2000) also offers tips to keep in mind when booktalking. While the term *booktalking* implies that one must only talk about books, this is not true. A good way to grab the attention of teens is to start off a booktalk presentation with formats of interest to them. Bring along magazines as well as new audio or video titles to show. Take advantage of the captive audience and use the time with the students to show off all parts of the YA collection. An enthusiastic presentation will allow you to generate excitement about what you have to offer in the library.

Table 4. Booktalking Resources

Bodart, Joni Richards. *Booktalk! Booktalking and School Visiting for Young Adult Audiences*. New York: H. W. Wilson, 1980.

———. *Booktalk! 2*. New York: H. W. Wilson, 1985.

———. *Booktalk! 3*. New York: H. W. Wilson, 1988.

———. *Booktalk! 4*. New York: H. W. Wilson, 1992.

———. *Booktalk! 5*. New York: H. W. Wilson, 1993.

———. *Booktalking with Joni Bodart* (video). New York: H. W. Wilson, 1985.

———. *Booktalking the Award Winners 1992–1993*. New York: H. W. Wilson, 1994.

———. *Booktalking the Award Winners 1993–1994*. New York: H. W. Wilson, 1995.

———. *Booktalking the Award Winners 3*. New York: H. W. Wilson, 1997.

———. *Booktalking the Award Winners 4*. New York: H. W. Wilson, 1998.

———. *Booktalking the Award Winners: Young Adult Retrospective Volume*. New York: H. W. Wilson, 1996.

———. *Booktalker's Companion 1 and 2*. Bookhooks Publishing, 1995–1996.

———. *Index to the Wilson Booktalking Series*. New York: H. W. Wilson, 1997.

Jones, Patrick. *Connecting Young Adults and Libraries*, 2d edition. New York: Neal-Schuman, 1998.

PROMOTIONAL MATERIALS

Printed materials such as flyers, pamphlets, brochures, bookmarks, news-letters, and booklists can also draw attention to the YA collection. The primary purpose of any type of printed material is to communicate information to the patron. Certain design elements should be examined carefully to enhance the readability of a publication. These include font, flow, graphics, white space, paper, and ink. Any type of publication requires the following basic elements in order to be useful:

- Focus—This is usually a large, bold display type or graphic.

- Balance—The type and graphics should not be overcrowded.

- Flow—A directional flow is created on the page with lines, type, and paths of white space. Consider that the eye moves from the top left to the top right, then bottom left to the bottom right.

- Unity—This involves the use of consistent type and graphic motifs.[5]

The mention of white space is especially important when developing any printed material. Empty space on a page gives the eye a place to rest and keeps graphics uncluttered. White space must be grouped together to have an impact. It does not work well if it is scattered across a page.[6] Typeface or font can set the tone and style of the piece. Typically no more than two typefaces should be used per printed matter. Avoid combining similar typefaces. To add emphasis to certain words or phrases, the same typeface can be used, however, the font style can be changed. A large-size typeface allows for easier readability, and the type should not be smaller than ten points.[7]

Graphics will enhance any printed material and make it more exciting to teens. To maintain credibility with teens, be certain that the graphics are appealing and appropriate for those you are trying to reach. Anything too childish or graphics depicting kids younger than teens will be an instant turn-off to your target audience. Photocopying the flyer on brightly colored (neon) paper instead of muted pastels also will create more excitement. All printed material from the YA department should contain library information such as address, phone, YA librarian's name and e-mail address, hours of operation, and the library's Web address. If the library uses a logo, it too should always be included to reinforce recognition.

A newsletter can be an effective way to communicate YA library services to teens. It can be a productive assignment for a teen advisory board under the direction of the YA librarian. Teens can use a computer to create the format and graphics. The original can simply be photocopied and distributed. Distribution can take place at the library, the school, and also through direct mail. Keeping a list of past registrants for programs or contests will provide an instant mailing list. More teens will probably prefer that a newsletter be e-mailed to them. The YA newsletter can contain student reviews of materials, notices for upcoming programming and events, new materials, star YA spotlights, contests, surveys, and anything else you can think of that would be of interest to teens. It would be ideal for this YA newsletter to be targeted only to teens and be kept as a separate publication from the library's regular newsletter that covers all departments and services. Young adults should be able to contribute to the YA department's section in the all inclusive library newsletter. The same reviews published in the YA newsletter can appear here along with other information. This will demonstrate to the entire library community that teens can contribute to the "common good" and places them in a positive light. It never hurts to highlight new YA materials. Adults may be interested in some of the items as well. Do not just limit the mailing of these newsletters to library patrons. Adults who work with youth in the community and youth group leaders will be interested to receive them as well.

Places where teens hang out may be willing to provide a space to distribute YA-related materials. This tactic will allow you to reach nonusers who may become future users of library services. It is important to remember when using places outside of the library for distribution to make a constant effort to refill items when necessary and remove items as they become dated. This is the library staff's responsibility, not the staff of the organization who approved the placement and distribution.

Cooperatively working with the city's recreation department has advantages. The recreation department may be willing to accept information about library services for submission into its newsletter or community calendar of events. The library can reciprocate in their newsletter. When the recreation department distributes information about its summer programs, make sure the library's information is included as well. Also, why not submit a list of good summer reads to be included?

BOOKLISTS

Booklists provide yet another strategy to increase awareness of the YA collection. Providing booklists to patrons has the value of making particular works more visible and physically accessible. Booklists also help alleviate overload by focusing patron attention on a smaller group of titles in which they might be interested.[8] It should be mentioned that booklists are less effective at increasing use of library materials than actual point-of-purchase displays. This is due to the fact that patrons must make an effort to examine a booklist, comprehend the information, find the item in the library, and then check it out. Displays only require that the patron notice the item, pick it up, and check it out.[9] Despite this fact, research has shown that booklists can be used successfully under certain circumstances. It has been found that booklists significantly increase patron selection of the materials they contain, only when they are distributed widely and in a manner requiring little patron effort to obtain them.[10] One researcher's attempt at using booklists to increase circulation failed. The failure was attributed to the fact that the booklists were not actually distributed to the patrons. Instead, they were left out on the second floor of the library in hopes they would be picked up by patrons who desired to do so.[11] Many patrons did not visit the area where the booklists could be found, while others who noticed them had to comprehend the information and consciously pick up the list to use it as an aid to selection.[12]

Research on the use of booklists has shown that there are three effective distribution techniques that will increase the use of titles on the list:

1. Handing the booklists to patrons ensures they come into visual contact with them without having to make an effort to locate it and pick them up.

2. Placing the lists with a large accompanying sign in a well-trafficked area of the library.

3. Asking staff to distribute booklists to patrons who ask relevant reference or reader's advisory questions.[13]

It would seem that the behavior of teens would support these research findings. Odds are that teens will not willingly pick up a booklist. Having circulation staff insert them into their pile of books at checkout is a good idea. Using YA or reference staff to distribute them to those asking relevant questions should be effective also. Don't forget to keep bookmobiles and other service outlets stocked with YA booklists for the same reasons. Any time that a librarian makes a booktalking presentation, a booklist should be distributed to every member of the audience. It should not only have the titles that were booktalked, but also library contact information. Providing a copy of this booklist to staff in the library alerts them to titles that will be requested as a result of the booktalk presentation.

When designing a booklist and finding titles for inclusion, many things should be considered. It is a good idea to use titles of which the library owns multiple copies. Consider using authors who have written several works rather than just one or two titles. Think about using subject headings and general call numbers of popular nonfiction. These three suggestions can help patrons avoid trying to find works that have already been checked out.[14] This gives the patron an option of finding other things if the original item is not on the shelf. He or she can always pick up another book by the same author or find a nonfiction title with the same general call number or subject heading.

While most YA librarians read quite a few books, it is virtually impossible for someone to read all of the books included in the library's collection. When creating a booklist there is probably a good chance that you may have not been able to read every book that will be printed on it. While this is not a problem, it may be difficult to find different titles eligible for a booklist. Therefore it may be necessary to use the following steps as a quick guide to help provide you with a basic description of any book:

• Examine the cover. It should give you an indication of the book's content.

• Read the blurb. Will it hook a young adult without revealing the whole story?

• Look at the print type. Full pages of text usually means there is a great deal of description, while bits of white space usually means more dialogue.

- Read the first chapter or first five pages, then skip to the middle and read five pages and then read the end. Does it seem as if the story flows?

- Determine if the book has YA appeal.

- Think of other books the YA reader may like to read. Does the book tie into a movie, television show, or real life event?[15]

You will need to decide if the list will contain annotations. Annotated and unannotated booklists on a single subject or genre have both been shown to increase the use of the promoted titles. When more than one genre or subject is featured on a single list, annotations are more helpful to patrons.[16]

A reader's annotation should be written using no more than three sentences. The annotation should pique someone's interest about a book and make him or her want to read it. It should not give away the ending. Often reading the blurb or back cover of an item will provide a good starting point. Catchy phrases and action words can create excitement about the title. Beginners to annotation writing may want to consider the following questions to use as a framework for the annotation:

1. Who is the central character? Make a list of identifying characteristics, such as age, occupation, and ethnic background.

2. Who are significant others? This list should include with whom, or what, the central character interacts.

3. What or where is the setting of the work?

4. When does the story take place?

5. What challenges are the characters facing in the story?[17]

When finding titles for inclusion on a booklist, think small. It is not necessary to include every book in a genre or on a subject. Nonfiction works belong on booklists also. A good number to have on any list is ten titles. Just because it is called a booklist does not mean that only books should be included. Related websites, CD-ROMs, audio, and video can also be included. Graphics and borders can add pizzazz to the list and make it more attractive.

A popular list that can be found in many libraries is the "If you liked [insert title], try these other titles." These types of lists can allow teens to help themselves, especially when they become hooked on a certain genre. Special lists can be created to target specific groups within the teen community. A list of college materials can be compiled and distributed to local schools to be given to the entire junior class, for example. If a tour is being conducted for a certain group, develop a booklist that matches their interests in some way. Distributing it to the group will provide a visual reminder of their visit and of you as a library staff member. Booklists should also be made to accompany point-of-purchase displays. These lists can be displayed among everything else in the display. An advantage to this is that a teen can have a list of what was displayed. This can be helpful if he or she finds that, upon returning to the library, the display has been disassembled or certain items have been checked out from the display.

WEBSITES

Library websites offer yet another opportunity to create awareness of the YA collection. Few people can dispute the popularity of using this technological medium with young adults. Forty-two percent of those teens who participated in the SmartGirl.com Teen Read Week survey responded "online websites or webzines" when asked about types of materials they read.[18] A website identifies YA library services and helps to build and sustain an image of those services by disseminating information. The current generation of teens and those younger have grown up with computers. They view the Net as a cool thing compared to the bricks and mortar library that houses (in their eyes) mostly boring books. More and more librarians are encountering students who would prefer to find resources for homework on the World Wide Web as opposed to in books.

With teens experiencing such hectic schedules, a library's Web presence needs to be a way to reach out to those who are pressed for time to visit the actual building during the time that it is open for operation. Often library hours of operation clash with the actual time that young adults have to spend doing homework. Most often, the minute the final bell rings signaling the end of the school day, teens are off and running to extracurricular activities (often more than one) or jobs. Dinner may not get eaten until late and by the time it takes to settle down and start homework it is often the time when libraries begin to close. This is one of the many reasons a library's website should act as another outlet of the library. It would be helpful to teens if the library's website makes available such things as online encyclopedias, periodical databases, homework help, the library's catalog, and circulation functions such as renewals and the reserving of materials. Many libraries are activating twenty-four-hour reference desks over the Web to field patron requests. Allowing the submission of reference questions on-line is a tremendous service to offer, especially to teens who would feel more comfortable asking for help using their computer as opposed to asking in person or over the phone.

Hopefully, if your library has a website, the YA department has its own page as well. After examining teen Web pages in libraries across the country and surveying the librarians that developed them, Patrick Jones concluded that the elements of success for a YA area are the same in cyberspace as in physical space.[19] First, young adults should be involved in the site development. The area should be attractive looking, loaded with high interest materials, and most of all, the area should be made distinct from other parts of the library's site. This can be done by clearly defining its audience and giving it an identifiable appearance, content, and scope.

Whether your library creates its Web page in-house or uses an outside source, make sure that teens are asked what they would like to see included. They will probably have many ideas to contribute to the design and maintenance of the site. Some caution is necessary, however, when taking into consideration their opinions. For instance, teens may request the use of lots of Web animation and other glitzy bells and whistles. Too many of these additions, while making the site cool and graphically pleasing, can make the page too difficult to load. Nothing is more frustrating for the teen (or the adult, for that matter) than waiting for images to load. Not everyone uses a T-1 or T-3 line that can be found in many libraries and offices, so keep this in mind. In the business world, companies are discovering the faster their pages download, the more likely their customers will stick around. Slow pages translate into unimpressive revenues. Businesses prefer to follow a rule that a page load should be no slower than six to eight seconds.[20]

Another important point to remember when considering graphics is to make the site more easily readable for disabled young people. Sites with different colored text and patterned backgrounds can be particularly difficult to read for those with poor vision or colorblindness.[21]

In Patrick Jones's survey, only half of the librarians reported that young adults were involved in the creation or maintenance of the YA Web page. Of those who involved teens, they were able to document positive results. Since YA suggestions were used in choosing a site's content, some had fears that young adults might provide questionable links, but only one library reported an intellectual freedom challenge.[22] Young adults can contribute book reviews to be shared on the website. Do not forget to include links to other sites that offer book reviews. Booklists can also be placed on the library's website. Provide a section on the site for teen comments on any type of material, such as music, games, and videos. These can be linked from the list of materials.

Before beginning any attempt to put up a YA website for the library, do some homework. First visit other library websites to begin developing ideas and to discover things that are likable and those to avoid. Next, develop a complete outline of the site and its content. Remember this should be simple and clear. Ninety percent of site visitors will spend ninety seconds or less looking at your page.[23] This means text should be presented in a clear, organized way. Any text longer than a paragraph should be broken up with visual symbols such as bullets for easier readability. Also make sure that the YA page is easily accessible from the library's home page, instead of forcing teens to navigate through a couple of pages. Under no circumstance should the teen page be listed under the children's services section nor should the teen have to go through the children's page to access the teen page. This is the equivalent to housing the YA room in the physical library building right next to or within the children's room.

Decide what the purpose of the site will be. What information will it provide to teens? Most YA Web pages contain one or all of these five elements:

1. Book reviews

2. Links

3. Resource lists

4. Program information

5. Information on library services[24]

When providing links, include some to the local community. Schools (including colleges and universities, the department of education), radio stations, and community agencies should be included and linked. Organizations such as crisis centers, shelters, and hot lines are also necessary. These are places where teens can go to for help, but they might not be comfortable asking a library staff member for the information. Caution should be taken to avoid linking to obvious sites. Sites such as www.wwf.com and www.backstreetboys.com are ones that teens can get to on one click as opposed to going to the library site, clicking on the teens section, clicking on the music section, and then finding the link.[25] Any external links should be monitored on at least a monthly basis to confirm their existence. While a staff member can be in charge of this effort, special software products can be purchased to facilitate it.

Graphics found on the website should follow the same rule as any type of display or promotional material. Graphics need to be age appropriate. If your library uses a logo or special sign to identify the YA area, include its use on the website as well. If real teen patrons are included in any of the pictures, be sure to follow the library's policy in posting photographs and/or names of patrons on anything viewed by the public. A parent or legal guardian's signature may be required before photos or names can be posted.

Once the website is up and running, make sure that it is maintained on a regular basis. Any information highlighting contests, displays, or new materials should be monitored and removed when their presence is no longer needed or outdated.

To develop awareness of the website's existence, the Web address should be included on all promotional printed materials. If a website is a new service, send out press releases to notify the public, but also place advertisements in local papers and the school newspaper sharing the information. Anything and everything should be done to make your Web presence, or for that matter any new service, known to the community and to your target audience—teens.

All of the techniques discussed in this chapter provide examples of activities that can easily be performed every day to increase the awareness of and excitement for the YA collection. Teen librarians need to take advantage of every opportunity to "toot their horn" and highlight special collections and displays. Do not think that none of this is necessary because most everyone already knows what the library has to offer. This is simply not true. Continually be on the lookout for methods to show teens and those who work with them that the YA collection and library services can meet their needs, whether they be educational or recreational. It is important to make the point that the library has many services and programs to offer that will meet their needs and make them feel welcome.

NOTES

1. www.SmartGirl.com

2. Gayle Skaggs, *Bulletin Boards and Displays: Good Ideas for Librarians and Teachers* (Jefferson, NC: McFarland, 1993), 1.

3. Ibid., 2.

4. Patrick Jones, *Connecting Young Adults and Libraries,* 2d ed. (New York: Neal-Schuman, 1998), 246.

5. Anne C. Tedeschi, *Book Displays: A Library Exhibit Handbook* (Fort Atkinson, WI: Highsmith, 1997), 46.

6. Ibid., 47.

7. Ibid., 48.

8. Sharon L. Baker, *The Responsive Public Library Collection: How to Develop and Market It* (Englewood, CO: Libraries Unlimited, 1993), 267.

9. Ibid.

10. Sharon L. Baker, "Overload, Browsers, and Selection," *Library and Information Science Research* 8 (October 1986): 325.

11. Ibid.

12. Ibid., 326.

13. Baker, *The Responsive Library Collection*, 267.

14. Ibid., 268.

15. C. Allen Nichols and Mary Anne Nichols, " How to Read and Annotate a Book in Five Minutes" (A handout from various seminars and classes conducted on YA library services around the United States, 1995.) Adapted from a handout prepared by Connie Fillinger and Deborah Madigan of the Rocky River (OH) Public Library.

16. Ibid.

17. Mary K. Chelton, "Read Any Good Books Lately? Helping Patrons Find What They Want," *Library Journal* 116 (May 1, 1993): 35.

18. www.SmartGirl.com/results/trwreadingpref.html

19. Patrick Jones, "A Cyber Room of Their Own: How Libraries Use Web Pages to Attract Young Adults." *School Library Journal* 43, no. 11 (November 1997): 34.

20. Laura Wonnacott, "Site Savvy: The Speed of Business, If Your Pages Are Slow, Your Customers Will Go." *InfoWorld* 22, no. 37 (September 11, 2000): 80.

21. Walter Minkel, "Become Enabled," *NetConnect: The Librarian's Guide to the Internet* (Summer 2001): 30.

22. Jones, "A Cyber Room of Their Own," 37.

23. Walter Minkel, "Tis a Gift to Be Simple: Designing a Library Web Site That Makes Sense." *School Library Journal* 46, no. 6 (June 2000): 29.

24. Jones, "A Cyber Room of Their Own," 35.

25. Sara Ryan, "It's Hip to be Square: Library Web Sites for Teens May Never Be Cool, but They Can Be Effective," *School Library Journal* 46, no. 3 (March 2000): 140.

9

Library Services to Enhance Your Merchandising Efforts

The ultimate goal of any young adult library services merchandising plan is to place the library's materials in the teens' hands. Successful merchandising assumes that the young adults have actually entered the library to have access to the materials in the first place. While it has been said that an inviting library interior, a collection that appeals to teens and meets their needs, and programs geared just for them make teens feel welcome, one aspect of library service is vitally important and cannot be left out of the mix. Teens will not feel welcome and become repeat customers, if all library staff do not provide them with excellent customer service at *all* times.

Libraries are service organizations and that service is usually viewed as a library's strength. It is important that the same exemplary library service be given to patrons of all ages. Many librarians and support staff, while very knowledgeable on the technical aspects of their job, work best with materials and adult patrons only. In other words, their teen people skills leave much to be desired. Because of their mode of dress and hairstyles as well as their tendency to travel in groups, teens can be intimidating customers to library staff. This, in conjunction with the negative stereotypes of teens portrayed in the media, can make staff wary of teen customers. The media tends to lead some people to believe that all teens are rude and/or violent and have no contribution to add to society. This scares some adults, and thus they feel intimidated by teens. The truth of the matter is that for the most part, the teens who enter your library building are good kids who need help using the library and finding materials. They may be loud and obnoxious, may look funny to you, and seem to be challenging your library's quiet rules, but in reality none of those reasons is so grave that teens should be denied respect just like every other patron.

Too often staff members do not like young adults and do not provide them the same level of customer service that other patrons receive. Some staff may feel that it is not their job to help young adults with homework questions (but helping an older individual with crossword questions is justified) or that teens cannot possibly be getting anything out of the library experience if they are just sitting around talking with their friends. While some staff members do not voice these opinions outright, their negative body language, tone of voice, facial expressions, and other nonverbal communication make it obvious that teens are not valued nor welcome in the library. While teens at times appear to be unperceptive or flighty, they most certainly pick up on these clues and hence harbor a poor image of the library. They most likely feel that the library staff is not any different than suspecting storeowners and clerks. Many times teens are closely watched and followed in retail establishments to ensure that they act in a way the adult feels they should and do not steal anything. It is the responsibility of the young adult librarian to work with other staff to put them at ease and offer a place in the library where teens can feel welcome and receive respectful customer service.

It is important for any YA librarian to create a plan of service for young adults. This can be done formally or informally. YALSA has developed a set of competencies that YA librarians should incorporate into their plan of service.[1] While it is necessary for a YA librarian to develop his or her vision of YA service, it is even more necessary to share that vision not only with supervisors and administrative staff, but more importantly with all staff in the library. The employees who work daily with the public, which includes teens, need to be aware and mindful of the plan in order to execute it. Also, the staff who work behind the scenes, such as those who process and catalog items, need to know that paperbacks are a high priority in your collection development and that including a series note in the computer will help teens find these books more quickly. Customer service and respect does not only apply to patrons. Co-workers and colleagues need to be respectful of each other and work together to offer a comprehensive and successful plan of service.

Often, as new library staff are hired in any capacity, they are trained in the technical aspect of the job. That is, they are taught how and when to use certain resources to answer patron inquiries, how the computers work, and routines of the workplace. The concept of customer service is often addressed as a staff development day topic or a short program at a state, regional, or national library conference. It is often assumed that library staff practice exemplary customer service skills. The fact is that a high level of customer service skills should not be taken for granted, but should be included in every library training program.

In the retail world, sales personnel can have a major impact on consumer purchases. The effectiveness of sales efforts is influenced by the salesperson's knowledge, skill, and authority as well as the customer-salesperson relationship that develops during the transaction.[2] Customers in retail establishments are regularly asked, "Did you find everything you needed?" One marketing question—"Do you want fries with that?"—has probably generated more sales of fries than anyone could ever count.[3] This question reminds the customer that fries are available and most people will think, "Mmm, fries do sound good." These questions create a positive experience for the buyer and make him or her aware of other products for sale. While library patrons do not take part in a sales transaction in the literal sense, the service they experience affects their willingness to return. When questions such as "Did you know the library has DVDs now?" or "Did you need to place a reserve for anything that you could not find?" are asked of library patrons, the same concept is applied. It is a form of marketing the library's materials and services while reminding patrons what the library is all about.

Customer service has many facets. A friendly and approachable staff is probably the one aspect of service that everyone agrees is necessary. That staff must be able to provide accurate information to fill patron needs. It is important that it is done in the most speedy and expeditious manner. Simplifying policies and offering services that make the patron's library experience easy and enjoyable are two other components of customer service.

Communication is the heart of customer service and involves many different forms. First, anyone who works with the public needs to practice active listening; that is, he or she needs to pay attention, concentrate, and focus on what the customer is saying. Too often, while one person is talking, the other person is planning what he or she will say next. The other person's message therefore has a hard time getting through.[4] Show patrons that you understand by genuinely listening and carefully asking clarifying questions or rephrasing their requests.

A study involving library school students posing as library users seeking reference help sheds light upon negative behaviors practiced by librarians. These behaviors led users to negatively assess the reference transaction. Only 54 percent of the users in the study said that they would be willing to return to the same librarian with another question.[5] Many users in the study encountered unwelcome body language on the librarian's behalf. This form of nonverbal communication is one that teens usually experience the most. Pursed lips or a curt tone and unfriendly eye contact can make the teen feel that his or her query is an interruption as opposed to a request for service. A user in the study felt that the librarian's pursed lips and rolled eyes said "Why did I get stuck with this question?"[6]

In order to provide successful service to teens, a librarian must possess the quality of approachability. No matter how many other skills a librarian possesses, if the teen does not feel that the librarian wants to help (through body language or out-right behavior) the other skills will not be used.[7] Approachability means smiling at teens, making eye contact, and giving them a friendly greeting. Sometimes a librarian may appear to be busy working behind the desk so much so that patrons do not want to disturb him or her. While many librarians view down time at the reference desk as an ideal opportunity to catch up on paperwork, and so forth, appearance-wise it can turn patrons off. Working at the desk may provide a better opportunity to read a YA book or, better yet, to browse through teen magazines, as they do not require so much of your attention that you cannot lift your head from the pages as teens approach or walk by. Remember, as customers approach, they become the most important piece of work to be tended to at the desk. Approachability shows teens that you are willing to help them and like them. Instead of sending a teen to the stacks with a call number, accompany the young adult to the shelves to help him locate material. Get out from behind the desk! Be willing to approach teens that look like they may need help, but do not be upset if they refuse your help.

Listening to a patron's request shows her that you value her service. Ask follow-up questions that are open-ended. Rephrase and repeat what you have heard to make sure you and the patron are on the same page. Users in the aforementioned study were turned off by librarians who listened to part of the question and then "dashed off into the stacks" or who quietly, without comment, began typing without asking for more details.[8] Asking the right questions may result in a shorter time spent to answer the request. The extra details may reveal a different search strategy than you originally thought.

Once helpful materials have been located in the computer, relay to the patron what has been found. Do not just bolt for the stacks leaving teens at the desk alone wondering where you have gone. Explain what you are doing and either ask them to accompany you or tell them you will be right back with the items. Do not take for granted that patrons know how to find items on their own or use reference materials without some guidance. If you are too busy to accompany them to the stacks and have to hand them a list of titles and call numbers, make sure you create a free moment when you can see if they found the materials they needed.

Be respectful of YA requests. Keep an open mind. Just because your library may have encountered some troublesome teens does not mean that every other one follows the same pattern of behavior. Treat each new young adult with respect, and even those who may have been in trouble before need a clean slate to start anew. Treat all YA questions as important. This may be difficult, especially when teens may require help with school assignments or need a 150-page book about an obscure subject by tomorrow. Be especially aware of those teens who are pressed for time when they come in ten minutes before closing time to pick out needed materials. It is a good idea to walk around the building near closing time to inform patrons that time is running out and ask if they require any final assistance.[9] School assignments can produce obscure requests that may take some creative reference work to fulfill. Teens will get turned off if the librarian right from the start implies that a search will be futile or difficult. If a computer search does not give you any ideas, browse through some resources and exhaust all references, including colleagues. Do not declare that you cannot help them and then promptly return to your magazine reading.

Lastly, good customer service requires follow-up. Invite teens to return if what you found for them is not helpful. Check in with patrons who have gone into the stacks to search for materials. Ask questions such as "Does this completely answer your question?' Or make a comment such as "If you need anything else, I will be right here, just ask."

Darlene Weingand, author of *Customer Service Excellence: A Concise Guide for Librarians*, mentions the following magic phrases of customer service:

- "Of course we can try to get it for you." Never end a transaction with "No, we do not have it." A customer should be made to feel as if everything possible has been done to meet his/her request—even if it requires borrowing materials from another library.

- "How may I help you?" This open-ended question encourages dialogue.

- "Of course we will waive the fines . . . and I hope you are feeling better." This statement implies that library policies need not be followed too rigidly. Often the goodwill created by "bending the rules" goes a lot further than turning people away with the phrase "That is the policy." Being flexible with the rules can help young adults feel that the library is really trying to help them. A young adult with no money will appreciate a free photocopy of a page that will help complete an assignment. Policies, while critical to library operations, should not become a reason to deny service.

- "I'll be happy to make that call to _____ for you." If the library cannot directly answer a request, going the extra mile to find another agency that can is necessary.

- "Did you locate what you wanted? Is there something else I can find for you?" These questions are good to ask of those who are browsing.

- "Is this what you are looking for, or shall I investigate further?" This question makes sure that the customer is satisfied with what you have found.

- "There are several possible ways to address the question. Can you give me a little more background?" This allows the patron to give you more detail regarding the query.

- "I am with a customer at the moment. May I call you back in just a few minutes?" Customers will gain an understanding that you are busy and each customer is important.

- "Yes that item is in and I will be happy to hold it for you for forty-eight hours." Teens, like adults, are often too busy to come in and conduct searches on their own. Calling ahead makes perfect sense and saves them time.

- "Thank you for using the XYZ library." This expresses gratitude to people for their patronage.[10]

Customer service is the heart of any service organization. Every interaction with a patron results in marketing of sorts for the library and its services. This establishes an image for the patron to grasp. Often library staff become overwhelmed in busy situations or in dealing with teens, and customer service suffers as a result. Training in customer service can help to reinforce positive behaviors. Employers should include interview questions that objectively address an applicant's attitudes regarding public service. In addition, customer-service attitudes and effectiveness should be included as categories on employee performance evaluations.[11] An investment in regular training for all new and existing staff on customer-service practices and procedures can go a long way in helping staff members feel comfortable working with teens.

Focusing on the customer is also important when developing policies and services. As customers, we are used to the convenience of quickly prepared food at fast food restaurants and using an ATM at any hour of the day rather than having to visit a bank during certain hours. Services should offer maximum convenience for teens. Think of a teen's schedule, which is overloaded and hectic. Often just at the time a library is closing, a teen is finally free from extracurricular activities and jobs. Therefore, offering services, such as reference, referral, and reserves, over the Web makes accessing the library's collection a twenty-four-hours-a-day, seven-days-a-week possibility. Think about what the service at drive-up windows in fast food restaurants and banks has done for a time-pressed society. Libraries too need to offer this convenience for the quick drop off and retrieval of items. Teens should be able to call ahead and have items waiting for them at the drive-up window for a speedy transaction. A library system containing branches or satellites needs to provide for the easy and rapid transfer of reserve materials from one location to another.

As previously mentioned, policies are sometimes discriminatory against teens. Management should allow for times when exceptions to the rules are accepted. For example, younger teens may have difficulty obtaining rides to pick up reserve materials. If a teen tells staff of this predicament, it would create much goodwill to extend the holding time for the items until the young adult can pick them up a day or so later, rather than stating that the policy that items not picked up before a certain date are returned to the shelf.

Libraries often require patrons to verify their identity, including their address, when checking materials out, using certain reference resources, or placing items on hold. If a teen has forgotten his or her library card and has yet to obtain a driver's license, this can be problematic. Most teens that do not drive do not carry identification that shows their address. Alternatives should be found in order to allow teens to access items. Sometimes a student ID can be accepted or even just the verification of a name written in a school notebook or textbook. Obviously there are abusers to every policy, and steps should be taken to make sure that the library does not fall prey to those who purposely deceive library staff in order to steal materials. For the most part, bending the rules every once in a while for a teen in dire straits will be appreciated.

Practicing exemplary customer service with the public is just a part of over-all service. Positive working relationships with other staff members and colleagues must be established in order to reach the overall goal of service to everyone who enters the library's door. Your role as a librarian serving teens is to be an advocate for all teens in your community and beyond, as well as for the services geared toward them.

A key element of customer service is to focus on the customer. It is vitally important that all staff understand the developmental needs of young adults in order to understand what services they need and to appreciate them as customers. One way to educate staff about these needs is to have an outside trainer come into the library as a staff development speaker. As of the year 2001, YALSA has commissioned over sixty such trainers who reside all over the United States. YALSA received funding from a number of sources to host "Serving the Underserved" seminars. These sessions graduate trainers who are prepared to lead workshops and sessions on teenagers and the services libraries can provide to them. They are geared to YA generalists, specialists, or staff members with any background. For a complete listing of "Serving the Underserved" trainers, contact the YALSA office at 1-800-545-2433 ext. 4390, or www.ala.org/YALSA.

As a teen advocate, you must always be prepared to defend teens and the YA services of the library. It is common for a library to have only one staff member responsible for providing services to young adults. Some libraries are lucky to even have one. As the person serving teens, do all that you can to help fellow staff members feel at ease when serving teens. As a one-person show, it will be impossible to be available to serve teens every hour that the library is open. Obviously, there will be times when the YA librarian is unavailable and other staff members must answer YA questions. Keep all staff informed of upcoming YA events. Working with local schools, keep a notebook of assignments so that staff is alerted to possible reference questions. Also, keep a notebook of YA titles you have read, and make it available for staff members. This will make recommending unfamiliar YA books a little easier. Keeping a notebook of teen recommendations that staff can refer to is even better. Encourage staff members to read, listen to, and view YA materials. Use every opportunity available to promote these items at staff meetings, in the lunchroom/staff lounge, and so forth. Staff members who are more informed may not feel so overwhelmed working with teens.

Incorporating the concept of merchandising in the YA collection will require communication with staff members. Displays and exhibits often generate new demands on staff, such as increased business at the circulation desk. This can burden the circulation staff. Curiosity about materials related to a display can burden the reference staff as well. Booklists and displays may cause more holds or reserves to be placed on items.[12] As weeding is constantly performed, those who handle the deletions and "unprocessing" of weeded materials also may react to the added workload.

The person planning and making a display is the only one directly involved, yet others' work time is affected as well. Before starting any merchandising effort, it may be a good idea to train staff members in basic marketing or merchandising concepts so they can fully understand the philosophy behind them and participate in the process. A speaker can be hired to educate staff on the reasons why merchandising works and how it can be applied in the library setting. It would be ideal to find a speaker who is from another library and who has successfully incorporated merchandising into his or her service plan. If no budget allows for such a speaker, create a session yourself using resources such as this one. Taking the time to educate those staff members whose workload will be affected can help them be less resistant to change. A place to introduce these concepts would be at staff meetings, where people can ask questions about possible problems and solutions can be worked out together.

Staff attitudes must change in order to keep ongoing merchandising a success. As more items are displayed at various places, locating them becomes more difficult because they are out of the traditional Dewey Decimal/alphabetical order. The status of display items should be changed in the computer to show that they are in a temporary location. Reference staff assisting patrons and staff searching for items placed on reserve will appreciate this small task that makes their job less frustrating. It may also make them more accepting of the fact that materials will be out of the standard order. Clerks and pages will need to be trained in the art of display. The staff who reshelve items will need to be aware that materials in need of repair do not belong in a display. Shelvers must pay more attention to detail, and everyone will need to take charge and help restock displays. Staff must be informed that poorly shelved items discourages teens from browsing. The overall appearance of the display is important. For example, an empty display that houses a sign, props, and one lone item will look neglected, while on the other hand, a display that has too many items in disarray will need to be cleaned up in order to look appealing. All staff members need to be aware that merchandising requires a constant effort—a display should be revisited almost every hour or so as time permits.

Encourage other staff to help in merchandising efforts. Include them in brainstorming for ideas and assembling the props and materials needed or even in creating annotated lists. Staff who share ownership in an idea will embrace it more excitedly. Your colleagues may appreciate their inclusion in the merchandising process as long as they already do not feel overburdened with extra projects. Some staff, such as pages, may appreciate this avenue to think creatively because their normal tasks do not allow for such thinking. If you sense that staff is already overburdened and will be reluctant to deal with the extra work involved, start small and slowly build up a merchandising plan. Throwing too much at people all at once will make staff members resent any effort you put forth.

Those staff members who do not actively take part in setting up a display or creating a booklist for you still have a job to do. Children's room staff as well as adult reference staff should work on offering YA titles to their patrons in order to bridge the gap from department to department. The whole library staff needs to work as a team. While they are not expected to be well versed in YA literature, staff members from other departments should have YA booklists and award lists available to distribute. They should also know when to turn the patron over to the YA specialist if they find they cannot fully answer the query. This creates a need to include YA-related reference sources, especially of the reader's advisory type, in the collection. They can be helpful to those staff members who do not work with teens very much.

READER'S ADVISORY FOR TEENS

Offering reader's advisory to teens can be another way to promote titles in the collection. While this type of service cannot simultaneously promote as many titles as a display, it can be an opportunity to provide assistance to teens, offering them three or four titles. Patrick Jones states the goals of reader's advisory service to be the following:

1. Match YA reading interests with the library collection.

2. Provide access for readers to the library collection.

3. Learn the likes and dislikes of YA readers.

4. Promote reading through the use of documents.

5. Find the right book for the right young adult at the right time for the right reason.[13]

For the most part, teens would not be caught dead asking a librarian for help in finding reading material. Be assured that those who do are a special breed, so take time to spend with them if they are willing. Show them by your actions, body language, and tone of voice that you are sincere in wanting to help them find something they would like. Your actions will show that you like to read YA literature and that you have a good knowledge of it. Barbara Auerbach found in her library that most opportunities for reader's advisory occur when she shelves mass market paperbacks on the floor. She feels that she is much more approachable as she kneels among the books and displays than when she is seated behind the reference desk.[14]

Reader's advisory service in the YA area can be a sort of handselling. Not as in-depth as booktalking, handselling entails finding ways to suggest books to customers when they really are not looking for anything in particular. These short selling opportunities, also called jacket talks, do not dwell on the plot of a book. They are just a presentation of short sentences that relate the "feel" of a book. They are not as long as booktalks, and it may take some practice before you feel comfortable using them. When selling a book to a patron, describe action from the book that will grab the reader's attention. Choose materials that match the type of book for which he or she is looking.

In any reader's advisory transaction the librarian, as a reader's advisor, has to accomplish four things. You must elicit information about the reader's interests. You must have already developed a way of thinking about books that looks for similarities between titles. The advisor must be able to establish links between titles based on the reader's interest and the advisor's knowledge of titles and reader's advisory sources. Lastly, the advisor should be able to present titles and communicate how each title relates to the reader's interest.[15]

In order to find out what a teen is interested in, it is necessary to conduct a reader's advisory interview. When working with teens, it is best to keep the interaction low key. This will help them feel comfortable in rejecting any of your suggestions.[16] Also, it is important to *suggest* books rather than recommend them.[17] For example, going on about how much you loved a book and how he or she would too, makes it hard for someone to say, "No thank you, this is not what I am looking for."

When asking questions of a teen, make sure that they are of the open-ended variety. A good question to ask is "What was the last book you enjoyed reading?" This will give you an author or genre with which to start. You can then suggest titles that share a similar author, style, or theme. Any questions that are asked of the teen should help both him/her and you develop an idea of what the patron is looking for.[18] You may find that teens are really good at articulating what they are not looking for. Any information they can provide is helpful. Some teen requests may be specific enough so that you can show them how to find a book using the electronic catalog. Other requests may be more general, and the transaction can be moved to where the YA materials are located. You can then begin choosing items that you think fit the request. Some questions to ask in the beginning stages of the reader's advisory interview are the following:

- Are you looking for any particular type of book?
- What books or authors have you enjoyed reading?
- Are you looking for something to read for fun or for an assignment?
- Is this the type of thing you are looking for?[19]

If after asking these questions the teen still has no response, try asking what television shows or movies he or she enjoys.[20] Think of anything that will at least give you an idea of where to start. The aim of the reader's advisory interview is to get the reader to tell you what kinds of things he likes to read. It may actually be easier to find a title for a young adult who does not have a big interest in reading, but needs something for an assignment. He or she may be more likely to accept the first book that catches his or her eye. It is far more demanding to find something for a young adult who has strong opinions, likes and dislikes, or reads a single genre exclusively.[21] To further pinpoint the YA patron's likes and dislikes, consider asking some of the following questions:

- Do you like lots of action or a more leisurely pace?
- Do you like the story set in the past or in the present?
- Are there subjects you do not enjoy?
- Why did you like the last book you read?[22]

After asking clarifying questions and gaining an idea of the type of books the teen might enjoy, it is time to start suggesting titles. Be aware of the pitfall of assuming the teen wants another book by the author of a title he or she has just finished. Also do not assume that the young adult wants the next installment of a series. Do not be quick to suggest a title with characters of the same race or ethnicity as the patron or as characters of the book just finished. The key issue in suggesting titles is to con- sider the moods of the patrons. What do they feel like reading now? Their moods can vary. If they are busy or under stress they may want reassuring books such as ones they have already read or new books by trusted authors. If their lives are less stress- ful, they may be willing to take a risk and pick books on sheer impulse.[23] Therefore a statement to make before the standard "Tell me about a book you have read and enjoyed" would be to say "Tell me what you are in the mood for."[24] The latter statement is a better query in case the patron is looking for something different than the last item read. It can make the difference between suggesting something light and quick, such as *Hostage* by Willo Davis Roberts, versus something a little more detailed, such as *The Killer's Cousin* by Nancy Werlin.

Becoming adept at advising teens on what materials they would like takes practice. It requires a broad knowledge of the characteristics and elements of all genres, even the ones that are not your own preference. A familiarity with the library's collection, as well as any titles in the adult and children's collection, is essential. The best way to feel comfortable suggesting titles to teens is to read, view, and listen to as much in the collection as you can. If reading a whole work is not possible, read enough of it to get a good feel for the material. Make it a part of your job each day to look over new materials after they are processed but before they are put on the shelves or displays for circulation. Try to read whenever and wherever you can, while on duty at the service desk, during your free time, or while waiting for an appointment. If you have a long commute to and from work, use that time to listen to YA books on tape or CD. Audio geared to young adults can also help a long power walk or time on a stair climber or treadmill seem much shorter.

As you read or listen to as much as you can, you will soon develop a list of suggestions that you can rely on when asked certain things. You may know of several authors to suggest in each genre or certain titles that will fit specific teen requests. It may be helpful to keep a notebook or database of titles that you have read, listened to, or viewed. In addition to each title's bibliographic information and a brief plot summary, it would be advantageous to note genre, subject headings, geographical setting, series, appeal, and similar authors or titles. A file or reading log such as this can help to jog your memory when thinking of titles. Other staff members can use your suggestions when you are not present. Teens can also use the log to help them in choosing titles. As previously mentioned, allow teens to add titles they have read to the notebook or database. Table 5 provides a sample reading log form that could be copied back-to-back. It is adapted from one used by the staff of the Rocky River (Ohio) Public Library.

Table 5. Sample Reading Log Form

PACING	CHARACTERIZATION
• Nonstop action or a slow unfolding?	• How are characters presented?
• Grips you right away or builds in action?	• If singly, is there a long section devoted to each or does the character appear and is then developed over time?
• More dialogue or more description?	
• Depth of writing?	• Stereotypical characters?
• Lots of detail or minimal language?	• Does vision of characters change?
• Multiple plot lines or flashbacks?	• Likeable characters?
• Length of sentences, paragraphs, chapters?	• Single or multiple characters?
• Words, important in their own right or a vehicle for the action?	• Are characters like television or movie characters? (bigger than life)
• Do characters react to events or are they more involved in action?	• Prevailing trait of main character? Physical, social, psychological?
	• Most emphasized trait?

Table 5 continues on next page.

- Least emphasized trait?

- Depth of character?

- Do you know the inside or just the outside of characters?

- Is the character in control of action or does action control characters?

- What is the author's intent?

- Is the author concerned most about relationship between characters?

- How do the characters react to plot complications?

- How do the characters react to setting?

- Characters developed through description or action?

- Point of view? (Whose story is it?)
  1st or 3rd person? Omniscient?
  Is there an obvious narrator?

- Role of secondary characters?

STORYLINE/PLOT

- Serious drama, soap opera, romantic, comic, dark, etc.?

- Emphasis on people or situations?

- Emphasis on characters or plot?

- Amount of dialog vs. description?

- Multiple plots or straight line plot?

- Is the story developed through action or description?

- What is the focus of the story?
  Suspense, romance, historical period, murder, social/moral issues?

- Chronology of story?

Episodic?
Parallel plots?
Does the book unfold in layers?

- Surprise ending?

- Reader involvement?
  Is story related to or experienced by reader?

SETTING OR BACKGROUND

- Atmosphere?
  Minimal or detailed?

- Plot set in a frame?
  A train, one room in a house, etc.?

- Tone reflected through atmosphere?
  Dark, romantic, comic, cheerful, bleak, menacing, etc.?

- Background?
  Rich and famous, alien worlds, country, time period, etc.?

GENERAL/SIMILAR AUTHORS/TITLES

- Does one feature dominate?
  Pacing, characters, atmosphere, story?

- Story type? (Genre?)

- Cerebral vs. action?

- More than one time period?

- Quality of writing?

- Focus of the book?

- Unusual devices?
  Allusions, literary references?

- Who else writes like this author?

- Is there a similar title and why?

Author: SUMMARY:

Title:

CHARACTERISTICS:

Pacing

Characterization

Storyline/Plot

Setting or Background

General/Similar Authors

Date Read:

Pub. Date:

In order to be successful at reader's advisory service, it is necessary to be able to articulate a book's appeal. You will need to relay to a patron how a book "feels" (the tone of the book) in order to sell it to him or her. Elements to consider when exploring a book's appeal are pacing, characterization, storyline, and frame.

PACING

Pacing is one of the first elements readers become aware of, often unconsciously.[25] Points to consider are:

- Are characters and plot quickly revealed?

- Is there nonstop action, or does the storyline unfold as the book progresses?

- Is there more dialogue or description?

- Are sentences, paragraphs, and chapters short? These pull the reader along more quickly.

- Are there multiple plot lines, flashbacks, or alternating chapters from different points of view? This trend has become more popular with YA fiction.

- Do characters act or react to action?[26]

CHARACTERIZATION

Points to consider when studying characters are:

- Is the focus on a single character or several characters whose lives are intertwined?

- What is the point of view from which the story is told?

- Are the characters more important than the plot or setting?

- Are the characters developed over time or do we quickly recognize their stereotype?

- Do the characters seem familiar right away?[27]

STORYLINE

Points to consider about the storyline are:

- Does the story emphasize people or events?

- What did the author intend the storyline to be?[28]

FRAME

Frame includes setting, atmosphere, background, and tone. Points to consider about the frame of a book include:

- Is there a special background frame? For example, a story set in a historical period needs details from the life and thoughts of people from that era.

- Is the background detailed or minimal? In other words, could the book take place anywhere else without altering its effect?[29]

Occasionally you will be required to talk about a book or genre that you have not read. This may be a time to rely on others' comments, as well as reviews and information from the book's jacket or blurb. If it is a book that you have read but did not personally enjoy, you can still suggest it. Talk about what the author does best; just do not relay any negative comments.

Answers to reader's advisory questions most often come from your own personal knowledge of the collection. Reading reviews and journal articles, as well as keeping up with booklists, enhances this knowledge. Paying attention to teens' comments on materials is helpful. Relying on personal knowledge may not be enough. Over the years, different reader's advisory sources have been published to help answer reader's advisory questions. Because many of these resources can be costly, you may have to be choosy as to which ones can fit into your meager YA budget. Librarian and author Joyce Saricks suggests looking at the following points when considering a commercially produced reader's advisory reference source:

1. Access points and indexes.

2. Plot summaries.

3. Evaluative material about books such as characteristics of an author's works, best and/or most representative titles, where to start new readers.

4. Point of view from which the book is written.[30]

Do not be afraid to use reader's advisory reference sources. After all, you bought them, so do not let them collect dust on the shelf. Teach teens to use the sources as well. Reference sources are good browsing material to give that parent of a teen who insists on doing all of the talking and choosing of materials without any regard to what the teen wants or needs. If a parent walks in with his or her teen son or daughter and begins to take over, try to separate the two. Address all comments to the teen, while the parent looks through the reference source. Also hand any materials you find to the teen. It may be difficult to find something that meets the parent's criteria and appeals to the teen as well, but you cannot disregard a parent's restriction. Table 6 is a selected list of reader's advisory reference sources that might be helpful in a transaction involving teens.

Table 6. Selected Reader's Advisory Sources for YA Librarians

Adamson, Lynda G. *American Historical Fiction: An Annotated Guide to Novels for Adults and Young Adults.* Oryx, 1999.

———. *World Historical Fiction: An Annotated Guide to Novels for Adults and Young Adults.* Oryx, 1999.

Ammon, Bette D., and Gale W. Sherman. *Worth a Thousand Words: An Annotated Guide to Picture Books for Older Readers.* Libraries Unlimited, 1996.

Anderson, Vicki. *Fiction Index for Readers 10 to 16: Subject Access to Over 8200 Books (1960-1990).* McFarland, 1992.

———. *Fiction Sequels for Readers 10 to 16: An Annotated Bibliography of Books in Succession.* McFarland, 1998.

Barron, Neil (ed.). *Anatomy of Wonder: A Critical Guide to Science Fiction,* 4th ed. Bowker, 1995.

———. *Fantasy and Horror: A Critical and Historical Guide to Literature Illustrations, Film, Radio, and the Internet.* Scarecrow, 1999.

Bodart, Joni, R. *One Hundred World Class Thin Books: Or What to Read When Your Book Report Is Due Tomorrow.* Libraries Unlimited, 1993.

———. *What to Read When Your Book Report Is Due Tomorrow: The World's Best Thin Books.* Scarecrow, 2000.

Calvert, Stephen (ed.). *Best Books for Young Adult Readers.* Bowker, 1997.

Carter, Betty, Sally Estes, Linda Waddle, and the YALSA staff. *Best Books for Young Adults.* American Library Association, 2000.

Coffey, Rosemary. *America as Story: Historical Fiction for Middle and Secondary Schools.* American Library Association, 1997.

Cooper-Mullin, Alison, and Jennifer Marmaduke Coye. *Once Upon a Heroine: 450 Books for Girls to Love.* Contemporary Books, 1998.

Day, Frances Ann. *Lesbian and Gay Voices: An Annotated Bibliography and Guide to Literature for Children and Young Adults.* Greenwood, 2000.

Dodson, Shireen. *100 Books for Girls to Grow On.* HarperCollins, 1998.

Estell, Don, et al. *Reading Lists for College Bound Students,* 3d ed. Arco/Thomson Learning, 2000.

Fonseca, Anthony J., and June Michele Pullium. *Hooked on Horror: A Guide to Reading Interests in Horror Fiction.* Libraries Unlimited, 1999.

Gillespie, John T. *Best Books for Young Teen Readers, Grade 7–10*. Bowker, 2000.

Helbig, Alethea. *Many Peoples, One Land: A Guide to New Multicultural Literature for Children and Young Adults*. Greenwood, 2000.

Herald, Diana Tixier. *Teen Genreflecting*. Libraries Unlimited, 1997.

———. *Fluent in Fantasy: A Guide to Reading Interests*. Libraries Unlimited, 1999.

Herz, Sarah K., and Donald R. Gallo. *From Hinton to Hamlet: Building Bridges Between Young Adult Literature and the Classics*. Greenwood Press, 1996.

Kutenplon, Deborah, and Ellen Olmstead. *Young Adult Fiction by African American Writers, 1968-1993: A Critical and Annotated Guide*. Garland, 1996.

Makowski, Silk. *Serious About Series: Evaluations and Annotations of Teen Fiction in Paperback Series*. Scarecrow Press, 1998.

Matulka, Denise J. *Picture This: Picture Books for Young Adults, a Curriculum Related Annotated Bibliography*. Greenwood Press, 1997.

Middle and Junior High School Library Catalog, 7th ed. Wilson, 1995.

Odean, Kathleen. *Great Books for Girls: More than 600 Books to Inspire Today's Girls and Tomorrow's Women*. Ballantine, 1997.

———. *Great Books for Boys: More than 600 Books for Boys 2–14*. Ballantine, 1998.

Ramsdell, Kristin. *Romance Fiction: A Guide to the Genre*. Libraries Unlimited, 1999.

Rand, Donna. *Black Books Galore!: Guide to More Great African American Children's Books*. Wiley and Sons, 2001.

———. *Black Books Galore! Guide to Great African American Children's Books About Boys*. Wiley and Sons, 2000.

———. *Black Books Galore! Guide to Great African American Children's Books About Girls*. Wiley and Sons, 2001.

Rothschild, Aviva. *Graphic Novels: A Bibliographic Guide to Book-Length Comics*. Libraries Unlimited, 1995.

Samuels, Barbara (ed.). *Your Reading: A Booklist for Middle School and Junior High*, 10th ed. National Council of Teachers of English, 1999.

Saricks, Joyce G., and Nancy Brown. *Reader's Advisory Service in the Public Library*, 2d ed. ALA, 1997.

Senior High School Library Catalog, 1st ed. Wilson, 1997.

Table 6 continues on next page.

Sherman, Gale W. *Rip-Roaring Reads for Reluctant Teen Readers*. Libraries Unlimited, 1993.

———. *More Rip-Roaring Reads for Reluctant Teen Readers*. Libraries Unlimited, 1999.

Spencer, Pam. *What Do Young Adults Read Next?* 4 vols. Gale, 1994, 1997, 1999, 2001.

Stover, Lois, and Stephanie Zenker (eds.). *Books for You: An Annotated List from 1994–1996 for Senior High Students*, 13th ed. National Council of Teachers of English, 1997.

Sullivan, Edward T. *The Holocaust in Literature for Youth*. Scarecrow, 1999.

Walker, Barbara J. *Developing Christian Fiction Collections for Children and Adults: Selection Criteria and a Core Collection*. Neal-Schuman, 1998.

Weiner, Steve, and Keith R. A. Decandido. *The 101 Best Graphic Novels*. NBM Publishing, 2001.

What Inspirational Literature Do I Read Next? Gale Group, 2000.

Zvirin, Stephanie. *The Best Years of Their Lives*, 2d ed. American Library Association, 1996.

Reading Rants. http://tln.lib.mi.us/~amutch/jen/

Teen Genreflecting. http://www.genrefluent.com/teen.html

YALSA booklists (ALA). http://www.ala.org/yalsa

Kay Vandergrift's Young Adult Literature Page. http://scils.rutgers.edu/~kvander

Virtual YA Index: Public Libraries with Young Adult Web Pages. http:yahelp.suffolk.lib.ny.us/virtual.html

Teen Series and Sequels. http://www.rbls.lib.il.us/bpl/services/series.htm

The Book Report Network. http://www.teenreads.com

D. Aviva Rothschild's The Comics Get Serious site. http://www.rationalmagic.com

Horrornet. http://www.horrornet.com

Tor, Forge, and Orb Science Fiction Books. http://www.tor.com

Online Reader's Club (a reader's advisory site from the Public Library of Charlotte and Mecklenburg County, North Carolina). http://www.readersclub.org

Recommended Graphic Novels for Public Libraries. http://my.voyager.net/~sraiteri/graphicnovels.htm

Booklists for Young Adults on the Web. http://www.seemore.mi.org/booklists/

As with any reference in this digital age, do no forget to use the Internet and electronic mailing lists as resources for reader's advisory. Some websites can be very useful while others can be of no use at all. Publisher sites can be very accurate but difficult to navigate because of elaborate graphics or confusing layouts.[31] Listservs are probably familiar to those with Internet access. In a listserv, you sign up with a group of like-minded people in order to discuss a particular topic, and everyone's comments are e-mailed to everyone else.[32] YALSA has a listserv called YALSA-BK where teens, librarians, media specialists, authors, and other unknown "lurkers" discuss specific titles and other issues concerning YA literature. It is also a place where subscribers can learn what has been nominated to the YALSA lists of Best Books for Young Adults, Popular Paperbacks for Young Adults, and Quick Picks for Reluctant Young Readers. The books are also discussed here. Fellow YALSA-BK subscribers can help solve a reader's advisory query or be an avenue to learning about new and old YA literature. The useful part about the listserv is that everyone is so willing to share information. A librarian may post a request for titles written in diary format. Fellow subscribers respond with one or several titles, and then the person who posted the original request may compile and post the whole list for everyone. Other discussions may center around a certain title and how those who read it feel about it. Whether you actively respond to queries or discussions or lurk anonymously, taking all the information in, this type of resource can be a big help. To subscribe to YALSA-BK send a message to listproc@ala.org. Leave the subject line blank. For the message type "Subscribe YALSA-BK first name last name."

Many publisher websites contain book discussion guides, while others will e-mail you information on new titles. In addition to an upcoming publishing schedule and dates for author appearances, features may include sample chapters from upcoming books. Other sites such as amazon.com and barnesandnoble.com not only offer reviews from trade journals, but also provide useful customer comments. These sites also offer titles related to the one in the original search.

No matter what sources are used to find titles for the teen, conclude the transaction by saying, "Look at these and let me know if I am on the right track."[33] This gives the patron an opportunity to return for additional assistance. You may also want to tell the teen to let you know when he or she returns the items if they were what he or she was looking for. This is done because the teen might not know if your suggestions were on the right track until after he or she has read them.

NOTES

1. www.ala.org/yalsa

2. Del Hawkins, Roger J.Best, and Kenneth A. Coney. *Consumer Behavior: Implications for Marketing Strategy*, 6th ed. (Chicago: Richard D. Irwin, 1995), 505.

3. Peter Eager, " 'Do You Want Fries with That?' Use Marketing Questions to Promote Library Materials and Services," *The Unabashed Librarian* 92 (1994): 11.

4. Darlene E. Weingand, *Customer Service Excellence: A Concise Guide for Librarians* (Chicago: ALA, 1997), 82.

5. Catherine Sheldrick Ross and Patricia Dewdney, "Best Practices: An Analysis of the Best (and Worst) in Fifty-two Public Library Transactions," *Public Libraries* 33 (September/October 1994): 261.

6. Ibid., 263.

7. Patrick Jones, *Connecting Young Adults and Public Libraries* (New York: Neal-Schuman, 1998), 180.

8. Ross and Dewdney, "Best Practices," 263.

9. Peter Lisker, "The Ties That Bind: Creating Great Customer Service," *Public Libraries* 39, no. 4 (July/August 2000): 191.

10. Weingand, *Customer Service Excellence*, 93–95.

11. Don Sager, "Customer Service and Public Libraries," *Public Libraries* 40, no. 2 (March/April 2001): 89.

12. Anne Tedeschi, *Book Displays: A Library Exhibits Handbook* (Ft. Atkinson, WI: Highsmith Press, 1997), 19.

13. Jones, *Connecting Young Adults*, 196.

14. Barbara Auerbach, "Young Adult Reader's Advisory: Recommending the Right Reads," in *Young Adults and Public Libraries: A Handbook of Materials and Services*, edited by Mary Anne Nichols and C. Allen Nichols. (Westport, CT: Greenwood Press, 1998), 123.

15. Kenneth Shearer, ed., *Guiding the Reader to the Next Book* (New York: Neal-Schuman, 1996), 103.

16. Tom Reynolds, "Connecting with the Young Adult Reader: A Reader's Advisory Strategy," in *Young Adults and Public Libraries: A Handbook of Materials and Services*, edited by Mary Anne Nichols and C. Allen Nichols. (Westport, CT: Greenwood Press, 1998), 115.

17. Joyce Saricks and Nancy Brown, *Reader's Advisory Service in the Public Library*, 2d ed. (Chicago: ALA, 1997), 58.

18. Jones, *Connecting Young Adults*, 197.

19. Renee Vaillancourt, *Bare Bones Young Adult Services: Tips for Public Library Generalists* (Chicago: ALA, 2000), 49.

20. Jones, *Connecting Young Adults*, 197.

21. Reynolds, *Connecting with the Young Adult Reader*, 115.

22. Mary K. Chelton, "Read Any Good Books Lately?: Helping Patrons Find What They Want," *Library Journal* 116 (May 1, 1993): 34.

23. Catherine Sheldrick Ross and Mary K. Chelton. "Reader's Advisory: Matching Mood and Material," *Library Journal* (February 1, 2001): 52.

24. Ibid., 54.

25. Saricks and Brown, *Reader's Advisory Service*, 38.

26. Ibid., 39–42.

27. Ibid., 44–47.

28. Ibid., 48.

29. Ibid., 49–50.

30. Ibid., 19.

31. Roberta Johnson, "The Global Conversation: Reader's Advisory on the Web," *Booklist* (January 1 and 15, 2001): 912.

32. Ibid.

33. Shearer, *Guiding the Reader*, 33.

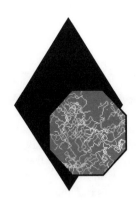

10

A Running Start! Ideas to Begin Your Merchandising Efforts

The ideas found in this chapter are meant to give any librarian interested in incorporating point of purchase or POP displays into his or her merchandising efforts a running start. Each display idea has a title, an explanation of the theme, decorating ideas, and an annotated list of materials that can be used in the display. A conscious effort has been made to include as many titles published between 1998 and 2001 as possible. Some items have titles or subtitles that are self-explanatory, so in those instances no annotation is given. Since reading tastes and collections reflect the preferences and diversity of the community, you may well find that titles listed cannot be found in your collection. While these titles are suggested to fit the theme of the display, feel free to add your own favorites as you see fit. These titles are provided to give you a starting point—with so many books published each year, it is likely some of your favorites are missing. Fiction and nonfiction titles have been included. Many of the fiction titles are also available as books-on-tape. Do not forget to incorporate those in your displays as well. In addition, you must constantly be aware of all media in your collection that can fit with your display theme. Often music CDs and videos fit well with the theme; these too should be added. While it is necessary to have a minimum of fifteen to twenty titles in the core list to be displayed, including all types of materials can help expand the list and offer more titles to display.

It should go without saying that titles in any display should reflect diversity in all levels, beliefs, ethnicities, and opinions. There should also be representations from all genres. A display becomes much more effective and appealing when it is that inclusive. A display of just one genre or of characters of a single ethnicity, for example, may elicit stereotypes and further the negative preconceived notions held by some patrons, while rendering the display unappealing to others. A well-thought-out display encourages a patron to select materials that he or she normally may not have chosen. The patron focuses on the theme of the display as well as the similarity of the materials contained in it—not the individuality of each item. While singling out a genre for a display may seem easy, remember that patrons can also identify genre fiction if a technique such as genre spine labels is used in the collection. It is a better idea to incorporate genre fiction into displays with different themes. For example, a teen may have a preconceived notion that science fiction is not for him or her. However, incorporating a time travel book in a general theme of travel or a book such as *Dancing with an Alien* by Mary Logue in with books on relationships broadens the appeal of the material and lessens the idea that it is a "science fiction" book.

As displays become an integral part of your merchandising efforts, you will find that they are not that difficult to create and assemble. The more YA material you are able to read, the easier it will be to find similar themes among items. Listservs such as YALSA-BK can provide you with titles and ideas. Also websites such as Reading Rants (http://tln.lib.mi.us/~amutch/jen) and Booklists for Young Adults on the Web (www.seemore.mi.org/booklists), just to name two, offer an indispensable place to start.

GENERAL THEMES

Some display ideas do not require titles with a similar plot line or literary theme. When time is of the essence and a display is needed, be creative. Construct a colorful sign stating "Colorful Covers" and choose titles whose book jackets have vibrant colors. Use a painter's dropcloth, paint cans, rollers, brushes, and an artist's palette as props. Do not forget to use splatters of paint as a finishing touch. Other ideas for materials not connected by a theme per se include "Too Good to Miss," "These Don't Fit on the Shelves," or even "These Fell on the Floor." Keep an open mind and take a look at the calendar to see what events are happening—it may lead to a display entitled "Books to Read While Your Boyfriend Watches the Super Bowl." These types of displays allow you to put unique material on display that may never have been given a chance for circulation.

SPECIFIC THEMES

Following are eighteen specific displays with annotated lists of appropriate titles. Then, there are two displays that not only have titles for display but are also interactive in nature. Teens can vote for their favorite characters in various categories. The categories and the nominees can be made into ballots and distributed near the display. The winners can be announced via the library's website, on a bulletin board, or a sign posted in the YA area. Teens can nominate their own characters and books or the librarian can prepare the list. The titles/characters given are examples, but the librarian can certainly substitute his or her favorites that may be more appropriate in the local setting.

Go to Jail . . . Go Directly to Jail

Explanation of theme: So many novels geared toward young adults depict teens in trouble with the law. Teens like to read these novels as a way to live dangerously along with the main character while keeping their own record clean. This type of story also reinforces their need for boundaries.

Props: Handcuffs, police line tape, face behind bars. In my locality orange is the universal color of the uniform for those who are incarcerated. Adapt a Monopoly theme without infringing on copyright.

Annotated list of titles:

Cadnum, Michael. *Rundown.* Viking, 1999. In order to gain attention because she is feeling alienated by her family, Jennifer Thayer reports an attempted rape that did not occur.

Cormier, Robert. *Tenderness.* Delacorte, 1997. Fifteen-year-old Lori is in love with eighteen-year-old serial killer Eric, who is about to be released from a detention center after murdering his mother and stepfather.

Deuker, Carl. *Night Hoops.* Houghton Mifflin, 2000. Does Nick really want to help the troubled classmate who lives across the street?

Dowell, Francis. *Dovey Coe.* Antheneum, 2000. In 1928, plucky mountain girl Dovey Coe finds herself in a courtroom pleading innocent to the charge of murdering her sister's suitor, the snobbish and wealthy Parnell Caraway.

Ferris, Jean. *Bad.* Farrar, Straus & Giroux, 1998. Dallas learns things about herself and life in a women's correctional center, where she meets drug dealers, gang members, and a fourteen-year-old prostitute.

Haddix, Margaret Peterson. *Among the Hidden.* Simon & Schuster, 1998. Thirteen-year-old Luke, the third of his parents' children, must hide in the attic from the population police in order to survive in a society where couples are allowed to have only two children.

Heynan, Jim. *Cosmos Coyote and William the Nice.* Henry Holt, 2000. Cosmos chooses a year in exile over jail time and falls in love with a religious girl who causes him to examine his values and beliefs.

Hobbs, Will. *The Maze.* Morrow, 1998. Rick escapes from juvenile detention and travels to Canyonlands National Park, where he ends up helping a biologist reintroduce condors into the wild.

Hoffman, William. *Tidewater Blood.* Algonquin, 1998. To prove his innocence, Charles becomes a fugitive when accused of blowing up his family's estate and most of his family.

Konigsburg, E. L. *Silent to the Bone.* Atheneum, 2000. After being struck dumb when dialing 911 to report his baby sister not breathing, Branwell lands in a juvenile detention center where his friend Connor helps him break down the silence to find out what happened and clear his name.

143

Lubar, David. *Hidden Talents*. TOR, 1999. Martin befriends a group of misfits with psychic powers when he arrives at an alternative school.

McDonald, Joyce. *Swallowing Stones*. Delacorte, 1997. Depression, guilt, and fear plague Michael's dreams after he accidentally kills a man and then hides the gun and feigns ignorance.

Myers, Walter Dean. *Monster*. HarperCollins, 1999. While standing trial as an accomplice to murder, sixteen-year-old Steve Harmon records his prison and courtroom experiences in the form of a film script.

Olson, Gretchen. *Joyride*. Boyds Mills Press, 1998. Instead of spending the summer as he had planned, a joyride turned bad forces Jeff to work on a strawberry farm to avoid criminal charges.

Plum-Ucci, Carol. *The Body of Christopher Creed*. Harcourt, 2000. High school junior Torey finds his seemingly perfect life in trouble as he becomes involved in the case of the mysterious disappearance of freaky classmate Christopher Creed.

Rottman, S. L. *Hero*. Peachtree, 1998. Freshman Sean performs community service at a farm owned by an old man who teaches Sean to take charge of his life.

Sachar, Louis. *Holes*. Farrar, Straus & Giroux, 1999. Stanley Yelnats is wrongfully accused of stealing a baseball star's sneakers and must spend six months digging holes in a dry lake bed under the watchful eyes of a wacko warden.

Strasser, Todd. *Give a Boy a Gun*. Simon & Schuster, 2000. What led Gary and Brandon to take their classmates hostage and methodically destroy their school and lives?

Sweeney, Joyce. *Players*. Winslow, 2000. A new player on Corey's basketball team is an evil and destructive force.

Tomey, Ingrid. *Nobody Else Has to Know*. Delacorte, 1999. Webber's grandfather perpetuates a lie to keep Webber out of trouble—will Webber let him?

Vande Velde, Vivian. *Magic Can Be Murder*. Harcourt, 2000. Nola, a teenage witch, and her mother seem to be able to evade witch-hunting authorities until she witnesses a murder and finds herself in such danger that even magic may not save her.

———. *Never Trust a Dead Man*. Harcourt, 1999. Left for dead after being wrongly convicted of murder, Selwyn must work with the obnoxious ghost of the victim to find the guilty party.

Walter, Virginia. *Making Up Megaboy*. DK Publishing, 1998. Everyone who knows Robbie, a quiet thirteen-year-old, struggles to understand why he shot an old man in a liquor store.

Wells, Ken. *Meely LaBauve*. Random House, 2000. Motherless Meely tries to avoid the trouble his often absent and in trouble father sends his way.

Werlin, Nancy. *The Killer's Cousin*. Delacorte, 1998. After being acquitted of murder, seventeen-year-old David goes to stay with relatives in Cambridge, Massachusetts, where he faces his past and encounters his strange cousin Lily.

Get Over It!

Explanation of theme: According to *Chase's Calendar of Events* (Contemporary Books, 2001), January is International "Get Over It" month. It is a month devoted to letting go of the past and getting over whatever is bugging you about anyone or anything for a renewed optimism about life (p. 67). This display features self-help books for teens, which have been published in great abundance and in interesting and appealing formats.

Props: A copy of the masterpiece *The Scream* by artist Edvard Munch and matching fabric. This famous artwork depicts a man screaming on a bridge holding his hands to his cheeks. Poster-sized copies of this masterpiece can be purchased on the Internet for less than $10. Inflatable scream dolls ranging in size from 19 inches to 8 feet can also be purchased in the same price range.

Annotated list of titles:

Brous, Elizabeth. *How to Be Gorgeous: The Ultimate Beauty Guide to Hair, Makeup and More.* HarperCollins, 2000.

Brown, Bobbi, and Annemarie Iverson. *Bobbi Brown Teenage Beauty: Everything You Need to Look Pretty, Natural, Sexy, and Awesome.* HarperCollins, 2000.

Canfield, Jack, ed., Mark V. Hansen, comp., and Kimberly Kirkberger. *Chicken Soup for the Teenage Soul Letters: Letters of Life, Love, and Learning.* Heath Communications, 2001.

———. *Chicken Soup for the Teenage Soul III: More Stories of Life, Love, and Learning.* Heath Communications, 2000. Collections of writings that supply inspiration and guidance.

———. *Chicken Soup for the Teenage Soul II: 101 More Stories of Life, Love, and Learning.* Heath Communications, 1998.

———. *Chicken Soup for the Teenage Soul: 101 Stories of Life, Love, and Learning.* Heath Communications, 1997.

Daldry, Jeremy. *The Teenage Guy's Survival Guide.* Little Brown, 1999.

Drill, Esther. *Deal with It! A Whole New Approach to Your Body, Brain, and Life as a Gurl.* Pocket Books, 1999.

Gottlieb, Lori. *Stick Figure: A Diary of My Former Self.* Simon & Schuster, 2000. You can be too thin and not really know it.

Greenberg, Gary. *Pop-Up Book of Phobias.* William Morrow, 1999. Everyone is afraid of something.

Irwin, Cait. *Conquering the Beast Within: How I Fought Depression and Won . . . and How You Can Too.* Random House, 1998. How you can fight depression and win—I did!

Kirkberger, Kimberly. *Teen Love: On Relationships, a Book for Teenagers*. Heath Communications, 1999. A book to help you sort out your thoughts and confusion about love and relationships.

Mannarino, Melanie. *The Boyfriend Clinic: The Final Word on Flirting, Dating, Guys, and Love*. HarperCollins, 2000.

Packer, Alex J. *Highs! Over 150 Ways to Feel Really, Really Good . . . Without Alcohol or Other Drugs*. Free Spirit, 2000. Offers suggestions (simple and those requiring time and money) on attaining serenity and social, spiritual, and physical highs.

Pinsky, Drew, and Adam Carolla. *The Dr. Drew and Adam Book: A Survival Guide to Life and Love*. Dell, 1998.

Piven, Joshua, and David Borgenicht. *The Worst Case Scenario Survival Handbook*. Chronicle, 1999. A humorous presentation of survival skills.

Raine, Alison, and Emma Harrison. *Ultimate You! 365 Days to a More Daring, Deep, and Adorable You*. Scholastic, 2001.

Rubens, Susan. *The Complete Idiot's Guide to Dating for Teens*. Alpha Books, 2001.

Schreibman, Tamar. *Kissing: The Complete Guide: Everything You've Always Wanted to Know About Kissing and Were Afraid to Ask*. Simon & Schuster, 2000.

Shaw, Tucker, and Fiona Gibb. *. . . Any Advice?* AlloyBooks, 2000. Questions about love, life, and more, with answers on how to deal with them.

Stine, Megan. *Trauma-rama: Life's Most Embarrassing Moments*. Avon, 2001. The experts at *Seventeen* offer advice on how to handle mortifying moments for teens.

Tom, Karen, and Kiki, eds. *Angst! Teen Verses from the Edge*. Workman, 2001. A collection of teens' thoughts and frustrations with a final chapter that defines the different types of poetry and how to get started writing your own verse.

Wann, Marilyn. *Fat!So?: Because You Don't Have to Apologize for Your Size*. Ten Speed Press, 1998. Learn to be comfortable—no matter how much you weigh.

Watson, Esther Pearl, and Mark Todd, eds. *The Pain Tree and Other Teenage Angst-Ridden Poetry*. Houghton Mifflin, 2000. Poetry and artwork presented in a straightforward, brutally honest way.

Who Do You Think You Are?

Explanation of theme: Many young adults spend their teen years struggling to fit in and searching for themselves. Items in this display depict teens doing just these things or speaking out about who they are.

Prop: Huge mirror hung on a wall with words cut out and attached to mirror.

Annotated list of titles:

Bauer, Joan. *Backwater.* Putnam, 1999. Who is the reclusive aunt no one speaks about but everyone thinks is just like Ivy?

Bauer, Marian Dane. *Am I Blue? Coming Out from the Silence.* HarperCollins, 1995. Popular young adult authors present short stories from the gay and lesbian perspective that explore pride, individuality, and struggle.

Calhoun, Dia. *Aria of the Sea.* Winslow, 2000. A dangerous rivalry with the star of the School of the Royal Dancers leads to self-discovery for thirteen-year-old folk healer Cerinthe.

Ferris, Jean. *Eight Seconds.* Harcourt, 2000. John confronts his own sexuality at summer rodeo camp when he meets Kit who is smart, tough, complicated, and gay.

Flake, Sharon. *The Skin I'm In.* Hyperion, 1998. Outcast Maleeka thinks her extremely dark complexion makes it easy to be made fun of until her teacher shows her that she can accept herself.

Frank, E. R. *Life Is Funny.* DK, 2000. The lives of teens in a Brooklyn neighborhood become intertwined over a seven-year period.

Gallo, Donald R. *On the Fringe.* Dial, 2001. Acclaimed young adult authors write short stories about those often ridiculed high school students who do not seem to fit in with the more popular mainstream teenagers.

Gaskins, Pearl Fuyo, ed. *What Are You? Voices of Mixed Race Young People.* Henry Holt, 1999. Forty-five mixed race young people talk about themselves and growing up.

Gayatri, Patnaik, and Michelle Shinseki. *The Secret Life of Teens: Young People Speak Out About Their Lives.* HarperCollins, 2000. Teens offer insight in the form of letters on issues such as who they are, friendships, love, sexuality, and substance abuse.

Gray, Mary. *In Your Face: Stories from the Lives of Queer Youth.* Haworth Press, 1999. Honest narratives by gay, lesbian, and bisexual teens who share their experiences of coming out, their search for love, and their hope for the future.

Kalergis, Mary. *Seen and Heard: Teenagers Talk About Their Lives.* Stewart Tabori, 1998. A cross-section of American teens talk about their lives and beliefs.

Kehret, Peg. *I Am Not Who You Think I Am.* Dutton, 1999. Ginger is stalked by a deranged mother who believes that Ginger is her daughter.

Klass, David. *You Don't Know Me*. Farrar, Straus & Giroux, 2001. John creates alternative worlds to deal with his mother's abusive boyfriend.

Lessa, Christina, Teresa Edwards, and Peggy Fleming. *Women Who Win: Stories of Triumph in Sport and in Life*. Universe, 1998. Twenty champion athletes share their views on life and sports.

Lynch, Chris. *Slot Machine*. HarperCollins, 1995. Can Elvin find his slot in his new sports-oriented high school?

Mastoon, Adam. *The Shared Heart*. William Morrow, 1997. Essays and photographs present the lives of four dozen gay, lesbian, transgendered, and bisexual teens.

Myers, Walter Dean. *Bad Boy: A Memoir*. HarperCollins, 2001. Author's biography of how his bad-boy Harlem childhood and life after dropping out of high school made him one of the strongest voices in children's and young adult literature today.

Peters, Julie Anne. *Define Normal*. Little, Brown, 2000. Antonia, who considers herself normal, learns that normal can mean different things when she peer counsels Jazz, a perceived druggie with body piercing, tattoos, and hair that changes colors.

Randle, Kristen. *Breaking Rank*. Morrow, 1999. Can Baby think for himself or does the Clan control his every move?

Shandler, Sara. *Ophelia Speaks: Adolescent Girls Write About Their Search for Self*. HarperPerennial, 1999. Essays, poems, and comments from teenage girls throughout the country.

Werlin, Nancy. *Locked Inside*. Delacorte, 2000. It is so much safer for Marnie to be a sorceress in an adventure game on the Net than to survive in a locked basement.

Whittlinger, Ellen. *What's in a Name?* Simon & Schuster, 2000. As their home town considers changing its name to improve its image, ten teens explore their own identity.

This Is Happily Ever After?
Dump Your Significant Jerk Day

Explanation of theme: According to *Chase's Calendar of Events* (p. 119) Dump Your Significant Jerk Day is celebrated annually the Tuesday of the week before Valentine's Day. Take this opportunity to highlight materials featuring relationships gone bad. This can also be a chance to display informative series books on date and acquaintance rape along with pamphlets from the Battered Woman's Shelter or those agencies who counsel teens and provide assistance.

Props: Heart broken in half (with jagged edges) with a 3-D arrow in the middle of it or a heart-shaped dartboard with a teens face (male or female) as a bullseye and a dart in the forehead.

Annotated list of titles:

Bauer, Joan. *Thwonk!* Delacorte, 1995. Cupid's arrow turns Peter, the guy of AJ's dreams, into an obnoxious and annoying nuisance.

Block, Francesca Lia. *Violet and Claire*. HarperCollins, 1999. The story of two teenage friends, one who becomes a successful screenwriter and one who becomes obsessed with her teacher.

Dessen, Sarah. *Dreamland*. Viking, 2000. Will Caitlin ever leave her dream-like state to face the ugly facts about gorgeous wealthy Rogerson?

Flinn, Alex. *Breathing Underwater*. HarperCollins, 2001. Wealthy and popular Nick meets beautiful Caitlin, who is in love with him, and looks forward to a long relationship—until everything changes.

Haddix, Margaret Peterson. *Just Ella*. Simon & Schuster, 1999. Prince Charming and palace life are not all that it's cracked up to be.

King, Stephen. *Rose Madder*. Viking, 1995. After fourteen years of being beaten, Rose finally walks out on her husband Norman and starts a new life at a women's shelter only to find that 800 miles is not far enough to move away from Norman.

Lehman, Yvonne. *A Fighting Chance*. Bethany House, 1997. Ruthie is embarrassed to tell anyone about Sean's abusive behavior—what if she is making a big deal out of nothing?

Miklowitz, Gloria. *Past Forgiving*. Simon & Schuster, 1995. Alex can forgive her popular boyfriend Cliff when he hits her, but after he rapes her she realizes that she cannot change him.

Naylor, Phyllis Reynolds. *Alice Alone*. Atheneum, 2001. Alice and Patrick's relationship starts to crumble, along with her self-confidence, as new girl Penny, who is perky and petite, comes into town.

Platt, Randall Beth. *The Likes of Me*. Delacorte, 1999. In the summer of 1918, fourteen-year-old Cordy, who is half-Chinese, half-Caucasian, and all albino, runs away to

Seattle to follow Squirl, the first boy she ever kissed and while there meets an interesting cast of carnival workers and the unwelcome truth about Squirl.

Plummer, Louise. *A Dance for Three*. Delacorte, 2000. Hannah's world is shattered when she tells her wealthy boyfriend, Milo Fabiano, that she is pregnant.

Quindlen, Anna. *Black and Blue*. Random House, 1998. A battered wife takes her son and leaves an abusive marriage but must live with the daily fear that the husband/father might track her down.

Sparks, Beatrice. *Treacherous Love: The Diary of an Anonymous Teenager*. HarperCollins, 2000. The fictional diary of a fourteen-year-old girl in love with her sexually abusive teacher.

Stratton, Allan. *Leslie's Journal: A Novel*. Annic Press, 2000. From the outside Leslie's relationship with Jason seems romantic, but Leslie's journal knows the truth.

Tamar, Erika. *Fair Game*. Harcourt, 1993. How can it be rape when the girl is willing?

Tarbox, Katie. *Katie.com*. Dutton, 2000. In this true story, nothing in Katie's relationship and romance found on the Internet is what she thought it would be.

Are We There Yet?

Explanation of theme: These materials all have someone embarking on a journey. Time-travel books should also be included. This can be used in summer, when most people do their traveling. If this is the season in which it is used, be sure to include audio versions of books, as well as related music to make a long drive seem shorter.

Props: Large stop sign or road signs are easy to recreate. Four can be made—one for each word in the title of the display. Signs can be a red-and-white upside down triangle, a red stop sign, a yellow diamond, and a white square (like where speed limits are posted). Omit the words, such as *yield*, and substitute a word from the display title. Other props include suitcases, maps, used airline tickets, and so on.

Annotated list of titles:

Adams, Douglas. *The Hitchhiker's Guide to the Galaxy*. Harmony Books, 1983. Arthur Dent and his friend Ford Prefect travel to various galactic civilizations while gathering information for a hitchhiker's guidebook.

Almond, David. *Heaven Eyes*. Delacorte, 2000. Erin, January, and Mouse escape from the Whitegates orphanage on a raft and meet a strange old man and an even stranger girl with webbed fingers named Heaven Eyes.

Armstrong, Jennifer. *Shipwreck at the Bottom of the World: The Extraordinary True Story of Shackleton and the* Endurance. Crown, 1998. It's not a good idea to winter in Antarctica.

Avi. *The True Confessions of Charlotte Doyle*. Avon, 1990. While sailing from England to America in 1832, Charlotte finds herself involved in a plot to overthrow the ship's villainous captain.

Bauer, Joan. *Rules of the Road*. Putnam, 1998. Sixteen-year-old Jenna drives the elderly owner of a chain of successful shoe stores from Chicago to Texas to help her confront the son who is forcing her to retire, while gaining her own strength to face her alcoholic father.

Bennett, Cherie. *Anne Frank and Me*. Putnam, 2001. On a Holocaust-related field trip, Nicole is transported to 1942 and becomes a Jew in Paris who must help her family survive.

Blackwood, Gary. *Shakespeare's Scribe*. Dutton, 2000. After the queen closes the Globe theater due to the Black Plague, Widge travels with Shakespeare and his players across England to perform and along the way learns the value of sticking up for himself and others.

Calabro, Marian. *The Perilous Journey of the Donner Party*. Houghton, 1999. Proper planning is essential for any trip to be successful.

Coman, Carolyn. *Many Stones*. Front St., 2000. Berry and her estranged father travel to South Africa to attend a memorial service for her murdered sister, Laura, and look beyond their own grief to search for peace and reconciliation.

Creech, Sharon. *Walk Two Moons*. HarperCollins, 1994. As she travels in a car with her grandparents, Sal tells the story of her friend, Phoebe, whose life is similar to Sal's since her mother's disappearance.

———. *The Wanderer*. HarperCollins, 2000. Sophie's hidden past is revealed through journal entries on her ship voyage with her male uncles and cousins.

Curtis, Christopher Paul. *Bud, Not Buddy*. Delacorte, 2000. Sometimes the person you start out looking for is not always who you find.

———. *The Watsons Go to Birmingham—1963*. Delacorte, 1995. Kenny and his family drive from Detroit to Birmingham to see Grandma, who can hopefully straighten out Kenny's brother Byron, who quite often finds himself in trouble.

Etchemendy, Nancy. *The Power of UN*. Front Street, 2000. Middle-schooler Big is given a magical device called an Unner that will allow him to travel back in time to undue the chain of events that led to his sister's accident.

Fleischman, Paul. *The Mind's Eye*. Henry Holt, 1999. In a nursing home, sixteen-year-old Courtney, paralyzed from an accident, learns to shed self-pity as she takes an imaginary trip to Italy with a fellow nursing home resident.

———. *Whirligig*. Henry Holt, 1998. To pay for his crime of killing a teenage girl in an automobile accident, Brent must travel to the four corners of the United States to build whirligigs in her memory.

Goodman, Joan Elizabeth. *Peregrine*. Houghton Mifflin, 2000. After losing her much older husband and infant daughter, Lady Edith pilgrimages to Jerusalem while confronting her sorrow.

Heneghan, James. *The Grave*. Farrar, Straus & Giroux, 2000. When construction workers unearth a mass grave site at his school, Tom falls through a grave and travels back to Ireland during the time of the Potato Famine.

Peck, Richard. *A Long Way from Chicago*. Dial, 1998. Life is amusing, to say the least, for brother and sister Joey and Mary Alice when they spend summers during the Depression visiting their wacky grandma in the country.

———. *Year Down Yonder*. Dial, 2000. In this sequel to *A Long Way from Chicago*, the Depression has ended and Mary Alice is sent alone to the country where she once again experiences grandma's shenanigans.

Price, Susan. *The Sterkarm Handshake*. HarperCollins, 2000. Twenty-first-century elves underestimate the primitive sixteenth-century Sterkarm clan in this time travel adventure involving blood, guts, deceit, and love.

Temple, Frances. *The Ramsay Scallop*. Orchard, 1995. Fourteen-year-old Elenor and eighteen-year-old Thomas, betrothed even though they barely know each other, set out on a pilgrimage from their English village through France to Spain in 1299.

Working for a Living

Explanation of theme: These titles help teens find a job and offer information on different careers. In addition, fiction titles that depict teens working are included. Also, Jobs for Teens Week is celebrated annually during the week containing the first day of spring. Jobs for Teens Week encourages young adults to better prepare themselves for their future career through practical experience in the workplace. For a free kit from Highsmith Press contact www.hpress.highsmith.com/jobweek.htm

Props: Use the classified ads from the local newspaper as background, job applications from different places (do not forget the library!), fake money, and time cards.

Annotated list of titles:

Anderson, Joan. *Rookie: Tamika Whitmore's First Year in the WNBA.* Dutton, 2000. Tamika's determination and willingness to learn takes her from a skinny thirteen-year-old who would practice with anyone, including the neighborhood boys and her mom, to becoming the top rookie for the New York Liberty of the WNBA.

Anderson, Matthew T. *Burger Wuss.* Candlewick Press, 1999. The story of Anthony's brief first love and a humiliating summer.

Bartoletti, Susan Campbell. *Kids on Strike.* Houghton Mifflin, 1999. Your situation at work is nothing like it was for these kids.

Block, Francesca Lia. *Violet and Claire.* HarperCollins, 1999. The story of two teenage friends, one who becomes a successful screenwriter and one who becomes obsessed with her teacher.

Bauer, Joan. *Hope Was Here.* Putnam, 2000. In this hilarious novel, sixteen-year-old Hope and her aunt move to Wisconsin to work as waitress and cook in a rural diner and end up in a political campaign to oust the mayor.

———. *Rules of the Road.* Putnam, 1998. Sixteen-year-old Jenna sells shoes and ends up driving the elderly owner of the shoe store chain from Chicago to Texas to help her confront the son who is forcing her to retire, while gaining her own strength to face her alcoholic father.

Dessen, Sarah. *Keeping the Moon.* Viking, 1999. While spending the summer with an aunt, Colie, who has low self-esteem, finds friends in two waitresses and love with a shy teenage artist.

Hawk, Tony, and Sean Mortimer. *Hawk: Occupation Skateboarder.* HarperCollins, 2000. How's this for a job—world champion skateboarder?

Hobgood, Debby, and Cindy Pervola. *How to Get a Job If You're a Teenager.* Alleyside Press, 2000. An easy-to-read job skills guide for teens.

Holland, Isabelle. *Paperboy.* Holiday House, 1999. Kevin, a poor Irish immigrant in the 1800s, works for *The Chronicle* and as a result gains an interest in journalism.

Ireland, Susan. *The Complete Idiot's Guide to Cool Jobs for Teens*. Alpha Books, 2001.

Leibowitz, Jay. *Wall St. Wizard: Advice from a Savvy Teen Investor*. Simon & Schuster, 2000. The author, an investor since he was thirteen, shares his wisdom on the basics of getting rich through wise investing.

Mazer, Anne. *Working Days: Stories About Teenagers and Work*. Persea Books, 1997. A multicultural collection of short stories about teenagers at their jobs.

Paulsen, Gary. *The Beet Fields: Memoirs of My Fifteenth Summer*. Delacorte, 2000. Running away from home, a boy learns about life from the interesting people he meets working his way from back-breaking job to back-breaking job.

Silvey, Anita, ed. *Help Wanted: Short Stories About Young People and Work*. Little Brown, 1997.

Vernon, Naomi. *A Teen's Guide to Finding a Job*. New-Bee-ginnings, 1999.

What in the World?

Explanation of theme: Titles in this display reflect a multicultural theme. Teens will be happy to find that teens living in another country often experience similar situations. Other titles enlighten teens on traditions of other cultures.

Props: World map, passport, globe (inflatable versions are available from US Toy—www.ustoy.com). Also contact local travel agents.

Annotated list of titles:

Abelove, Joan. *Go and Come Back.* DK Ink, 1998. (Peru) Alicia, an Indian teenager, wonders what the two female anthropologists are doing in her village.

Almond, David. *Kit's Wilderness.* Delacorte, 2000. (England) Kit's family moves in with his recently widowed grandfather in a small coal-mining town haunted by ghosts of the past.

Alshalabi, Firyal. *Summer, 1990: A Young Adult Novel.* Aunt Strawberry Books, 1999. (Kuwait) The Persian Gulf War through the eyes of Danah, a thirteen-year-old Kuwaiti.

Bo, Ben. *The Edge.* Lerner, 1999. (Canada) Declan is sent to the Canadian Rockies in lieu of juvenile detention and while working and snowboarding learns he cannot escape his past.

———. *Skullcrack.* Lerner, 2000. (Ireland) Jonah surfs off the coast of Ireland where he sees images of a girl swirling in the mist.

Burgess, Melvin. *Smack.* Henry Holt, 1998. (England) Teens Tar and Gemma are runaways who experience the harrowing ups and downs of heroin addiction.

Coman, Carolyn. *Many Stones.* Front St., 2000. (South Africa) Berry and her estranged father travel to South Africa to attend a memorial service for her murdered sister, Laura, and look beyond their own grief to search for peace and reconciliation.

Farmer, Nancy. *The Ear, the Eye and the Arm.* Orchard, 1994. (Zimbabwe) When a general's three children are kidnapped in 2194, their mother hires the best detective team available.

———. *A Girl Named Disaster.* Orchard, 1996. (Africa) Nhamo flees her home in Mozambique to avoid a planned marriage.

Garland, Sherry. *Song of the Buffalo Boy.* Harcourt, 1992. (Vietnam) Loi, promised in marriage to a cruel military man, runs away with the boy she loves to find her American soldier father.

Kessler, Christina. *No Condition Is Permanent.* Philomel, 2000. (Sierra Leone) On a trip with her anthropologist mom, Jodie befriends Khadi and finds that she does not agree with aspects of her new friend's culture.

Lebert, Benjamin. *Crazy.* Knopf, 2000. (Germany) Autobiographical coming-of-age novel about a sixteen-year-old German boy at a remedial boarding school.

Levitin, Sonia. *Escape from Egypt.* Little Brown, 1994. (Egypt) A retelling of the biblical story of the exodus of the Israelites from Egypt to the Promised Land, as told through the eyes of Jesse, a Hebrew slave, and Jennat, a half-Egyptian, half-Syrian girl.

Mah, Adeline Yen. *Chinese Cinderella—The True Story of an Unwanted Daughter.* Delacorte, 1999. (China) Seen as bad luck when her mother dies, Adeline has everything taken away from her but triumphs over her isolation.

Marchetta, Melina. *Looking for Alibrandi.* Orchard, 1999. (Australia) Josie struggles to find her place in her family's secrets, cultural ties to Italy, and her Australian home.

Moriarty, Jaclyn. *Feeling Sorry for Celia.* St. Martin's Press, 2001. (Australia) Elizabeth's hilarious yet complicated teenage life is unveiled through communications to her mother and others by wacky notes.

Mori, Kyoko. *Shizuko's Daughter.* Henry Holt, 1993. (Japan) After her mother's suicide, Yuki gains an inner strength when coping with her distant father and painful memories.

Namioka, Lensey. *Ties That Bind, Ties That Break.* Delacorte, 1999. (China) In early-twentieth century China, Ailin rebels against the tradition of binding women's feet and achieves self-fulfillment after a difficult journey to America.

Rennison, Louise. *Angus, Thongs, and Full-Frontal Snogging: Confessions of Georgia Nicholson.* (England) HarperCollins, 2000. Georgia spills out her woeful life, which includes her crazy cat Angus, a baby sister that pees in her bed, prudish parents, and kissing (aka snogging) lessons.

———. *On the Bright Side, I Am Now the Girlfriend of a Sex God: Further Confessions of Georgia Nicholson.* (England) HarperCollins, 2001. In this hilarious sequel to *Angus, Thongs, and Full-Frontal Snogging*, Georgia finds that life is never perfect—even if you are dating a sex god named Robbie.

Reuter, Bjarne. *The Boys of St. Petri.* Dutton, 1994. (Denmark) A group of teenage boys fight the Nazi occupation of their hometown during World War II in a series of dangerous resistance missions.

Staples, Suzanne Fisher. *Haveli: A Young Woman's Courageous Struggle for Freedom in Present-Day Pakistan.* Knopf, 1993. (Pakistan) In this sequel to *Shabanu*, a young woman struggles with the rigid cultural tradition women must follow in Pakistani society as she searches for freedom for herself and her daughter.

———. *Shabanu: Daughter of the Wind.* Knopf, 1989. (Pakistan) Coming-of-age story of Shabanu, a member of a nomadic tribe in the Pakistani desert.

———. *Shiva's Fire.* Farrar, Straus & Giroux, 2000. (India) Parvati's destiny is the world of sacred Hindu classical dance.

Taylor, Theodore. *Timothy of the Cay.* Harcourt, 1993. (Caribbean) Using alternating chapters, this prequel/sequel to *The Cay* illustrates how Timothy and twelve-year-old Phillip's lives are intertwined.

Taylor, William. *The Blue Lawn.* Alyson Books, 1999. (New Zealand) A fifteen year old acknowledges his attraction to an older rugby teammate.

Temple, Frances. *Grab Hands and Run.* Orchard, 1994. (El Salvador) When Jacinto, who opposes the oppressive government of El Salvador, disappears, his family flees north to Canada, not knowing if he can ever join them.

Whelan, Gloria. *Homeless Bird.* HarperCollins, 2000. (India) Thirteen-year-old Koly is abandoned by her dreadful stepmother and left on her own after her husband from an arranged marriage dies.

Short on Time? . . . Try One of These

Explanation of theme: Titles featured are short story collections for teens. Titles could also include thin books. For a resource for "thin" books use *What to Read When Your Book Report Is Due Tomorrow: The World's Best Thin Books* by Joni Bodart (Scarecrow, 2000).

Prop: A large clock—this is attention grabbing because everyone is conscious of the time.

Annotated list of titles:

Appelt, Kathi. *Kissing Tennessee and Other Stories from the Stardust Dance*. Harcourt, 2000. The night of the big dance means different things to the students of Dogwood Junior High.

Asher, Sandy, ed. *With All My Heart with All My Mind: Thirteen Stories About Growing Up Jewish*. Simon & Schuster, 1999.

Block, Francesca Lia. *Girl Goddess #9: Nine Stories*. Harper Trophy, 1998. Short stories about love.

———. *The Rose and the Beast*. HarperCollins, 2000. Modern, magical landscapes are the settings for the retelling of these classical fairy tales.

Blume, Judy, ed. *Places I Never Meant to Be: Original Stories. Censored Writers*. Simon & Schuster, 1999.

Brooks, Bruce. *All That Remains*. Atheneum, 2001. Three novellas explore how young people deal with the aftermath of the death of a family member.

Carlson, Lori M., ed. *American Eyes: New Asian-American Short Stories for Young Adults*. Henry Holt, 1994. A look into the life of Asian-American adolescents.

Cart, Michael. *Love and Sex: Ten Stories of the Truth for Teens*. Simon & Schuster, 2001. Various adult and young adult authors write about the complexities, pressures, and joys teenagers encounter in their romantic lives.

———. *Tomorrowland: Stories About the Future*. Scholastic, 1999. Distinguished YA authors share their ideas of what the future will be.

Coville, Bruce. *Odder Than Ever*. Harcourt, 1999. Nine short fantasy stories.

Crutcher, Chris. *Athletic Shorts: Six Short Stories*. Greenwillow, 1991. Characters from Crutcher's novels deal with life issues.

Dahl, Roald. *Skin and Other Stories*. Viking, 2000. Satisfying stories with twisted endings.

Datlow, Ellen, and Terri Windling, eds. *A Wolf at the Door and Other Retold Fairy Tales*. Simon & Schuster, 2000.

Duncan, Lois, ed. *On the Edge: Stories at the Brink*. Simon & Schuster, 2000. Young people living on the edge—mentally, physically, or psychologically.

———. *Trapped!: Cages of Mind and Body.* Simon & Schuster, 1998. YA authors interpret the limitations of mind and body.

Faustino, Lisa Rowe, ed. *Dirty Laundry: Stories About Family Secrets.* Viking, 1998.

Gallo, Donald R., ed. *Join In: Multiethnic Short Stories by Outstanding Writers for Young Adults.* Bantam Paper, 1995. Problems faced by ethnic teens living in the United States.

———. *No Easy Answers: Short Stories About Teenagers Making Tough Choices.* Delacorte, 1997. YA authors write about teens facing ethical and moral dilemmas.

———. *On the Fringe.* Dial, 2001. Acclaimed young adult authors write short stories about those often ridiculed high school students who do not seem to fit in with the more popular mainstream teenagers.

———. *Time Capsule: Short Stories About Teenagers Throughout the Twentieth Century.* Delacorte, 1999. YA writers contribute short stories that span the decades.

Martin, Erick B., ed. *The Campfire Collection: Spine-Tingling Tales to Tell in the Dark.* Chronicle Books, 2000.

Mazer, Anne, ed. *Working Days: Short Stories About Teenagers at Work.* Persea, 1997.

Mazer, Harry, ed. *Twelve Shots: Outstanding Stories About Guns.* Delacorte, 1997. Stories about the ways guns are present in people's lives.

Myers, Walter Dean. *145th Street Stories.* Delacorte, 2000. Meet the people who live on 145th Street in Harlem.

Rochman, Hazel, and Darlene Z. McCampbell, eds. *Leaving Home.* HarperCollins, 1997. Stories by well-known writers on different ways to leave home.

Singer, Marilyn, ed. *I Believe in Water: Twelve Brushes with Religion.* HarperCollins, 2000. YA authors write about teens representing different religions.

———. *Stay True: Short Stories for Strong Girls.* Scholastic, 1998. Stories to empower girls.

Soto, Gary. *Petty Crimes.* Harcourt, 1998. The lives of Mexican-American teenagers in California's central valley.

Thomas, Rob. *Doing Time: Notes from the Undergrad.* Simon & Schuster, 1997. Ten vignettes about a high school's mandatory community service.

Van Belkom, Edo. *Be Afraid! Tales of Horror.* Tundra, 2000.

Vande Velde, Vivian. *The Rumplestiltskin Problem.* Houghton Mifflin, 2000. Rumplestiltskin retold five different ways.

Weiss, M. Jerry, and Helen S. Weiss, eds. *From One Experience to Another: Stories About Turning Points.* Forge, 1997. YA authors write about important turning points in their lives.

Wynne-Jones, Tim. *Lord of the Fries and Other Stories.* DK Ink, 1999. Thought-provoking stories of teens in different situations.

Yolen, Jane, ed. *Sherwood: Original Stories from the World of Robin Hood.* Philomel, 2000.

Can You Haiku?

Explanation of theme: National Poetry Month is celebrated in April. Recently many poetry collections for teens have been published, including collections written by teens.

Prop: A dry erase board allowing teens to create their own poems or a magnetic poetry board where a variety of words are written on paper and affixed to magnetic tape. Teens are able to arrange letters or words into free verse.

Annotated list of titles:

Adoff, Arnold, ed. *I Am the Darker Brother: An Anthology of Modern Poems by African Americans.* Simon & Schuster Paperbacks, 1997.

Carlson, Lori M., ed. *Cool Salsa: Bilingual Poems on Growing Up Latino in the United States.* Fawcett Juniper, 1995. Bilingual poems abut growing up Latino in the United States.

Fletcher, Ralph. *Relatively Speaking: Poems About Family.* Orchard, 1999. The experiences and relationships of a close-knit family.

Franco, Betsy, ed. *Things I Have to Tell You: Poems and Writing by Teenage Girls.* Candlewick Press, 2001. Poems written by teenage girls that reveal secrets that enabled them to overcome challenges they faced.

———. *You Hear Me? Poems and Writings by Teenage Boys.* Candlewick, 2000. Adolescent boys speak out on their issues of concern.

Glenn, Mel. *Foreign Exchange: A Mystery in Poems.* Morrow, 1999. Residents of a small lake-side community react to the murder of a new high school student.

———. *Jump Ball: A Basketball Season in Poems.* Dutton, 1997. Basketball players, parents, teachers, and friends tell the story of a high school's winning season.

———. *Split Image: A Story in Poems.* HarperCollins, 2000. Laura Li's seemingly perfect life, both inside and outside high school, is revealed through the thoughts and reflections of herself, her parents, teachers, librarian, and friends.

———. *The Taking of Room 114.* Dutton, 1997. A teacher holds seniors hostage on the last day of school.

———. *Who Killed Mr. Chippendale?* Dutton, 1996. An investigation into a high school English teacher's murder.

Herrera, Juan Felipe. *Crashboomlove: A Novel in Verse.* University of New Mexico Press, 1999. The painful experiences growing up as a fatherless Mexican-American high school student.

———. *Laughing Out Loud, I Fly: Poems in English and Spanish.* HarperCollins, 1998. The poet recalls his childhood.

Hesse, Karen. *Out of the Dust.* Scholastic, 1998. Fifteen-year-old Billie Jo deals with the hardships and tragedies of the Oklahoma dust bowl years.

Johnson, Dave, ed. *Movin: Teen Poets Take Voice.* Orchard Books, 2000. Brief glimpses into the varied interests of teens.

Koertge, Ron. *The Brimstone Journals.* Candlewick Press, 2001. Voices of high school students reveal violence existing and growing in their lives in interconnected poems.

Nye, Naomi Shihab. *What Have You Lost?* Greenwillow, 1999. The feeling of loss means different things to different people.

Okutoro, Lydia Omolola. *Quiet Storm: Voices of Young Black Poets.* Hyperion, 1999. Features poems from black youth ages thirteen to twenty-one from all over the world.

Shakur, Tupac. *The Rose That Grew from Concrete.* Simon & Schuster, 1999. Passion-filled poems from the rapper presented in his handwriting, as well as typeface.

Smith, Charles R., Jr. *Rimshots: Basketball Pix, Rolls, and Rhymes.* Dutton, 1999. Poetry set to the rhythm and motions of basketball.

Sones, Sonya. *Stop Pretending: What Happened When My Big Sister Went Crazy.* HarperCollins, 1999. Life after her older sister has a mental breakdown is hard to adjust to for her younger sister.

Vecchione, Patrice, ed. *Truth and Lies: An Anthology of Poems.* Henry Holt, 2001. Selections span more than 300 years and deal with all the sides of honesty.

Watson, Esther Pearl, and Mark Todd, eds. *The Pain Tree and Other Teenage Angst-Ridden Poetry.* Houghton Mifflin, 2000. Poetry and artwork presented in a straight-forward, brutally honest way.

Wolff, Virginia Euwer. *Make Lemonade.* Henry Holt, 1993. In order to make money for college, LaVaughn baby-sits for Jolly, an unwed teenage mother of two.

———. *True Believer.* Atheneum, 2001. In this sequel to *Make Lemonade*, fifteen-year-old LaVaughn lives in the inner city amidst guns and poverty and learns from friends and mentors that life is what you make it.

Wong, Janet S. *Behind the Wheel: Poems About Driving.* Simon & Schuster, 1999. From speeding tickets, to dead batteries, to backseat romance.

Psst . . .

Explanation of theme: Titles in this display depict a character who is hiding something or keeping a secret.

Props: A large ear made out of foam, cartoon balloons saying, "Don't Tell," "It's Between You and Me," "Promise You Won't Tell."

Annotated list of titles:

Almond, David. *Kit's Wilderness*. Delacorte, 2000. Who wins the game called Death?

————. *Skellig*. Delacorte, 1999. Who is the man hiding in Michael's garage that eats flies and Chinese takeout?

Anderson, Laurie Halse. *Speak*. Farrar, Straus & Giroux, 1999. Will Melinda find her voice and tell why she dialed 911 and ended a great party?

Aphin, Elaine Marie. *Counterfeit Son*. Harcourt, 2000. Fourteen-year-old Cameron takes on the identity of one of his father's murder victims in order to escape the nightmare that has been his life.

Atkins, Catherine. *When Jeff Comes Home*. Putnam, 1999. Was he or wasn't he? Everyone wants to know the answer once Jeff is released by his kidnapper after three years.

Bat-Ami, Miriam. *Two Suns in the Sky*. Front St., 1999. Chris cannot tell her anti-Semitic father of her relationship with Adam, a Yugoslavian Jew who lives in a refugee shelter in Oswego, New York, in 1944.

Bauer, Joan. *Backwater*. Putnam, 1999. Who is the reclusive aunt no one speaks about but everyone thinks is just like Ivy?

Cooney, Caroline. *Driver's Ed*. Delacorte, 1994. Was it their fault she ran through the stop sign and was killed?

Cross, Gillian. *Tightrope*. Holiday House, 1999. Who can she turn to for help when the stalker knows everything about her?

Flinn, Alex. *Breathing Underwater*. HarperCollins, 2001. Never having told anyone of his father's abusive temper, the truth comes out when Nick is ordered to keep a journal while undergoing counseling for hitting his girlfriend.

Garden, Nancy. *Holly's Secret*. Farrar, Straus & Giroux, 2000. After moving from Manhattan to a small town in Massachusetts, Holly wants to make a fresh start with a new identity, so she doesn't tell anyone about her parents.

Glenn, Mel. *Split Image*. HarperCollins, 2000. Laura Li's seemingly perfect life, both inside and outside high school, is revealed through the thoughts and reflections of herself, her parents, teachers, librarian, and friends.

Grant, Cynthia. *Uncle Vampire*. Atheneum, 1994. If you believe that the worst thing your uncle can be is a vampire, you're wrong.

Haddix, Margaret Peterson. *Among the Hidden*. Simon & Schuster, 1998. Thirteen-year-old Luke, the third of his parent's children, must hide in the attic from the population police in order to survive in a society where couples are allowed to have only two children.

Herman, John. *Deep Waters*. Philomel, 1999. The mysterious drowning of a camp counselor leaves a camper with a moral dilemma.

Horrocks, Anita. *Topher*. Stoddart Publishing, 2000. Only Stacey knows the connection of her father's past and a dead boy named Topher.

Kindl, Patrice. *Owl in Love*. Houghton Mifflin, 1993. How will Owl share her life secret with the man she loves—her science teacher?

Levine, Gail. *Dave at Night*. HarperCollins, 1999. It's easier than you think to sneak out of the cruel Hebrew Home for Boys every night.

Lowry, Lois. *Gathering Blue*. Houghton Mifflin, 2000. Set in a futuristic society, Kira begins to wonder if the Council of Guardians is really there to help after her parents die or if they had a part in their death in order to control her extraordinary talent.

Lubar, David. *Hidden Talents*. TOR, 1999. Martin befriends a group of misfits with psychic powers when he arrives at an alternative school.

Matas, Carol. *In My Enemy's House*. Simon & Schuster, 1999. Keeping her identity a secret will keep her alive, but can she keep her secret from her Nazi boss?

Murphy, Rita. *Night Flying*. Delacorte, 2000. Georgia, like all the women in her family, can fly but becomes flustered when Aunt Carmen reveals infuriating secrets that cause Georgia to commit two serious offenses—flying alone and in daylight.

Naylor, Phyllis Reynolds. *Jade Green: A Ghost Story*. Atheneum, 2000. Judith doesn't make the connection between her hidden green silk frame and the appearance of the ghostly hand of Jade Green, a girl who supposedly committed suicide by chopping off her hand with a cleaver.

Randle, Kristin. *The Only Alien on the Planet*. Scholastic, 1995. When you are too afraid to ever speak, you must have a pretty good reason.

Rinaldi, Ann. *Girl in Blue*. Scholastic, 2001. Fourteen-year-old Sarah disguises herself as a boy to enlist in the Union Army and becomes a soldier on the battlefields of Virginia and later a Union spy.

Sparks, Beatrice, ed. *Treacherous Love: The Diary of an Anonymous Teenager*. Avon, 2000. The fictional diary of a fourteen-year-old girl in love with her sexually abusive teacher.

Tomey, Ingrid. *Nobody Else Has to Know*. Delacorte, 1999. Webber's grandfather perpetuates a lie to keep Webber out of trouble. Will Webber let him?

Van Dijk, Lutz. *Damned Strong Love: The True Story of Will G. and Stefan K.* Holt, 1995. The Nazis didn't just hate the Jews. . . .

Werlin, Nancy. *The Killer's Cousin*. Delacorte, 1998. After being acquitted of murder, seventeen-year-old David goes to stay with relatives in Cambridge, Massachusetts, where he faces his past and encounters his strange cousin Lily.

Williams, Lori Aurelia. *When Kambia Elaine Flew in from Neptune*. Simon & Schuster, 2000. Shayla does not know what to think of her new neighbor Kambia's fantastic stories and failing health but eventually realizes that what she does know can help Kambia survive.

Woodson, Jacqueline. *I Hadn't Meant to Tell You This*. Delacorte, 1994. When life is so bad that you can't tell your friend, then you have to do something.

Zindel, Paul. *The Gadget*. HarperCollins, 2001. In 1945, Stephen joins his physicist father at an army base in New Mexico and is caught in a web of intrigue revolving around a secret project to end World War II.

Make Yourself Heard

Explanation of theme: Characters in these stories are standing up for what they believe in or are fighting for their rights. Political activism and the support of social issues are of great importance to teens.

Props: Picket signs made out of poster board with a paint mixer stick as the holder for the sign. The colors red, white, and blue are appropriate since to many Americans, they symbolize freedom and independence.

Annotated list of titles:

Avi. *Nothing but the Truth.* Orchard, 1991. When Philip decides to hum the national anthem during homeroom, the incident sparks a national debate.

Bauer, Joan. *Hope Was Here.* Putnam, 2000. In this hilarious novel, sixteen-year-old Hope and her aunt move to Wisconsin to work as waitress and cook in a rural diner and end up in a political campaign to oust the mayor.

Boyers, Sara Jane. *Teen Power Politics: Make Yourself Heard.* Twenty-first Century Books, 2000. This nonfiction title empowers teens to get ready for political action and community service, both locally and globally, in order to made a difference—before they turn eighteen and are able to vote.

Cormier, Robert. *The Chocolate War.* Dell Paper, 1993. Do we really have to sell chocolates?

Crutcher, Chris. *Whale Talk.* Greenwillow, 2001. Smart, athletic T. J. shuns organized sports at his school and recruits a swimming team made up of some of the less popular students in order to find a place for them in school.

Freedman, Russell. *Give Me Liberty: The Story of the Declaration of Independence.* Holiday House, 2000. The events leading up to the writing of the Declaration of Independence and the people involved in its draft and redraft in order to create a document that all thirteen colonies would accept are all here.

Garden, Nancy. *The Year They Burned the Books.* Farrar, Straus & Giroux, 1999. High school newspaper editor Jamie must defend her controversial editorial against community backlash from a group called "Families for Traditional Values."

Jacobs, Thomas. *What Are My Rights? 95 Questions and Answers About Teens and the Law.* Free Spirit, 1997. Teens' rights within the family, at school, and on the job.

Klass, David. *California Blue.* Scholastic, 1994. Is that butterfly worth it?

Lynch, Chris. *Political Timber.* HarperCollins, 1996. Imprisoned racketeer Mayor Foley coaches his eighteen-year-old grandson to win the election and become his successor.

Meyer, Carolyn. *Drummers of Jericho.* Harcourt, 1995. Jewish Pazit joins the acclaimed Jericho High School marching band but objects to their playing of hymns and forming a cross on the field.

Myers, Walter Dean. *Malcolm X: By Any Means Necessary.* Scholastic, 1993. Tribute to the charismatic civil rights leader.

Namioka, Lensey. *Ties That Bind, Ties That Break*. Delacorte, 1999. In early-twentieth-century China, Ailin rebels against the tradition of binding women's feet and achieves self-fulfillment after a difficult journey to America.

Peck, Richard. *Last Safe Place on Earth*. Bantam Paper, 1996. Todd stands up against censorship and beautiful Laurel's fundamentalist beliefs about Halloween.

Perry, Susan K. *Catch the Spirit: Teen Volunteers Tell How They Made a Difference*. Franklin Watts, 2000. Twenty teens who received the Prudential Spirit of Community Award tell about their projects that won national recognition.

Reisfeld, Randi, and Marie Morreale. *Got Issues Much? Celebrities Share Their Traumas and Their Triumphs.* Scholastic, 1999.

Ruby, Lois. *Miriam's Well*. Scholastic, 1993. Miriam's life hangs in the balance, as her religious parents' beliefs do not allow for the use of chemotherapy to treat her bone cancer.

Singer, Marilyn, ed. *Stay True: Short Stories for Strong Girls*. Scholastic, 1998. Stories to empower girls.

Spinelli, Jerry. *Wringer*. HarperCollins, 1997. Palmer must accept the violence or find the courage to oppose it.

Taylor, Theodore. *The Bomb*. Harcourt, 1995. Sorry and his grandfather protest the use of Bikini Island as a test site for American bombs in the 1940s.

Thomas, Rob. *Slave Day*. Simon & Schuster, 1997. African-American students object to a fund-raiser called "Slave Day."

Winick, Judd. *Pedro and Me: Friendship, Loss, and What I Learned*. Henry Holt, 2000. Judd's story of his roommate on MTV's *The Real World*—the unforgettable Pedro, an AIDS educator, who taught millions of viewers about being gay and living with AIDS.

Wittlinger, Ellen. *What's in a Name?* Simon & Schuster, 2000. As their hometown considers changing its name to improve its image, ten teens explore their own identity.

That's Not the Way I Heard It!

Explanation of theme: These titles are revisions or continuations of fairy tales. Urban legends, always popular with teens, are also included.

Props: Shimmery fabric, knights/armor, jewels, crowns.

Annotated list of titles:

Block, Francesca Lia. *The Rose and the Beast: Fairy Tales Retold*. HarperCollins, 2000. Beauty and the Beast.

Card, Orson Scott. *Enchantment*. Del Ray, 1999. Sleeping Beauty.

Craughwell, Thomas. *Alligators in the Sewer and 222 Other Urban Legends*. Black Dog, 1999.

Datlow, Ellen, and Terri Windling. *Wolf at the Door and Other Retold Fairy Tales*. Simon & Schuster, 2000.

Donoghue, Emma. *Kissing the Witch: Old Tales in New Skins*. HarperCollins, 1997. Retold with a lesbian/feminist point of view.

Garner, James Finn. *Politically Correct Bedtime Stories*. Macmillan, 1994.

Geras, Adele. *The Tower Room*. Harcourt, 1992. Rapunzel.

———. *Troy*. Harcourt, 2001. Trojan War.

Haddix, Margaret Peterson. *Just Ella*. Simon & Schuster Paper, 1999. Cinderella.

Holt, David, and Bill Mooney, eds. *Spiders in the Hairdo: Modern Urban Legends*. August House, 1999.

Levine, Gail Carson. *Ella Enchanted*. HarperCollins, 1997. Cinderella.

McKinley, Robin. *Beauty: A Retelling of the Story of Beauty and the Beast*. HarperCollins, 1978.

———. *Rose Daughter*. Greenwillow, 1997. Beauty and the Beast.

———. *Spindle's End*. Putnam, 2000. Grimm's Briar Rose.

Napoli, Donna Jo. *Beast*. Simon & Schuster, 2000. Beauty and the Beast.

———. *Crazy Jack*. Delacorte, 1999. Jack and the Beanstalk.

———. *Spinners*. Dutton, 1999. Rumpelstiltskin.

———. *The Magic Circle*. Dutton, 1993. Hansel and Gretel.

———. *Zel*. Dutton, 1996. Rapunzel.

Ngaire, George. *Urban Legends: The As-Complete-As-One-Could-Be Guide to Modern Myths*. Three Rivers Press, 2000.

Pullman, Phillip. *I Was a Rat!* Knopf, 2000. The footman in Cinderella.

Roeper, Richard. *Urban Legends: The Truth Behind All Those Deliciously Entertaining Myths That Are Absolutely Positively 100% Not True.* Career Press, 1999.

Springer, Nancy. *I Am Mordrid: A Tale from Camelot.* Putnam, 1998.

———. *I Am Morgana LeFay: A Tale from Camelot.* Penguin Putnam, 2001.

———. *Rowan Hood: Outlaw Girl of Sherwood Forest.* Philomel, 2001.

Vande Velde, Vivian. *The Rumplestiltskin Problem.* Houghton Mifflin, 2000.

Yolen, Jane. *Twelve Impossible Things Before Breakfast.* Harcourt, 1997. Includes a variation of Peter Pan.

Yolen, Jane, and Robert J. Harris. *Odysseus and the Serpent Maze.* HarperCollins, 2001.

I Don't Need No Education

Explanation of theme: September is College Savings Month. According to *Chase's Calendar of Events*, this event is sponsored by College Savings Plan National Association of State Treasurers and encourages families to plan ahead for the cost of college attendance. More information can be found at www.collegesavings.org. In addition to college planning and text preparatory materials, include titles in which the main action of the story revolves around school.

Prop: Chalkboard with letters written in chalk.

Annotated list of titles:

Anderson, Laurie Halse. *Speak*. Farrar, Straus & Giroux, 1999. Will Melinda find her voice and tell why she dialed 911 and ended a great party?

Appelt, Kathi. *Kissing Tennessee and Other Stories from the Stardust Dance*. Harcourt, 2000. The stories that brought graduating eighth grade students to Dogwood Junior High's magical Stardust Dance.

Asher, Donald. *Cool Colleges for the Hyper-Intelligent, Self-Directed, Late-Blooming and Just Plain Different*. Ten Speed Press, 2000. Unlike typical guides providing costs, majors, and so forth, this explains what college life is like for students.

Boylan, James Finn. *Getting In*. Warner, 1998. The adventures of four teens and their week-long trek through New England for their entrance interviews.

Cabot, Meg. *The Princess Diaries*. HarperCollins, 2000. Mia's biggest problem is passing algebra until she learns she is the sole heir to the throne of Genovia.

Card, Orson Scott. *Ender's Shadow*. TOR, 1999. Bean is picked off the street by a nun and sent to war school to become a brilliant space-war strategist.

Efaw, Amy. *Battle Dress*. HarperCollins, 2000. Seventeen-year-old Allie struggles to get through the grueling six weeks of West Point's new cadet training known as the Beast.

Gallo, Donald R., ed. *On the Fringe*. Dial Books, 2001. Acclaimed young adult authors write short stories about those often ridiculed high school students who do not seem to fit in with the more popular mainstream teenagers.

Glenn, Mel. *Split Image*. William Morrow, 2000. Laura Li's seemingly perfect life, both inside and outside high school, is revealed through the thoughts and reflections of herself, her parents, teachers, librarian, and friends.

Haddix, Margaret Peterson. *Among the Imposters*. Simon & Schuster, 2001. In this sequel to *Among the Hidden*, Luke attends a boarding school under a fake identity which he is afraid to reveal, even to the other "thirds" because of a traitor working for the population police.

Herrera, Juan Felipe. *Crashboomlove*. University of New Mexico Press, 1999. The painful experiences growing up as a fatherless Mexican-American high school student.

Koertge, Ron. *The Brimstone Journals*. Candlewick Press, 2001. Voices of high school students reveal violence existing and growing in their lives in interconnected poems.

Lackey, Mercedes. *Brightly Burning*. DAW, 2000. Enrolled in merchant's school, sixteen-year-old Lavan encounters torment and torture until he realizes his gift as a firestarter.

Lubar, David. *Hidden Talents*. TOR, 1999. Martin befriends a group of misfits with psychic powers when he arrives at an alternative school.

Lynch, Chris. *Gold Dust*. HarperCollins, 2000. It isn't easy for Napolean when he moves from the Caribbean to a Catholic school in racially polarized Boston.

Neufeld, John. *Boys Lie*. DK Ink, 1999. When lies are spread, Gina must take matters into her own hands.

Pinkwater, Daniel. *The Education of Robert Nifkin*. Farrar, Straus & Giroux, 1999. High school in 1950s Chicago wasn't like *Leave It to Beaver* or *Happy Days*.

Rowling, J. K. *Harry Potter and the Chamber of Secrets*. Scholastic, 1999.

———. *Harry Potter and the Goblet of Fire*. Scholastic, 2000.

———. *Harry Potter and the Prisoner of Azkaban*. Scholastic, 1999.

———. *Harry Potter and the Sorcerer's Stone*. Scholastic, 1998. The adventures of Harry and his friends at the Hogwarts School of Witchcraft and Wizardry.

Scott, Cherie Carter. *If High School Is a Game, Here's How to Break the Rules: A Cutting Edge Guide to Becoming Yourself*. Delacorte, 2001. A self-help book for teens on the changes and challenges of high school.

Soto, Gary. *Buried Onions*. Harcourt, 1997. Living in the Fresno barrio, Eddie drops out of junior college and tries to support himself.

Spinelli, Jerry. *Stargirl*. Knopf, 2000. Boring Mica High has never had a student with such school spirit as Stargirl.

Thomas, Rob. *Doing Time: Notes from the Undergrad*. Simon & Schuster, 1997. Ten vignettes about a high school's mandatory community service.

———. *Rats Saw God*. Simon & Schuster, 1996. A high school counselor suggests that senior Steve York explore what went wrong when he moved from Texas to California.

———. *Slave Day*. Simon & Schuster, 1997. African-American students object to a fund-raiser called "Slave Day."

Wynne Jones, Dianna. *The Year of the Griffin*. Greenwillow, 2000. Elda arrives at the Wizards' University where she and her new friends encounter assassins and misused magic.

Got Guts?

Explanation of theme: Titles have characters who show exceptional courage or survival skills.

Prop: Adapting the idea from the famous Got Milk? billboards, use a black background with white lettering.

Annotated list of titles:

Armstrong, Lance, with Sally Jenkins. *It's Not About the Bike: My Journey Back to Life.* Putnam, 2000. Autobiography from the three-time winner of the Tour de France.

Arnoldi, Katherine. *The Amazing True Story of a Teenage Single Mom.* Hyperion, 1998. A teen mom struggles to support and educate herself.

Carbone, Elisa. *Stealing Freedom.* Knopf, 1998. A teenage slave escapes to Canada via the Underground Railroad in this novel based on fact.

Carter, Alden. *Between a Rock and a Hard Place.* Scholastic, 1995. While on their family's rite-of-passage canoe trip, diabetic Randy and his cousin Mark face adventure when Randy's insulin is lost in a boating accident.

Desetta, Al, and Sybil Wolin. *Struggle to Be Strong: True Stories by Teens About Overcoming Tough Times.* Free Spirit, 2000. Self-help book for teens on the power of resiliency.

George, Jean Craighead. *Julie of the Wolves.* HarperCollins, 1972.

———. *Julie's Wolf Pack.* HarperCollins, 1997. The adventures of an Eskimo girl raised by wolves in Alaska.

Hobbs, Will. *Down the Yukon.* HarperColllins, 2001. In 1899, Jason and his girlfriend Jamie face the grueling hazards of the Yukon River when they enter a race to Nome, Alaska, where gold has been discovered.

———. *Downriver.* Atheneum, 1991. It takes more than guts to go white-water rafting after stealing the raft.

———. *Far North.* William Morrow, 1996. Sixteen-year-old Gabe and his Dene Indian friend, Raymond, struggle to survive a winter in the wilderness of the Northwest Territories after their float plane is destroyed.

———. *Jason's Gold.* William Morrow, 1999. Fifteen-year-old Jason embarks on a 10,000-mile journey to strike it rich in the Yukon Territory gold rush in 1897.

King Stephen. *The Girl Who Loved Tom Gordon.* Scribner, 1999. You are alone and lost in the woods with a Walkman, no food, a stalker, and the nagging thought that you should have never left the trail.

Lessa, Christina, Teresa Edwards, and Peggy Fleming. *Women Who Win: Stories of Triumph in Sport and in Life.* Universe, 1998. Twenty champion athletes share their views on life and sports.

Lobel, Anita. *No Pretty Pictures: A Child of War.* Greenwillow, 1998. The famous children's book illustrator describes her experiences as a Polish Jew during World War II.

Maurer, Richard. *The Wild Colorado: The True Adventures of Fred Dellenbaugh, Age 17, on the Second Powell Expedition into the Grand Canyon*. Crown, 1999. White-water rafting at its most raw.

McPhee, Jenny, Laura McPhee, and Martha MePhee. *Girls: Ordinary Girls and Their Extraordinary Pursuits*. Random House, 2000.

Nieuwsma, Milton, ed. *Kinderlager: An Oral History of Young Holocaust Survivors*. Holiday House, 1998. Memoirs of the Jewish-American women who were sent to the children's section of Auschwitz.

Opdyke, Irene Gut. *In My Hands: Memories of a Holocaust Survivor*. Knopf, 1999. Young Irene risks her life countless times to help Jews escape the hatred of the Holocaust.

Paulsen, Gary. *Brian's Return*. Delacorte, 1999. Brian can no longer live in the city but must return to the place where he really belongs after being rescued from his adventure in the wilderness.

———. *Brian's Winter*. Delacorte, 1996. Brian must survive a harsh winter in the wilderness in this version of *Hatchet* with a rewritten ending.

———. *Guts: The True Story Behind Hatchet and the Brian Books*. Delacorte, 2001. Paulsen shares his personal experiences, including mistakes and mishaps, that are the real events that inspired the Brian Robeson stories.

———. *Hatchet*. Macmillan, 1987. After surviving a plane crash in the Canadian wilderness, Brian must fend for himself if he is to survive.

———. *Nighthjohn*. Delacorte, 1993. Slave Nightjohn's punishment for teaching Sarny to read and write is the mutilation of his feet—yet he continues to teach other slaves.

———. *The River*. Delacorte, 1991. In this sequel to *Hatchet*, Brian is responsible for saving someone else.

Piven, Joshua, and David Borgenicht. *The Worst Case Scenario Survival Handbook*. Chronicle, 1999. A humorous presentation of survival skills.

Schwager, Tina, and Michele Schuerger. *Gutsy Girls: Young Women Who Dare*. Free Spirit, 1999. Twenty-five young women share their adventures.

Taylor, Theodore. *The Cay*. Doubleday, 1969. Shipwrecked on a coral island, a blind boy and an old sailor are brought together.

Weaver, Will. *Memory Boy*. HarperCollins, 2001. After a chain of cataclysmic volcanic explosions brings food rationing, murder, and looting, sixteen-year-old Miles and his family flee the city into the wilderness and an uncertain future.

Whelan, Gloria. *Homeless Bird*. HarperCollins, 2000. Thirteen-year-old Koly is abandoned by her dreadful stepmother and left on her own after her husband from an arranged marriage dies.

Winick, Judd. *Pedro and Me: Friendship, Loss, and What I Learned*. Henry Holt, 2000. Judd's story of his roommate on MTV's *The Real World*—the unforgettable Pedro who taught millions of viewers about being gay and living with AIDS.

Just the Way You Are

Explanation of theme: So many of the teenage years are spent struggling with body image and changes. These titles depict characters dealing with changes in their body, as well as the normal progression of puberty. Some characters are experiencing the aftermath of an accident that changed their lives. Nonfiction titles on body image and sexual and emotional health should also be included.

Props: A collage of different teens (tall, short, thin, fat, blond, brunette, red-haired, disabled, from different races, etc.).

Annotated list of titles:

Belton, Sandra. *McKendree*. Greenwillow, 2000. In 1948, dark-skinned Tilara spends the summer at McKendree, a home for the elderly, and comes to learn that beauty has nothing to do with skin color.

Benjamin, E. M. J. *Takedown*. Banks Channel Books, 1999. Jacob deals with his newly diagnosed epilepsy and the state wrestling finals.

Bennett, Cherie. *Life in the Fat Lane*. Delacorte, 1998. Homecoming Queen Laura inexplicably gains weight and becomes a fat girl.

Bloor, Edward. *Tangerine*. Harcourt, 1997. Paul can see more with his thick glasses than people think.

Columbia University's Health Education Program. *The "Go Ask Alice" Book of Answers: A Guide to Good Physical, Sexual, and Emotional Health*. Owl Books, 1998.

Crutcher, Chris. *Staying Fat for Sarah Byrnes*. Greenwillow, 1993. Sarah's name could not be more true.

Daldry, Jeremy. *The Teenage Guy's Survival Guide*. Little Brown, 1999.

Drill, Esther. *Deal with It! A Whole New Approach to Your Body, Brain, and Life as a Gurl*. Pocket Books, 1999.

Fleischman Paul. *The Mind's Eye*. Henry Holt, 1999. In a nursing home, sixteen-year-old Courtney, paralyzed from an accident, learns to shed self-pity as she takes an imaginary trip to Italy with a fellow nursing home resident.

Gravelle, Karen. *What's Going on Down There?* Walker, 1998. Detailed here are the emotional and physical changes that occur in boys and, to a lesser extent, girls.

Haddix, Margaret Peterson. *Turnabout*. Simon & Schuster, 2000. An unauthorized medical experiment results in grave repercussions for those searching for the fountain of youth.

Holt, Kimberly Willis. *When Zachary Beaver Came to Town*. Henry Holt, 1999. Toby and his friend spend the summer getting to know the freak show star, a 600-pound teenager.

Johnson, Scott. *Safe at Second*. Philomel, 1999. Phil's best friend Todd is destined for the major leagues until a line drive causes him to lose an eye, and they both must find a new future for themselves.

Klaus, Annette Curtis. *Blood and Chocolate*. Delacorte, 1997. Life as a werewolf is much harder than you think.

Land, Jon. *Hope Mountain*. Forge, 1999. After a failed suicide attempt, Jamie heads for the mountains where an accident robbed him of his life as a champion skier.

Lawrence, Iain. *Ghost Boy*. Delacorte, 2000. Unhappy in a home seemingly devoid of love, a fourteen-year-old albino boy, Harold the Ghost, runs away to join the circus.

Lynch, Chris. *Extreme Elvin*. HarperCollins, 1998. Elvin continues to fight his weight as he tries to find a place among his peers.

———. *Slot Machine*. HarperCollins, 1995. Can Elvin find his slot in his new sports-oriented high school?

Madaras, Lynda, and Area Madaras. *My Body, My Self for Boys*, 2d ed. Newmarket Press, 2000.

———. *My Body, My Self for Girls*, 2d ed. Newmarket Press, 2000.

———. *What's Happening to My Body? Book for Boys: A Growing Up Guide for Parents and Sons*, 3d ed. Newmarket Press, 2000.

———. *What's Happening to My Body? Book for Girls: A Growing Up Guide for Parents and Daughters*, 3d ed. Newmarket Press, 2000.

Mosatche, Harriet S., and Karen Unger. *Too Old for This Too Young for That! Survival Guide for the Middle School Years*. Free Spirit, 2000.

Orr, Wendy. *Peeling the Onion*. Holiday House, 1997. Anna must face life after an automobile accident leaves her physically and mentally handicapped.

Peck, Robert Newton. *Extra Innings*. HarperCollins, 2001. After seeing his family, along with his hope to pitch in the majors, die, plane crash survivor Tate seeks solace in Great-Aunt Vidalia's stories of a childhood spent traveling with a Depression-era Negro baseball team.

Philbrick, Rodman. *Freak the Mighty*. Scholastic, 1993. When Maxwell Kane, a huge oaf, and tiny but brilliant Kevin, who has a birth defect, get together, they can accomplish mighty deeds.

Platt, Randall Beth. *The Likes of Me*. Delacorte, 2000. Fourteen-year-old half-Chinese albino Cordy runs away to Seattle and finds work in a carnival.

Wann, Marilyn. *Fat!So?: Because You Don't Have to Apologize for Your Size*. Ten Speed Press, 1998. Learn to be comfortable—no matter how much you weigh.

And You Think You Have It Bad

Explanation of theme: Teens love to read about other teens' predicaments. Reading about trauma in others' lives makes their life seem not so bad.

Props: Collage of photographs from magazines, newspapers, and other printed materials showing people in hospital beds, automobile accidents, guns, and so forth.

Annotated list of titles:

Abelove, Joan. *Saying It Out Loud*. DK Ink, 1999. Mindy, whose mother is dying of a brain tumor and whose father is uncommunicative, realizes she must depend on others for support.

Burgess, Melvin. *Smack*. Henry Holt, 1998. Teens Tar and Gemma are runaways who experience the harrowing ups and downs of heroin addiction.

Cole, Brock. *The Facts Speak for Themselves*. Front St., 1997. What happened in Linda's life that leads to murder?

Cormier, Robert. *We All Fall Down*. Dell Paper, 1991. Random violence in a small town.

Draper, Sharon. *Tears of a Tiger*. Atheneum, 1994. Andy cannot deal with the fact that his drunk driving has killed his friend.

Gallo, Donald R., ed. *No Easy Answers: Short Stories About Teenagers Making Tough Choices*. Delacorte, 1997. YA authors write about teens facing ethical and moral dilemmas.

Haddix, Margaret Peterson. *Among the Hidden*. Simon & Schuster, 1998. Thirteen-year-old Luke, the third of his parents' children, must hide in the attic from the population police in order to survive in a society where couples are allowed to have only two children.

Hesser, Terry Spencer. *Kissing Doorknobs*. Delacorte, 1998. Tara's life is filled with constant worrying, and it is starting to hurt the relationships around her.

Hurwin, Davida Wills. *A Time for Dancing*. Little Brown, 1995. Best friends Juliana and Samantha share so much, especially a passion for dancing, but Jules has something they cannot share—a diagnosis of cancer.

Lowenstein, Sallie. *Evan's Voice*. Lion Stone, 1999. Jake must take care of his plague-stricken brother Evan in a decimated future world.

McCormick, Patricia. *Cut*. Front St., 2000. While confined to a mental hospital, Callie must confront the family trauma that led to the destructive behavior of cutting herself.

McDonald, Joyce. *Swallowing Stones*. Delacorte, 1997. Depression, guilt, and fear plague Michael's dreams after he accidentally kills a man and then hides the gun and feigns ignorance.

McNamee, Graham. *Hate You*. Delacorte, 1999. Alice hates her father, who tried to strangle her but ended up damaging her voice.

Plummer, Louise. *A Dance for Three*. Delacorte, 2000. Hannah's world is shattered when she tells her wealthy boyfriend, Milo Fabiano, that she is pregnant.

Porter, Connie. *Imani All Mine*. Houghton, 1999. An unwed teenage mom tries her best to raise her daughter Imani, but the people and events around her lead to tragedy.

Rapp, Adam. *The Copper Elephant*. Front St., 1999. In post-apocalyptic America, Whensday struggles to survive amidst rape, dislocation, destruction, and poisoned rain.

Sones, Sonya. *Stop Pretending: What Happened When My Big Sister Went Crazy*. HarperCollins, 1999. Life after her older sister has a mental breakdown is hard to adjust to for her younger sister.

Trueman, Terry. *Stuck in Neutral*. HarperCollins, 2000. Fourteen-year-old Shawn McDaniel thinks his father is plotting to kill him and is helpless to try and stop him.

Voight, Cynthia. *When She Hollers*. Scholastic, 1994. With knife in hand, Tish decides the sexual abuse from her dad must stop.

Woodson, Jacqueline. *If You Come Softly*. Putnam, 1997. Two teens deal with other peoples' reactions to their interracial relationship.

———. *Lena*. Delacorte, 1999. Still mourning the death of their mother, Lena and her younger sister run away to escape their abusive father.

———. *Miracle's Boys*. Putnam, 2000. The story of three brothers, Tyree (twenty-two), who must keep the family together, bitter Charlie (sixteen), just released from being in prison for armed robbery, and Lafayette (thirteen), who still grieves and blames himself for their mother's death.

Yolen, Jane, and Bruce Coville. *Armageddon Summer*. Harcourt, 1998. Marina and Jed meet each other and the end of the world.

She Loves Me, She Loves Me Not

Explanation of theme: Love stories always appeal to teens because they too are looking for someone to go to the dance with or their first boyfriend or girlfriend.

Props: Daisy made out of craft paper with the yellow middle and stem, petals some on, some off, as if someone has already pulled them off.

Annotated list of titles:

Bat-Ami, Miriam. *Two Suns in the Sky*. Cricket, 1999. Chris cannot tell her anti-Semitic father of her relationship with Adam, a Yugoslavian Jew who lives in a refugee shelter in Oswego, New York, in 1944.

Bauer, Joan. *Thwonk*. Delacorte, 1995. Cupid's arrow turns Peter, the guy of AJ's dreams, into an obnoxious nuisance.

Block, Francesca Lia. *Weetzie Bat*. HarperCollins, 1989. Weetzie Bat and her punk friends share a special relationship.

Cart, Michael, ed. *Love and Sex: Ten Stories of Truth for Teens*. Simon & Schuster, 2001. Various adult and young adult authors write about the complexities, pressures, and joys teenagers encounter in their romantic lives.

Dessen, Sarah. *Keeping the Moon*. Viking, 1999. While spending the summer with an aunt, Colie, who has low self-esteem, finds friends in two waitresses and love with a shy teenage artist.

———. *Someone Like You*. Viking, 1998. Halley's first love is tempered by the death of her best friend Scarlett's boyfriend and Scarlett's announcement that she is pregnant.

Ferris, Jean. *Invincible Summer*. HarperCollins, 1987. Robin falls in love with Rick, a teen with leukemia, as he teaches her to survive her recent diagnosis.

Garden, Nancy. *Annie on My Mind*. Farrar, Straus & Giroux, 1982. Friends and families are uncomfortable with Lisa and Annie's relationship.

Garland, Sherry. *Song of the Buffalo Boy*. Harcourt, 1992. Loi, promised in marriage to a cruel military man, runs away with the boy she loves to find her American soldier father.

Goobie, Beth. *Before Wings*. Orca, 2000. At summer camp, Adrien is helplessly drawn to Paul, a boy with sixth sense.

Heynen, Jim. *Cosmos Coyote and William the Nice*. Henry Holt, 2000. Cosmos chooses a year in exile over jail time and falls in love with a religious girl who causes him to examine his values and beliefs.

Jordan, Sheryl. *The Raging Quiet*. Simon & Schuster, 1999. Set in the Middle Ages, villagers shun sixteen-year-old Marnie when she befriends the village mad man.

Kerr, M. E. *Hello, I Lied*. HarperCollins, 1997. Lang and Alex have a great relationship, but Lang is afraid to come out to his friends and confused about his feelings for a younger woman.

Kindl, Patrice. *Owl in Love*. Houghton Mifflin, 1993. How will Owl share her life secret with the man she loves—her science teacher?

Kirkberger, Kimberly. *Teen Love: On Relationships, a Book for Teenagers*. Heath Communications, 1999. A book to help you sort out your thoughts and confusion about love and relationships.

Klaus, Annette Curtis. *Blood and Chocolate*. Delacorte, 1997. Life as a werewolf is much harder than you think.

———. *The Silver Kiss*. Delacorte, 1990. Zoe and Simon fall in love—too bad he's a vampire.

Lane, Dakota. *Johnny Voodoo*. Delacorte, 1996. Dierdre learns about love when she meets Johnny Voodoo.

Logue, Mary. *Dancing with an Alien*. HarperCollins, 2000. Does Tonia love Branko enough to leave her life on Earth?

Mannarino, Melanie. *The Boyfriend Clinic: The Final Word on Flirting, Dating, Guys, and Love*. HarperCollins, 2000.

McNeal, Laura. *Crooked*. Random House, 1999. Will ninth-graders Clara and Amos ever realize they have a crush on each other?

McReynolds, Glenna. *Prince of Time*. Bantam, 2000. When Avallyn finally gets to meet her long-awaited soul mate, she finds he is a drunk and a thief.

Napoli, Donna Jo. *Sirena*. Scholastic, 1998. A Greek sailor is enchanted by the lovely mermaid Sirena.

Plummer, Louise. *Unlikely Romance of Kate Bjorkman*. Delacorte, 1995. Kate falls for former neighbor Richard and records the memories of her one-sided relationship with the assistance of *The Romance Writer's Phrase Book*.

Powell, Randy. *Is Kissing a Girl Who Smokes Like Kissing an Ashtray?* Farrar, Straus & Giroux, 1992. Once he gets up the nerve to speak to Heidi, it doesn't take Biff long to answer the question.

Rabens, Susan. *The Compete Idiot's Guide to Dating for Teens*. Alpha Books, 2001.

Randle, Kristin. *Breaking Rank*. Morrow, 1999. Casey falls for Baby but can he return the feeling? Does the Clan control his thoughts?

Schreibman, Tamar. *Kissing: The Complete Guide: Everything You've Always Wanted to Know About Kissing and Were Afraid to Ask*. Simon & Schuster, 2000.

Stoehr, Shelley. *Tomorrow Wendy*. Delacorte, 1998. How would you handle this? You have a boyfriend but you're in love with his sister.

Taylor, William. *The Blue Lawn*. Alyson Books, 1999. A fifteen-year-old acknowledges his attraction to an older rugby teammate.

Wersba, Barbara. *Whistle Me Home*. Holt, 1997. Noli thinks she and TJ would make a great couple but is totally shocked when she discovers he is gay.

Woodson, Jacqueline. *If You Come Softly*. Putnam, 1997. Two teens deal with other peoples' reactions to their interracial relationship.

Young, Karen Romano. *The Beetle and Me—A Love Story*. Greenwillow, 1999. Daisy deals with her love interest and the love of restoring a purple 1957 VW Beetle to running order.

This Is War!

Explanation of theme: The purpose of this display is to help teens place in context our current war on terrorism.

Props: Camouflage material, army men figurines, old parachute, dog tags. Visit an army surplus store for items or contact the local recruiting branch of the military.

Annotated list of titles:

Alshalabi, Firyal. *Summer, 1990: A Young Adult Novel.* Aunt Strawberry Books, 1999. The Persian Gulf War through the eyes of Danah, a thirteen-year-old Kuwaiti.

Bat-Ami, Miriam. *Two Suns in the Sky.* Front St., 1999. Chris can not tell her anti-Semitic father of her relationship with Adam, a Yugoslavian Jew who lives in a refugee shelter in Oswego, New York, in 1944.

Bennett, Cherie, and Jeff Goltesman. *Anne Frank and Me.* Putnam, 2001. On a Holocaust-related field trip, Nicole is transported to 1942 and becomes a Jew who must help her family survive in Paris.

Card, Orson Scott. *Ender's Game.* TOR, 1994. Man's nightmares haunt the world as alien creatures prepare for an all-out attack.

Clement-Davies, David. *Fire Bringer.* Dutton, 2000. The battle for dominion over the animal world leads Rannoch to the knowledge and courage to face his destiny in this epic.

Cormier, Robert. *Heroes.* Delacorte, 1998. Returning home without a face, but with a mission, Francis wants revenge on the hometown hero who he feels betrayed him.

Dickinson, Peter. *A.K.* Delacorte, 1990. Paul is forced to flee into the open countryside to avoid enemy soldiers who seek his life in his war-torn African country.

Fleischman, Paul. *Bull Run.* HarperCollins, 1993. The Civil War from a variety of views.

Gaeddart, Lou Ann. *Friends and Enemies.* Atheneum, 2000. William and his friend are at religious and political odds as Pearl Harbor is bombed.

Garner, Eleanor Ramrath. *Eleanor's Story: An American Girl in Hitler's Germany.* Peachtree, 1999. Eleanor is surrounded by war as her father moves the family to Germany after receiving a job offer.

Lobel, Anita. *No Pretty Pictures: A Child of War.* Greenwillow, 1998. The famous children's book illustrator describes her experiences as a Polish Jew during World War II.

Marsden, John. *Burning for Revenge.* Houghton Mifflin, 2000.

———. *Darkness Be My Friend.* Houghton Mifflin, 1999.

———. *The Dead of Night.* Houghton Mifflin, 1997.

———. *A Killing Frost.* Houghton Mifflin, 1998.

———. *Tomorrow, When the War Began*. Houghton Mifflin, 1995. Ellie and her friends must work underground to save their Australian homeland from an enemy invasion.

Matas, Carol. *In My Enemy's House*. Simon & Schuster, 1999. Keeping her identity a secret will keep her alive, but can she keep her secret from her Nazi boss?

Mazer, Norma Fox. *Goodnight, Maman*. Harcourt, 1999. A Jewish girl tells of her experiences in Europe during the Holocaust and later in a refugee camp in Oswego, New York.

Myers, Walter Dean. *Fallen Angels*. Scholastic, 1988. A seventeen-year-old African-American's experiences as a soldier in Vietnam.

Opdyke, Irene Gut. *In My Hands: Memories of a Holocaust Survivor*. Knopf, 1999. Young Irene risks her life countless times to help Jews escape the hatred of the Holocaust.

Paulsen, Gary. *Soldier's Heart*. Doubleday, 1998. A teenaged Union soldier experiences the mental and physical agonies of the Civil War.

Reuter, Bjarne. *Boys from St. Petri*. Dutton, 1994. A group of teenage boys fight the Nazi occupation of their hometown during World War II in a series of dangerous resistance missions.

Rinaldi, Ann. *The Coffin Quilt: The Feud Between the Hatfields and the McCoys*. Harcourt, 1999. Violence strikes when a McCoy daughter elopes with a Hatfield.

Salisbury, Graham. *Under the Blood Red Sun*. Delacorte, 1994. Japanese-American Tomi faces suspicion and hatred during World War II in Hawaii.

Spiegelman, Art. *Maus II: A Survivor's Tale: And Here My Troubles Began*. Pantheon, 1991.

———. *Maus: A Survivor's Tale: My Father Bleeds History*. Pantheon, 1986. The experiences of the author's father during the Holocaust—in graphic novel form.

Von Dijk, Lutz. *Damned Strong Love*. Holt, 1995. The Nazis didn't just hate the Jews. . . .

White, Ellen Emerson. *Road Home*. Scholastic, 1995. Rebecca's war doesn't end when she returns home from serving as an emergency room nurse in Vietnam.

Honorable Mentions

Explanation of theme: This display/contest can be used around the time of the Emmy awards (usually in spring) or in conjunction with the MTV movie awards. Multiple copies of the books would make it easier for teens to vote.

Props: Gold lamé, stars, pictures of the statues awarded at the Oscar's, Grammy's, MTV movie or video awards.

Categories and nominations:

Wackiest family or family member:

- Grandma in *A Long Way from Chicago* and *A Year Down Yonder* by Richard Peck
- Georgia's family in *Angus, Thongs, and Full-Frontal Snogging* by Louise Rennison
- The Breedlove family in *Backwater* by Joan Bauer
- The LaBauve family in *Meely Labauve* by Ken Wells

Biggest jerk:

- Rogerson in *Dreamland* by Sarah Dessen
- Milo Fabiano in *A Dance for Three* by Louise Plummer
- Eddie in *Tightrope* by Gillian Cross
- Jason in *Leslie's Journal* by Allan Stratton

Girl who would make the best girlfriend:

- Stargirl in *Stargirl* by Jerry Spinelli
- Georgia in *Angus, Thongs, and Full-Frontal Snogging* by Louise Rennison
- Mia in *The Princess Diaries* by Meg Cabot
- Razzle in *Razzle* by Ellen Wittlinger

Boy who would make the best boyfriend:

- Branko in *Dancing with an Alien* by Mary Logue
- Miah in *If You Come Softly* by Jacqueline Woodson
- Elvin in *Slot Machine* and *Extreme Elvin* by Chris Lynch
- Jay in *Playing Without the Ball* by Rich Wallace

Character with the most guts:

- Kit in *Kit's Wilderness* by David Almond

- Declan in *The Edge* by Ben Bo

- Trisha in *The Girl Who Loved Tom Gordon* by Stephen King

- Gina in *Boys Lie* by John Neufeld

Person you would most like to have as a friend:

- Shayla in *When Kambia Elaine Flew in from Neptune* by Lori Aurelia Williams

- Pedro in *Pedro and Me* by Judd Winick

- Lena in *The Sisterhood of the Traveling Pants* by Ann Brashares

- Torey in *The Body of Christopher Creed* by Carol Plum-Ucci

Worst parent/family member:

- The dad in *Stuck in Neutral* by Terry Trueman

- The dad in *Staying Fat for Sarah Byrnes* by Chris Crutcher

- The mom in *Tribute to Another Dead Rock Star* by Randy Powell

- The brother in *Tangerine* by Edward Bloor

Yearbook Memories

Explanation of theme: This display is taken from the superlatives that high school senior class members vote about their classmates. Again teens can do the voting and nominating and mulitple copies are a must in order to allow as many teens as possible a chance to read and vote. These categories and titles are just suggestions, feel free to use titles that you notice have been popular in your library.

Props: Mortar board, graduation supplies, color copies of the local school yearbook cover or the actual yearbook, rolled up paper tied with a ribbon to resemble a diploma, using the colors of the local school would be appropriate.

Categories and nominatons:

Most likely to succeed:

- La Vaughn in *True Believer* by Virginia Euwer Wolff
- Robert Nifkin in *The Education of Robert Nifkin* by Daniel Pinkwater
- Ellie in the *Tomorrow, When the War Began* series by John Marsden
- Jenna in *Rules of the Road* by Joan Bauer

Most fun to be around:

- Elvin in *Slot Machine* and *Extreme Elvin* by Chris Lynch
- Dave in *Dave at Night* by Gail Levine
- Georgia in *Angus, Thongs, and Full-Frontal Snogging* by Louise Rennison
- Ron in the *Harry Potter* series by J. K. Rowling

Most likely to get a detention:

- Jazz in *Define Normal* by Julie Anne Peters
- Charles Leblanc in *Tidewater Blood* by William Hoffman
- Amandine in *Amandine* by Adele Griffin
- Jeff in *Joyride* by Gretchen Olson

Most athletic:

- Travis Cody in *Roughnecks* by Thomas Cochran
- Tamika in *Rookie: Tamika Whitmore's First Year in the WNBA* by Joan Anderson
- Bridget in *The Sisterhood of the Traveling Pants* by Ann Brashares
- Austin in *Damage* by A. M. Jenkins

Most respected:

- Irene in *In My Hands: Memories of a Holocaust Rescuer* by Irene Gut Opdyke
- Marisa in *In My Enemy's House* by Carol Matas
- Nightjohn in *Nightjohn* by Gary Paulsen
- Janie in *The Face on the Milk Carton* series by Caroline Cooney

Most talented:

- Savion in *Savion: My Life in Tap* by Savion Glover
- Razzle in *Razzle* by Ellen Wittlinger
- Ashley in *Tightrope* by Gillian Cross
- Cosmos in *Cosmos Coyote and William the Nice* by Jim Heynen

Most masculine:

- The boy in *The Beet Fields* by Gary Paulsen
- Jacob in *Takedown* by E. M. J Benjamin
- Maxwell Kane in *Freak the Mighty* by Rodman Philbrick
- Baby in *Breaking Rank* by Kristin Randle

Most feminine:

- Lara in *Life in the Fat Lane* by Cherie Bennett
- Sophie in *What My Mother Doesn't Know* by Sonya Sones
- Claire in *Violet and Claire* by Francesca Lia Block
- Stargirl in *Stargirl* by Jerry Spinelli

Index